# Jews in Southern Tuscany during the Holocaust

# Sephardic and Mizrahi Studies

*Series Editors:* Jane Gerber and Judith Roumani

Being Sephardic has meant various things to various individuals at different times and in different places. In its narrowest definition "Sephardic" has defined Jews from the Iberian Peninsula and more specifically from al-Andalus or Muslim Spain. With the expulsion of Iberian Jewry in the fifteenth century and their dispersion throughout the Mediterranean world a broader definition of Sephardic Jewry has evolved. Today Sephardic Jewry denotes a global diaspora in which indigenous Jewries from many lands have retained distinctive cultures while sharing many customs and memories or associations with medieval Iberia. The role of the scholar is to try to capture these differences. Sephardi-Mizrahi studies lack the geographical concentration, of course, of regional or national studies. Even the supposed linguistic unity of a national culture is missing, though some languages do present themselves as candidates. Thus there can be endless debates about what fits into Sephardi-Mizrahi studies and what doesn't. What may not have fitted in the past may actually fit today. As a transnational field, influenced by a number of other cultures, Sephardi-Mizrahi studies fit in well with the current emphasis on multicultural, diaspora, and post-colonial studies.

We welcome prospective proposals and abstracts for monographs, edited collections, and occasional translations of important texts.

### Titles in the Series
*Jews in Southern Tuscany during the Holocaust: Ambiguous Refuge*, by Judith Roumani

# Jews in Southern Tuscany during the Holocaust

## Ambiguous Refuge

Judith Roumani

LEXINGTON BOOKS
*Lanham • Boulder • New York • London*

Published by Lexington Books
An imprint of The Rowman & Littlefield Publishing Group, Inc.
4501 Forbes Boulevard, Suite 200, Lanham, Maryland 20706
www.rowman.com

6 Tinworth Street, London SE11 5AL, United Kingdom

Copyright © 2021 by The Rowman & Littlefield Publishing Group, Inc.

*All rights reserved.* No part of this book may be reproduced in any form or by any electronic or mechanical means, including information storage and retrieval systems, without written permission from the publisher, except by a reviewer who may quote passages in a review.

British Library Cataloguing in Publication Information Available

Library of Congress Control Number: 2020947237

ISBN 9781793629791 (cloth) | ISBN 9781793629814 (pbk)
ISBN 9781793629807 (epub)

*In Memory of Jacques*
*To David, Elisa, Mo, Ace and Jewel*
*and*
*In Memory of a Dear Friend, Rut (Ester) Passigli Lichtner*

# Contents

| | |
|---|---:|
| List of Figures | ix |
| List of Sources | xi |
| List of Personalities | xv |
| Acknowledgments | xxi |
| A Short Introduction | 1 |
| 1 Pitigliano and Other Cities of Refuge for Jews in Southern Tuscany over the Centuries | 7 |
| 2 A Bolt from the Blue? Fascist Racial Laws of 1938 and Their Effects in Southern Tuscany | 27 |
| 3 Town versus Country, Conformity versus Defiance: Contrasting Behaviors Involving Jews | 49 |
| 4 Hiding like Animals, in Caves, Barns, and Farms; and the Righteous Gentiles of Southern Tuscany Who Risked Their Lives Protecting Jews | 65 |
| 5 At the Mercy of the Church and the Fascists: The Obligingly Hospitable Bishop Galeazzi of Grosseto and the Experience of Jews Who Turned Themselves In | 81 |
| 6 Foreign Jewish Refugees Who Fled to Tuscany: Early Experiences | 111 |
| 7 Last Days at the Bishop's Palace for Foreign and Italian Jews | 131 |

**8** Post War: The Search for a Return to Normal—For Jews, a
  Future of Virtual Judaism                                159

Bibliography                                               187

Index                                                      199

About the Author                                           203

# Figures

| | | |
|---|---|---|
| Figure 1.1 | Terraced Four-and-a-Half-Century-Old Jewish Cemetery in Pitigliano | 8 |
| Figure 1.2 | *Ketuba* from Pitigliano, 1714. A Marriage between the Gallichi and the Levi Families | 12 |
| Figure 1.3 | Parochet (Ark Curtain) of Pitigliano, 1834, Embroidered by Rachele Modigliani and Friends for the Festival of Shavuot | 15 |
| Figure 1.4 | Bar Mitzvah in Pitigliano, 1936 | 20 |
| Figure 3.1 | Pitigliano Street | 50 |
| Figure 3.2 | The Perugini Farm, One of the Farms on which the Paggi Family Hid | 57 |
| Figure 4.1 | Cave Dug Out by the Perugini and Bisogni Families for the Paggi Family | 67 |
| Figure 4.2 | Interviewing Elena Servi | 70 |
| Figure 4.3 | The Hospital in Pitigliano, in which a Few Elderly Jews Were Hidden | 74 |
| Figure 5.1 | Bishop Galeazzi of Grosseto on the Steps of the Cathedral, Surrounded by Fascist Leaders, 1940s | 87 |
| Figure 5.2 | Bishop's Seminary Near Roccatederighi, 2018. Used as a *campo di concentramento* for Local and Foreign Jews, 1943–1944 | 90 |
| Figure 6.1 | Painting by Egon Mosbach, Internee at Arcidosso, Prisoner in Camp of Roccatederighi, Died in Subcamp of Auschwitz Untitled, 1943 | 114 |

*Figures*

| | | |
|---|---|---|
| Figure 7.1 | First Page of Azeglio Servi's Diary, Included in *La Persecuzione degl ebrei nella Provincia di Grosseto nel 1943–1944*, Grosseto: ISGREC, 1996, 2002, p. 56 | 135 |
| Figure 7.2 | Second Page of Azeglio Servi's Diary, ibid., p. 57 | 136 |
| Figure 7.3 | Third Page of Azeglio Servi's Diary, ibid., p. 58 | 137 |
| Figure 7.4 | Fourth Page of Azeglio Servi's Diary, ibid., p. 59 | 138 |
| Figure 8.1 | Overgrown Sign Board at Entrance to Roccatederighi Seminary, Announcing Plan to Turn It into a Rest Home for Alzheimer's Patients | 162 |
| Figure 8.2 | Ariel Paggi Pointing Out Plaque Listing Holocaust Victims from Pitigliano, Next to Synagogue, During His Interview | 165 |
| Figure 8.3 | Plaque at Roccatederighi Seminary in Memory of Holocaust Victims Deported from the Camp | 177 |
| Figure 8.4 | Door to Former Jewish Home Next to Synagogue in Ghetto of Pitigliano | 178 |
| Figure 8.5 | Pitigliano's Synagogue, Interior | 179 |

# Sources

## ARCHIVES AND LIBRARIES

### Italy

- Camera dei Deputati, Armadio della vergogna, Ministry of Foreign Affairs, MAE correspondence (online).
- Archivio di Stato (ASG), Provincia di Grosseto. Regia Prefettura files.
- Archivio Centrale dello Stato (ACS), Rome.
- Istituto Storico Grossetano della Resistenza e dell'Età Contemporanea (ISGREC).
- Archivio Storico Diocesano, Pitigliano.
- Archivio Storico Comunale, Pitigliano.
- Archivio Storico, UCEI, Union of Italian Jewish Communities, Rome (Pitigliano files).
- Centro di Documentazione Ebraica Contemporanea (CDEC), Milan (online) access to Digital Library and Indice Generale degli Ebrei Stranieri internati in Italia 1940–1943) http://www.cdec.it/ebrei_stranieri/ (via Centro Primo Levi website, New York).
- Data bases and interview transcripts, private collection of Ariel Paggi.

### United States

- United States Holocaust Memorial Museum (USHMM) Library and Archives. The Jack, Joseph and Morton Mandel Center for Advanced Holocaust Studies.
- International Tracing Service Archive at Bad Arolsen, now known as the Arolsen Archive, consulted via the Holocaust Survivors and Victim

- Resource Center at USHMM, and the Benjamin and Vladka Meed Registry of Holocaust Survivors at USHMM.
- University of Southern California Shoah Foundation (Spielberg Foundation), Visual History Archive video testimonies (online).
- Library of Congress collections.
- Centro Primo Levi, New York (online).
- Jewish Museum, New York (online).
- The New York Public Library, Dorot Foundation.
- Bnai Brith Museum, Washington DC.
- American Jewish Joint Distribution Committee Archives in New York.

**Israel**

- National Library of Israel, Jerusalem.
- Yad Vashem Digital Collections, "The Righteous among the Nations," www.db.yadvashem.org/righteous/family.html and Central Database of Shoah Victims' Names (online)

## LIST OF CONVERSATIONS AND INTERVIEWS IN CHRONOLOGICAL ORDER

- Rut (Ester) Passigli Lichtner, and Israel (Rodolfo) Lichtner, Potomac Maryland, and Pitigliano, June 1999, July 2002
- Samuele Zarrugh, Livorno, July 2002
- Augusto Brozzi, Pitigliano, July 2002
- Rabbi Mino Bahbout, Pitigliano, July 2002
- Rabbi Gianfranco Di Segni, Pitigliano, July 2002
- Giuseppe Celata, Pitigliano, July 2002
- Robert Wistrich, Jerusalem, "Antisemitism, the World's Obsession," February, 2007 (with Barry Rubin)
- Marcella Servi Siegel, Jerusalem, December 2007 (with Jacques Roumani), and November 2009 (with Vivienne Roumani-Denn), August 2015
- Edda Servi Machlin, New York, September 2011 (with Vivienne Roumani-Denn)
- Elena Servi, Pitigliano, October 2011
- Ariel Paggi, Pitigliano, October 2011
- Angelo Biondi, Pitigliano, October 2011 (with Jacques Roumani)
- Giovanna Dainelli Mazzoli, Pitigliano, October 2011
- Bernard Cooperman, Potomac, Maryland, September 2014
- Rabbi Riccardo Di Segni, Rome, October 2014

- Luciana Rocchi, Grosseto, October 2014 (with Jacques Roumani) and April 2019
- Suzanne Brown-Fleming, Washington DC, March 2015
- Adolfo Turbanti, Roccatederighi, June 2018

- *Email correspondence with:*

Luciana Rocchi, October–December 2014, January 2019
Ariel Paggi, 2009 to 2018
Adolfo Turbanti, March 2015
Laura Paggini, August 2015, December 2017
Paola Bianciardi and Adriana Bargagli, November 2018.

# Personalities

## JEWS OF THE PROVINCE OF GROSSETO

### Azeglio Servi Family

*Azeglio Servi*, Assistant rabbi of Pitigliano for forty years during which there was no rabbi, volunteered to be interned in the local concentration/internment camp and kept a diary of events.

*Sara Di Capua Servi*, his wife, originally from Rome, also interned in camp, lost most of her own family in the October 16, 1943, deportation of Jews from Rome.

*Lello Servi*, eldest son, hid in the countryside with siblings in 1943–1944 and worked with the Resistance as a sapper, killed by a truck in Florence in his forties.

*Gino Servi*, second of the five siblings, hid in the countryside and fought with Resistance, moved to Florence after the war.

*Edda Servi Machlin*, third sibling, hid in the countryside and worked with Resistance, later moved to United States and authored a memoir of the war years and a number of cookbooks.

*Marcella Servi Siegel*, younger sister, hid in the countryside with siblings, and worked with Resistance, reclaimed family home from squatters after the war, eventually moved to United States, and later to Israel.

### Manlio Paggi Family

*Manlio Paggi*, Ariel's father, a high school teacher of mathematics who had a successful career teaching in an Italian school in Sofia until the 1938 racial laws deprived him of his position. He was interned as a subversive in the southern Italian internment camp of Tricarico. His family was the first to go into hiding with a succession of farming families.

*Dina Sadun Paggi*, Manlio's wife, an intelligent and skeptical woman according to her son. She gathered information about the progress of the war and the fate of Jews who were being deported; on behalf of her family refused the offer to go to the concentration camp.

*Ariel Paggi*, their eldest child, seven years old in 1943, survived with his family in hiding with several farming families, sometimes separated from his parents. After the war, he moved as a child to Grosseto and later Livorno and Milan, has authored two books on Jews in the province.

*Adele Paggi*, Ariel's aunt, owned a farm; her tenant farmer continued to supply the family with food while they were in hiding.

## Nunes Family

A Jewish family from Grosseto. Some of the first internees in the concentration camp of Roccatederighi. The parents were released early on the basis of false health diagnoses. The son *Cesare Nunes* was a friend of the leader of the Fascist militia guarding them. He helped foreign prisoners escape the camp and join the Resistance; soon after, together with his brother, and other internees, he escaped and joined the Resistance himself.

## Livio Servi Family

*Livio Servi* earned a medal for bravery in World War I. On amicable terms with some Fascists of Pitigliano and took the family into hiding among friendly farmers.

*Elena Servi* his daughter was a child in 1943–1944 and was hidden with her family in farms but mostly in a cave. All survived, and after the war Elena moved to Israel, married there and had a family. After her husband died, she moved back to Pitigliano with her son and founded the Piccola Gerusalemme organization, initiated contacts with Yad Vashem for honoring Righteous Gentiles and founded a Jewish museum.

## Cava/Moscati Family

*Abramo Moscati*, a prestigious person in Pitigliano in the early years of the century, adviser to the mayor. In 1943, the doctors hid him for months in the hospital. He lost his home in the Allied bombing and lost his daughter, son-in-law and grandchildren at Auschwitz.

*Elda Moscati Cava*, husband Aldo Cava, children Franca and Enzo, Abramo's daughter, son-in-law and grandchildren, took refuge in Pitigliano (all previously living in Livorno), voluntarily turned themselves in to be interned in the local camp. They were shipped from Roccatederighi camp to Fossoli transit camp, then to Auschwitz, where they were all murdered Abramo perhaps never knew.

### Tranquillo Servi Family

*Tranquillo Servi*, married to Lidia Servi, his cousin and sister of Azeglio. A talented mechanic and valued employee of the SIAT bus company, whose family spent only a few weeks in the concentration camp before they were freed. After his early release, Tranquillo undertook dangerous trips, along roads that were being strafed by the Allies, to bring supplies to the Fascist authorities of the province. Accused of being a collaborator, after the war he defended the behavior of Bishop Galeazzi.

*Eugenia Servi*, one of Tranquillo's daughters, was fifteen years old when interned briefly in the concentration camp. Considered it a "vacation"; after the war was one of the staunchest defenders of Bishop Galeazzi. Her older sister, *Bianca*, became engaged to and later married one of the guards. Her younger sister, *Carla*, published a memoir, defending their father.

## RESCUERS (A FULLER LIST OF RESCUERS MAY BE FOUND IN THE NOTES)

*Giuseppe Biondi and Rosa Biagi Family*, landowning farmers who lived in the area between Sorano and Sovana, and were the parents of Angelo Biondi, a historian and our informant, born after the war. They provided a refuge for a Jewish family from Grosseto.

*Pietro Felici and Marina Marchioni*, his wife, landowning farmers who were instrumental in rescuing and protecting twenty-two Jews of Pitigliano: eight Servis, nine Paggis, and five Pasermans. Marina was the daughter of a mixed marriage.

*Vincenzo and Adele Dainelli, and their son Luciano.* Luciano was receiving math tutoring from Manlio Paggi in 1943. He approached his father to ask him to hide the Paggis, the first family to go into hiding, and later found them a new hiding place when their own farm near the highway proved too risky. Soon after, other Jewish families such as that of Elena Servi sought refuge initially with the Dainellis.

*Dr. Italo Bruscalupi and Dr. Bruno Bognomini*, director and chief doctor respectively of the Pitigliano hospital, hid several Jews in the hospital and declared others too elderly to be transported.

*Agostino Guazzerotti and his son Piero*, tenant farmers of Adele Paggi, supplied the Paggis with produce even after the farm had been expropriated from them. Also hid Jews.

*Perugini family*, the second family to provide a refuge for the Paggi family. They had spent some years in the United States and then returned. Their son who was avoiding the Fascist draft was also in hiding.

*Marino Di Nardo family*, sheltered the young Servis plus partisans, deserters and Allied airmen who had been shot down near his farm in Pian di Conati.

*Eliseo and Angelo Conti family*, hosted the family of Livio and Elena Servi. The Jewish family had to leave in a hurry because they were denounced by a neighbor hostile to the Contis.

*Francesco Sonno and family*, managed the estate of a prominent Fascist, provided a long-term hiding place in a cave for the family of Livio Servi.

*Ilio Santarelli and family*, farming family in the area of San Martino on the Fiora river, sheltered many opponents of Fascism and three escaped Allied soldiers in a cave. The latter were betrayed and Fascists killed all three, as well as killing Ilio Santarelli himself, and burning down the farm.

## FOREIGN JEWISH REFUGEES

*Egon Mosbach*, a salesman from Germany, alone because all of his family had emigrated, mostly to the United States. In Italy he was first on the Adriatic side, perhaps hoping to head for Palestine. He was interned in a suburb of Arcidosso in the north of the province. An amateur painter, he expressed his gratitude by giving canvasses to his hosts and to the local shopkeeper. He was sent to Roccatederighi concentration camp in December 1943, was dispatched to Fossoli transit camp on the first transport, and eventually put on the last train from Fossoli to Auschwitz. He died in one of the sub-camps of Auschwitz.

*Edmund and Gertrude Turteltaub, and their sons* Hans and Walter, from Dornbirn, Austria. Edmund was a great raconteur, with excellent Italian, fled to Italy in 1939, with tickets to sail to Uruguay, but their voyage was cancelled. Interned in Ferramonti camp in the south, then in Arcidosso, then Roccatederighi camp, sent to Fossoli and finally Auschwitz, where the entire family, parents and two young children, perished.

*Moszek and Anna Paserman, and children* Davide, Leone, and Brucha, from Poland, interned near Viterbo. Moszek had been in the southern internment camp of Ferramonti, but applied for transfer to Pitigliano so their sons could attend the Jewish school. They lived near the Paggis in Pitigliano and Leone and Ariel Paggi were classmates. A local farmer, Pietro Felici, offered to hide them. They lived in a cave for the next eight months, emerging before the Allies arrived.

*Rosenfeld/Singer Family*: Ernesto and Edith Rosenfeld, his sister Serena Singer and her young daughter Edith, Jews of Hungarian origin who had been in Yugoslavia.

*David* and *Olga Pollak*, a childless couple from Vienna, interned in the area before being arrested and sent to the camp of Roccatederighi.

*Alberto, Franziska, Saul* and *Henriette Waldman* (as with all non-Italians, there is some confusion over the spelling of their names), a family of Polish origin who had been living in Paris, then interned in Ferramonti, Roccalbegna, and Roccatederighi, before being sent to Fossoli.

The *Waisborg* Family, related to the Pasermans, sent from Roccatederighi on the second bus, to Scipione camp rather than to Fossoli.

## ITALIAN JEWS FROM OUT OF THE AREA

*Natale and Berta Finzi and daughter Gigliola*, from Livorno. Gigliola was born in January 1944, in the local hospital while the family was interned in Roccatederighi, her parents having received special permission to go to the hospital. They were all deported and died at Auschwitz; Gigliola was three months old.

## FASCISTS

*Alceo Ercolani*, Fascist prefect (governor) of the province of Grosseto, set up an internment camp specifically for Jews, in November 1943, the earliest pre-deportation camp in Italy, before he had even received the order to do so. Signed a rental contract with the bishop. Ordered the executions of draft evaders. Ordered transport of Jews to Fossoli for deportation to Auschwitz. Fled north and became director of refugee operations in Milan for Mussolini's Salò government.

*Gaetano Rizziello*, appointed commander of the internment camp by Alceo Ercolani. Followed orders, ran the camp efficiently, harsh on some, lenient toward others, especially local Jews, and arranged for which Jews would be sent in each transport to Fossoli to be deported. His son was a local Resistance leader, and his daughter was engaged to a Jew.

## MEN OF THE CHURCH

*Bishop Stanislao Battistelli*, from Teramo near Ancona, Bishop of Pitigliano and Sovana. Publicly castigated local Christians in his sermons for socializing with Jews, but secretly protected some elderly Jews by arranging for the doctors to hide them in the hospital, and others by creating false baptismal certificates. Participated in four sessions of the Second Vatican Council, and may have voted on the liberal document "Nostra Aetate."

*Bishop Paolo Galeazzi*, from Umbria, Bishop of Grosseto for forty years. A conservative type whose passion was building churches, he cultivated good relations with important Fascist figures in Rome and accommodated the governor of the province when asked to rent out his summer seminary for use as a concentration camp. Some have claimed that he saved Jews, but we examine the record in detail.

*Don Omero Martino*, a priest in Pitigliano on friendly terms with Azeglio Servi and family.

# Acknowledgments

At the risk of forgetting someone who has been essential to the book, I would like to acknowledge profound debts to the following friends and colleagues who have helped along the way: first all those who have granted interviews and consented to conversations (see the attached list), often multiple times. I'd like to single out Ariel Paggi not only for granting a long two-part interview and conversations about his own experiences as a hidden Jewish child, but also for generously sharing his at the time unpublished research, summaries of his own interviews with rescuers and rescued, his statistical tables and lists of names of foreign and local Jews involved in the events of the time. In addition, Helen and Raffaello Marsili, loyal friends who have helped so much, Rut (Ester, Cristina) Passigli Lichtner z"l and Israel (Rudi) Lichtner who were the first people to invite and introduce us to Pitigliano, who hosted us on that occasion and subsequent visits, imbued me with their enthusiasm, and who helped in innumerable ways. Prof. David Meghnagi for advice and for the opportunity to lecture on this topic at the University Roma Tre, Program in Shoah Education; Elisabetta Peri (Pitigliano municipal archives), Dottoressa Adamati (church archives in Pitigliano), Dottoressa Gemini (state archives in Grosseto), Dr. Silvia Antonucci who introduced me to the Jewish archives in Rome, and several other people who have generously facilitated access to archives or otherwise helped: Dottoressa Luciana Rocchi of ISGREC (Istituto di Studi Grossetani sulla Resistenza e l'Epoca Contemporanea) who patiently shared her research and has supported my work in many ways; Adolfo Turbanti of ISGREC who has shared his wise opinions and took off several hours to take me to visit Ribolla and Roccatederighi; Mark Lazerson, a most helpful friend who drove me from Roccatederighi to Pitigliano and has helped in the search for Egon Mosbach's paintings; Khanh and Franco Batzella, generous friends and hosts; Judith Saphra and David Saphra z"l, more than cousins; the Mazzoli family of Pitigliano for many kindnesses and for making their Albergo della Valle Orientina feel like a second home; Jürgen Matthäus, Martin Dean, Jan Lambertz, Suzanne Brown-Fleming, Steven Feldman of USHMM (United States Holocaust Memorial Museum) for their initial encouragement of this project and expert advice; librarians at the Library of Congress and at the USHMM; as well as at the Dorot Foundation Division at the New York Public Library, and the American Jewish Joint Distribution Committee Archives in New York (in particular Isabelle Rohr). Professor Jane Gerber; Guido Guastalla of Belforte Press; Naor Meningher, film-maker; the late Marcella Servi Siegel z"l, for patiently granting several interviews, and for being above all a friend; Elena Servi, for interviews and unstinting support over two decades, and the staff of La Piccola Gerusalemme; the late mayor of Pitigliano, Augusto Brozzi; Angelo Piatelli; Laura Paggini; Deborah Manion; Giacomo Lichtner; Elaine Levine; Gabriella Pizzetti; Michael Gibson and Becca Beurer of Lexington Books and Ananth Rengaraj and Jehanne Schweitzer for their belief in my project and efficient shepherding of it through the publication process; the late Edda Servi Machlin z"l; Vivienne Roumani-Denn for generously sharing interviews and my daughter Elisa for transcribing them; and all the other friends and colleagues who have shown interest in this project. My anonymous readers and reviewers for all comments critical or laudatory, but especially for the former, which I hope will have been given the weight they deserve in my final version. To Dr. Annette Fromm, for her timely, critical and constructive comments. My patient children, Elisa and David, who found that many of what they thought were going to be family vacations in Italy instead turned into history hunts pursuing their mother's enduring obsession. Above all, to my dear late husband Jacques Roumani z"l, without whom none of this, starting with a connection with Italy, the Italian language, and the Italian Jewish community, could have ever been possible.

# A Short Introduction

As the few survivors of the generation of survivors of the Shoah gradually leave us, what do they leave us with? History pure and simple is very hard to find: some neo-Nazis, neo-Fascists, and Islamists say the Holocaust never happened; victims are no longer here to tell us what they suffered. Survivors, rescuers, witnesses, and bystanders as well as collaborators each has their own version of the facts. Many individuals fall under more than one of these categories. This book deals with a hitherto somewhat neglected corner of Holocaust history: the province of Grosseto, the southern tip of Tuscany. The myth-making about responsibilities, and about who exactly was a hero, and who a villain, has continued unabated over the seven decades since the end of World War II.

Not very much happened in the province of Grosseto, when compared with the rest of Europe, and yet everything happened in this corner of Italy. Holocaust history here has two faces. Local tenant farmers and their families risked their lives to hide the local Jews of Pitigliano during 1943 and 1944, when Fascists and Nazis were trying to arrest them, and many turned the other way pretending not to see the Jews. An internment or concentration camp (in Italian, campo di concentramento) was established, under the aegis of the Fascist head of the province and the bishop. Almost a hundred Jews, some local and many foreign, were arrested or presented themselves for arrest under the impression that the church would give them protection. This appears to have been one of the very few instances in Europe of church property that had not been requisitioned, being provided, or rented out for what was in fact a waystation to Auschwitz. And the local bishop was in residence and saw it all, perhaps even collaborated in deciding which Jews were to be handed over. About two-thirds of the Jews living in the camp were sent first to Fossoli de Carpi near Modena or to another nearby transit camp, Scipione, near Salsomaggiore, and then to Auschwitz, where almost forty perished. These numbers are infinitesimal compared with the murder of six million. The illusions of these Jews, however, and the emerging collaboration of local Fascists and others with the Nazi project, confirm why the original credence given to the "Italiani brava gente" ("We Italians are good folk") narrative has recently been called into question. A typical example of this narrative was expressed in a private letter now in the American Jewish Joint Distribution Committee Archives, from Harold Tittmann, a high-ranking American diplomat assigned to the Vatican who had been closely involved in wartime events, to a Mr. Leavitt, who in 1962 had just sent him the book *Jews under the Italian Occupation* (Piakov, 1955). Tittmann comments that the book "shows clearly that the Italians if left alone would not have persecuted the Jews." Such blanket absolutions were cherished for a long time, but have not held up to more searching scrutiny. Angelo Del Boca is one Italian scholar who in 2005 decisively punctured the myth, with his *Italiani, brava gente? Un mito duro a morire,* referring to Italy's mistreatment of her colonized populations and other overseas atrocities.[1] Michele Sarfatti, in an article entitled "Did the Germans do it all?" details many instances of deliberate Fascist policy close to home, such as the extreme racial laws starting in 1938, even before Mussolini's close alliance with Hitler. This was the sea change in Italians' attitudes to Jews after years of anti-Semitic propaganda, and culminated in active collaboration with Nazis on many levels to effect deportations and the Final Solution. One might also ask "Did Mussolini do it all?" with regard to Italian antisemitism. In answer to this David Kertzer has shown that indeed he did not; the foundations were laid over the centuries by anti-Jewish propaganda emanating from the Catholic church that enveloped Italians. Simon Levis Sullam's *The Italian Executioners: The Genocide of the Jews of Italy* (2018) virtually seals off the possibility of blaming it all on the Germans. Giacomo Lichtner in *Fascism in Italian Cinema since 1945* (2013), in a chapter entitled "Black Shirts, Hearts of Gold: Recurrent Memories" gives an excellent description of how the myth took hold after the war in Italy, inspired by and inspiring Italian cinema, thus perpetuating the narrative. The "brava gente" myth, though dented, survives today internationally, as well as in Italy both on a national level and on the local level, where even after three-quarters of a century old myths die hard, and personalities, relationships, loyalties, and feuds still have their hold. Lichtner makes the interesting point that forgetting (presumably the things of which one is ashamed) is also part of remembering, or of constructing memories.

Thus, this study, if it belongs to any genre of historiography, might fall into the well-trodden paths of the *Annales* school of history, prevalent for several generations in France and Italy. The school's focus is on regional microhistory, the relationship of geography to people, and is particularly well-suited to the subject matter herein.

Personally, I would have loved to subscribe to the truth of the "brava gente" narrative. In 2001, the Jewish Institute of Pitigliano was created to celebrate and propagate the Jewish culture of Pitigliano and the history of good relations between Jews and local Christians. Another goal was to help bring Jews to Pitigliano to revive Jewish culture. With the assistance of many kind people, Jews and non-Jews, several types of cultural activity were initiated. The most recent was this book, which has evolved from an uncritical celebration into an appreciation of the complexities of the past, the further twists fomented by stakeholders, and my eventual understanding that history and memory may never reveal the truth and neatly assign heroism and guilt. There are many humble heroes, some high-placed villains, and a large number who fit into neither category or perhaps both.

In fact, scholars over the last two decades or so have done a good job of discrediting the "brava gente" myth in the national field. I do not claim this effort as my intellectual achievement, except perhaps on a local level where relationships and motives have retained their continuity while merging with newer concerns extraneous to the Shoah. Since this book is a study in microhistory, it does not necessarily offer insights except in a very limited way into the big issues of the period, such as antisemitism, Fascism, the Vatican's view of Jews, or when or why Mussolini turned to totalitarianism, racism, and antisemitism. On the last topic, I offer some tentative thoughts in chapter 2. Certainly events in the Italian colonies did not directly impact the Jews in the province of Grosseto, but the latter clearly suffered the consequences of the growing atmosphere of racism and antisemitism. Many scholars maintain that it is not possible to pinpoint a specific cause for anti-Jewish sentiment and the turn to racism in Italy. Social and political forces merged with antisemitic rationalizations to scapegoat Jews and eventually conjure up images of a fifth column of internal enemies of the state.

I have tried to be cognizant of the many studies of Italian Jewry, the Fascist period, and the Holocaust, by both Italian and foreign scholars. My reading has extended among the former to Renzo De Felice, Michele Sarfatti, Giorgio Israel, Giovanni Miccoli, David Bidussa, Angelo Del Boca, Valeria Galimi, Liliana Picciotto, Carlo Spartaco Capogreco, Simon Levis Sullam, and others, and several local historians listed in the notes and bibliography. Renzo De Felice, publishing in 1961, only sixteen years after the end of the regime, first had the courage to confront the Fascist period. He has provided many occasions for later historians to correct his views, such as his belief that Mussolini was not a racist. Carlo Spartaco Capogreco, by bringing the world's attention to the buried history of Mussolini's network of internment camps, has done more than many to expose the erroneous basis of the "Italiani brava gente" myth, as have historians such as David Bidussa and Angelo Del Boca who have examined Italy's record as a colonial power. Guri Schwarz has memorably examined the "after Mussolini" postwar period in which healing came (if at all) with great difficulty for Jews, in an uncomprehending Italy. Foreign historians such as Susan Zuccotti, Alexander Stille, David Kertzer, Michael Livingston, Shira Klein, have also addressed the myth of the good Italian and Italy's record as an Axis power as well as competing assessments of Pope Pius XII's behavior. Shriller moral assessments have given way to an effort to understand the context of the time, without necessarily making excuses.

Much of this volume is based on interviews, eye-witness accounts, and oral histories. These have become, over the decades, one of the most important sources of Holocaust history.[2] But witnesses can edit, sugarcoat, and romanticize their testimony. While empathizing with those who kindly allowed me to interview them, I have tried to be aware of the limitations of oral testimonies, especially those recorded many years after the events.

This book is a study of a very restricted area, the province of Grosseto, the southernmost province of Tuscany. Other locations are largely not included, except insofar as certain phenomena might have been expected to impact our province. For example, there is some discussion of Livorno, because the Jewish community of Pitigliano has been closely linked with it, and Florence is mentioned as the capital of the region and a city where many Catholic clergy mobilized to help Jews. It is largely for the reader, or historian, to make comparisons with other areas that were under the control of the Nazis or Nazi allies. I only refer in passing for example to Poland, where 90 percent of Jews perished, including those who had sought to hide. One could more fruitfully compare Italy with France where 75 percent of Jews, both foreign and French, survived. In Italy, 80 percent of Jews survived the Nazi occupation and deportations to death camps. This figure is, indeed, a relatively high number of survivors compared with Germany and Eastern Europe. It is, however, on a par with France,[3] which was under the Nazis for five years, while Italy was occupied by Germany for only eighteen months. Many of the cases Jacques Semelin describes in France are similar to the Italian situation: a helping hand here and there; an ostensible collaborator who deep down resents the German occupation and is a French patriot; totally dedicated, fearless Jewish and Christian volunteers; rescue networks set up by Jewish organizations and sometimes involving clerics. We shall see how much of this applies also to Italy, and specifically to the province of Grosseto.

Memory has played a most important role in the making of history in recent decades, hence in public awareness, in its relation to *"lieux de mémoire"* (places of memory) created or restored all over Europe. So has selective amnesia, however. Thus, mention should be made of Enzo Traverso's classic *Le Passé, modes d'emploi: Histoire, mémoire, politique* (2005),[4] a little text that summarizes and explains this trend. In Grosseto province, the synagogue of Pitigliano, and the former Jewish community's premises, have become one of those places of memory, whereas the internment camp at Roccatederighi has become in contrast a place of forgetting. As Giacomo Lichtner has stated, "Amnesia was the cardinal ingredient of German and Italian memory. And, thanks to this rigorous and unwavering effort, the defeated countries thrived, building new identities on a mixture of denial, selective remembering, and invention, of a carefully managed historical legacy."[5] Both the positive and the negative sides of local memory and history with regard to refuge provided for Jews have contributed to this situation, and led to our chosen subtitle, "ambiguous refuge."

Holocaust memory over the past seven decades since 1943–1944 has been affected by the culture of the Holocaust both in the United States and Italy. In this study, I deliberately bring in references to Italian literature of the Holocaust and Fascism by writers such as Alberto Moravia, Ignazio Silone, Giorgio Bassani, Primo Levi, and Elsa Morante, as well as novelists writing sensitively for newer generations, such as the prize-winning Lia Levi and the new Livornese novelist Laura Paggini. Literary historians develop a sensitivity to textual incongruities and even silences that can be applied equally to archival documentation in which an official may be concealing the real facts and trying to produce something in conformity with the expected narrative of the time. A memoir by a former child eyewitness written many years later can slide into drawing upon archives or published sources, and next into unsubstantiated assertions, based on a narrative established later.

Holocaust literature, including fiction, however, also has an important role in education for the next generations. The same, perhaps even more so, applies to film. It is no longer possible for a historian to view the past through completely innocent or objective eyes, given the reams of written and filmed cultural production over the intervening decades. Even survivors and eyewitnesses have had their own memories unconsciously colored and influenced by others, or by the rhetoric of the media, in the meantime. But the injustice, the pain, and the suffering were horribly real, as were the lingering consequences for damaged lives. Under our guise of modern relativism, even when we examine the Holocaust on such a microlevel as the province of Grosseto, we cannot allow the intervening culture to rob us of our compassion and outrage.

## NOTES

1. Personally I had been made aware of Italian cruelty to colonized populations, in particular the setting up of concentration camps for rebellious Libyan tribes in Cyrenaica and starvation of the population, by Jacques Roumani's research in Italian

colonial archives, published in his Ph.D. dissertation, "The Emergence of Modern Libya: Political Traditions and Colonial Change," Princeton University, 1987.

2. Annette Wieviorka in *L'ère du témoin* 1998 (Paris: Fayard/Pluriel, 2013) shows us how from the earliest witness accounts, testimony, even when influenced by later trends, has become paramount, especially exemplified by the Spielberg Archives. The "wonder of their voices" of the earliest recorded testimonies (Alan Rosen, *The Wonder of their Voices: The 1946 Holocaust Interviews of David Boder*, Oxford: Oxford University Press, 2010) has given way to repeated interviews and set formats. But we still need and value the immediacy and personal contact of interviews and testimonies. Some who have remained silent for many decades decide in their last years to open up and share their memories. Who knows what may be still learned at this late hour?

3. For France, see Jacques Semelin, *Persécutions et entreaides dans la France occupée: Comment 75% des juifs en France ont échappé à la mort* (Paris: Seuil—Les Arènes, 2013), passim.

4. Enzo Traverso, *Le Passé, modes d'emploi: Histoire, mémoire, politique* (Paris: La Fabrique, 2005).

5. Giacomo Lichtner, *Fascism in Italian Cinema Since 1945: The Politics and Aesthetics of Memory* (Basingstoke and New York: Palgrave Macmillan, 2013), p. 11.

*Chapter 1*

# Pitigliano and Other Cities of Refuge for Jews in Southern Tuscany over the Centuries

### ORIGINS

A muffled, bent-over figure bestride a donkey struggles up the last turns of the zigzag path that leads into Count Orsini's fortress, which glowers darkly over the surrounding Tuscan landscape.[1] Behind comes another donkey, on which the rider's equally muffled wife sits, tears still drying on her cheeks. A servant or porter with a donkey loaded with pots and pans, blankets and, incongruously, many books follows behind them. To the walls of the fortress cling small lean-to hovels, the houses of the feudal lord's peasants. It is 1556, and the renowned Jewish physician and rabbi David De Pomis is fleeing persecution by the pope in Rome and arriving with his young wife at the invitation of Count Niccolo Orsini to take refuge and residence in Pitigliano. The count, who is delighted to have a family doctor and experienced financial adviser, grants the couple the right to stay. They are soon joined by their family and other Jewish refugees. The wife, whose name has not come down to us, dies a few years later in Pitigliano despite her husband's tender care. Like the patriarch Abraham, the rabbi purchases a field (actually a precariously steep hillside) near the fortress, in which to bury his wife (figure 1.1). Since he soon receives an invitation to reside elsewhere, he moves on a few years later, ultimately to Venice, where he will write with gratitude in his memoirs about Pitigliano, his "città-rifugio" (city of refuge). Rabbi Doctor David De Pomis has founded the Jewish community of Pitigliano.[2]

Such is the narrative of the founding of this community, but researchers have recently discovered that the actual situation was far more complex. It is not surprising that this founding legend has adhered to the figure of the eminent rabbi and doctor. Historians now tell us, though, that Jews were living, perhaps intermittently, in these wild borderlands at least a hundred years

**Figure 1.1** Terraced Four-and-a-Half-Century-Old Jewish Cemetery in Pitigliano.
*Source*: Photo by Judith Roumani, 2018.

earlier. The marshy, hilly, and forested region of Maremma lies just north and west of the Papal States, at the southernmost tip of Tuscany bordering on the flatter Lazio region of Rome, the Latium of Roman times. The hillsides were long the lands of the Etruscans, who obviously gave their name to Tuscany. Their ruined fortresses and sunken roads still scatter the landscape in abundance. By the Middle Ages the area was a magnet for small warlords who would occupy a hill and pile up rocks into a fortress from which to command their surroundings. One nickname for Pitigliano is "la Rocca." These hills and forests harbored smugglers and bandits, too. The Orsini counts[3] were preceded by the Aldobrandeschi, who may have also provided refuge to Jewish refugees. For example, there was a certain Abramo di Aleuccio in Pitigliano in 1430, a century before David De Pomis.[4]

It is hard to imagine that Jews would migrate to such places unless they felt themselves in real danger. Jews generally, then as now, have needed a community for all their ritual, spiritual, and physical needs. A Jewish settlement existed in Castro at that time, just across the border in Lazio, in papal lands, as well as others in a number of small towns, now villages, along the border, such as Farnese, Latera, Onano, Sorano, Sovana, Piancastagnaio, and in Scansano toward Grosseto. All were documented as having Jews both before and after the presence of David De Pomis in Pitigliano.

Several semi-independent fiefdoms, in defiance of both the popes in Rome and the archdukes of Tuscany (based in Florence), ruled the border area. The Orsini ruled in Pitigliano and surrounding towns, the Farnese family ruled the duchy of Castro and Farnese, the Sforza family held the hilly area of Scansano, and the Ottieri held yet another area (Castellottieri).

The current provincial capital, Grosseto, in the lowlands northeast of Pitigliano, must have been a tiny village; it has remained rather small. It is located in a marshy, malarial area that had declined greatly since Roman times and suffered great loss of life in the Black Death. It does not seem to have attracted any Jews at this time. Travelers to Rome in the Middle Ages always preferred to travel the Roman Via Cassia through the central hills, rather than risk the route through insalubrious marshes near the coast.

The eminent doctor was from Spoleto and had recently been living and teaching at the yeshiva of Magliano, just north of Rome. What drove him to leave was the infamous papal bull, "Cum nimis absurdum" issued by Pope Paul IV in 1555.[5] The pope found it absurd that Jews should be living freely in his realms, which stretched as far east and north as the port city of Ancona. He must have wished to follow in the footsteps of the Venetians, who had imposed the first ghetto in 1516, a "success" in terms of suitably humiliating and restricting Jews. All Jews in papal lands were forced to sell their property and cluster into the ghetto of Rome or Ancona. They were also forbidden to engage in any profession except rag-trading. Thus, they were reduced to poverty. Many fled the repressive conditions, finding refuge in the small towns of the independent fiefdoms north of Lazio and south of the Duchy of Tuscany, as we have seen. David De Pomis encouraged a number of relatives to follow him to Pitigliano and, though he left after five years, the relatives stayed on. Sixty years later two of his nephews and their families are documented in the area.[6] The counts and marquises of the area found their Jewish guests invaluable; they provided loan banks, medical care, crafts, and stimulated trade in such merchandise as grain and textiles.

By the end of the sixteenth century about a hundred Jews were living in Pitigliano. Under the Orsini they were able to own animals, houses, and even land. They built a synagogue in 1598. The independence of the Orsini was threatened, though, as the local municipality had petitioned Archduke Cosimo I to remove the family, due to mismanagement and corruption,[7] already in 1561; they were finally removed in 1608.[8] Niccolo Orsini was eventually put on trial, and a Jew called Cherubino was one of those who testified against him:

> Count Niccolo IV Orsini was a very, shall we say, disconcerting character. He obtained rule over the county in 1547 by means of a *congiura* (ban) banishing his father. After that he ruled somewhat as a tyrant, committing crimes and abuses of various kinds. He chased away the monks from the monasteries and turned churches into warehouses and stables for horses, and things of that sort. And he also had Jewish lovers. There was a young Jewish girl from Sorano called Brunetta, the only daughter of a mother called Ricca, and others, including some from the family of Cherubino. The latter seems to have been a sort of pawnbroker, and Niccolo sequestered all his possessions, and forced him to go away. So these were some of the crimes for which Niccolo was put on trial.[9]

## GHETTO PERIOD

Under the Medici archdukes Talmud burnings began to be staged in Tuscany, the privileges of the Jews were reduced and, since the Medici wanted to please the popes, ghettos were introduced in some towns in southern Tuscany: in Sorano in 1619, and in Pitigliano finally in 1622. Pitigliano's Jewish loan bank had been closed down in 1608, to be replaced by a Christian-managed Monte Pio, and other restrictions were placed on Jewish businesses. The Jews of Pitigliano had to pay the expenses for building two large fountains, the soaring archways carrying the aqueduct to the fountains, the walls and gates necessary to create a ghetto, and to cap it all, *il colmo*, as Italians say, six *scudi* every month for the salaries of two *sbirri* (policemen) to guard them.[10] At least the Jews of Pitigliano and Sorano were not forced to move into the ghettos of Siena or Florence, though their main sources of business were forbidden, and they became steadily impoverished. Also during the latter half of the sixteenth and the early seventeenth centuries, the other numerous Jewish loan banks of the region were shut down, and replaced by church-run *monti di pietà*. Though some Jews left, the community of Pitigliano continued to grow, as Jews abandoned the smaller, older nearby communities and moved in. In particular, the town of Castro just across the border with Lazio was destroyed in war, and the entire community moved to Pitigliano.[11]

Some of the harsher measures were later relaxed. Despite their apparent severity, the Medici appreciated the economic contribution the Jews were making in Pitigliano. They probably saw some value in the community as a way-station on the route to the new Medici port town of Livorno in northwest Tuscany. There, Spanish and Portuguese former and current Jews had been invited to participate in creating the important new trading center and port, without the requirement or restrictions of living in a ghetto.

The relative proximity of this vibrant multiethnic port city must have already provided economic and cultural incentives for Jews in rural southern Tuscany, too, between the late sixteenth and the late nineteenth century. Jews in Livorno maintained trading networks all over the Mediterranean and as far as India for several centuries. Members of the community established outposts in Tunisia and Libya. Their synagogue was the second largest Sephardic synagogue in Europe and the *Collegio Rabbinico* supplied teachers for far-away communities. The Jewish publishing houses issued texts in Hebrew, Italian, Ladino, and Judeo-Arabic for the Mediterranean world and beyond. Indeed, the prayerbooks printed in Livorno were used in Pitigliano. When the small community no longer had a rabbi in the twentieth century, it became officially dependent on Livorno for its religious needs.

Though the Jews of Pitigliano at times benefited from isolation, they also soon become part of the vibrant trading, cultural, and social networks of Tuscany, centered on Florence and the bustling port of Livorno, a situation which lasted into the nineteenth century and beyond. Though the origin of many Pitigliano Jewish families was the ancient community of Rome, it is probable that some of the descendants of Sephardim from Iberia also made their way to southern Tuscany over the centuries and integrated into Pitigliano life. Thus local ties and more far-reaching ties combined to form their particular local Jewish culture.[12]

But becoming an off-shoot of the Livorno Community is still far in the future. Over the seventeenth century, some Jews of Pitigliano benefited from individual privileges that the Medici granted piecemeal, such as the right to own land, to live outside the ghetto if there was no suitable house within the ghetto, and to be exempted from the requirement to wear distinguishing clothing or signs. These individual exemptions seem to have been liberally granted, without affecting the overall Medici policy. In 1704, for example, Abramo Pergola was allowed to live outside the ghetto and also allowed to bear arms. It appears from the evidence of the elaborate 1714 Pitigliano ketuba[13] (figure 1.2) that several families, such as the Levis, the Gallichi, and the Pergolas, must have been comfortably well off by the early eighteenth century. The majority of the Jewish community members, however, were simple, relatively poor craftsmen. During the eighteenth century, when the House of Lorraine took over from the Medici and ruled with interruptions until the mid-nineteenth century, the liberalization continued and expanded.

Among the various small Jewish communities of the borderlands, Sorano as well as others near Pitigliano were still in existence in the 1700s. Sorano's ghetto had been installed in 1619 by Duke Cosimo II. The small Jewish

Figure 1.2 *Ketuba* from Pitigliano, 1714. A Marriage between the Gallichi and the Levi Families. *Source*: Courtesy of Bnai Brith Klutznick Museum, Washington DC, gift of Joseph B. and Olyn Horwitz.

community consisted of textile sellers, artisans, and an occasional money lender. A Jewish loan bank there as well as a few others dotted around the county and surrounding areas still existed about fifty years after the church's *monte di pietà* had been set up. Sorano's simple synagogue is in a private house.[14]

Sovana, another small nearby town, had also had a Jewish community in late medieval times and the sixteenth century, with a similar economic focus: textiles, crafts, and a loan bank. Sovana suffered greatly from war and malaria in the late sixteenth century. The grand dukes invited Jews to come and settle there in an attempt to revive the town, as Jews had been invited to settle in the insalubrious mosquito marshes of northern Tuscany to create the port town of Livorno. Manciano, a hill town near Pitigliano, had a small but flourishing Jewish community that persisted into the nineteenth and early twentieth century, even having a Jewish mayor in the late eighteenth century. Paggi,

Sorani, Servi, and Sadun were the main families, mostly related in some way to families with the same names in Pitigliano.[15] Manciano, however, does not seem to have had a synagogue. There were even a few Jews living from a later date in Grosseto, the provincial capital; they looked to Pitigliano for their religious needs, as we see below in the interview with Marco Servi of Grosseto. Almost all these small communities of southern Tuscany revolved around and eventually were largely absorbed into Pitigliano.

At this time, documentation exists of the Catholic Church elsewhere in Italy abducting and converting Jewish women and children. In 1673, in the nearby town of Piancastagnaio, Sara la Ebreina, a six-year-old Jewish girl, wandered into a church and was abducted by Christians. The local people became so enflamed about her potential conversion that they took up arms against the local Jews, who had to take refuge in the synagogue. A struggle over jurisdictions ensued between the local authorities, the church, and the archduke in Florence, who demanded that the child not be converted but be brought to Florence (where converted Jews often attended his court). The Jews did not dare reclaim the little girl. The child Sara was subsequently raised by an aristocratic family in Florence and eventually converted to Christianity at the age of twenty-four.[16]

Some attempted forced conversions in 1593 and 1602[17] are recorded in Pitigliano. There were several known instances of the local clergy there conducting extensive investigations into whether presumed candidates for conversion came forward of their own free will, and of the local church's reluctance to proceed in these cases.[18] Christians and Jews seem to have had close social relations at certain times in Pitigliano. Fraternizing did go on, judging from the regulations that were often introduced to forbid it.[19] It seems that as the Jewish community grew, and the townspeople also prospered, their general economic well-being allowed them to relate more as equals, though this is obviously only a partial explanation.

The Pitiglianese dialect of Tuscan included many words based on Hebrew, such as the word "gadollu" which means "good, big," or "schiahor" which means "bad," and these words were freely used even by local non-Jews. The story is still told of a peasant from Pitigliano who walked into a Jewish clothier's shop in Rome, asking for some material to make a wedding suit. He was shown some coarse, low-quality fabric that he rejected saying that he didn't want that "schiahor" (black, bad) stuff, he wanted some of the good fabric from up on the top shelf.[20] We can imagine the amazement of the Jewish shopkeeper when he heard Hebrew words coming from the mouth of the country peasant from Tuscany.

The incident most cited to emphasize the good relations between local Christians and local Jews occurred in 1799, as the French army was withdrawing. Though the French had inflicted hardship and famine, Napoleon had emancipated Italian Jews. A "Tree of Liberty" stood in the main square of Pitigliano. As the French withdrew and turned their attention to Egypt, the Viva Maria backlash—"I moti del Viva Maria"—swept in and mobs came in from Arezzo and Orvieto, attacking the small Jewish communities. In Pitigliano thirty-four people, either Jacobins or Jews accused of Jacobinism were arrested. The Siena Jewish community suffered particularly hard, as the mob attacked the ghetto, murdering and burning to death about thirteen Jews. The rabble moved south; more recruits were picked up in Orvieto. They arrived prepared to attack again in Pitigliano where they vandalized the synagogue and Jewish homes and insulted the rabbi by pulling his beard. Local Christian farmers returning from the fields rose to the defense of the Jews of Pitigliano. They fought off the out-of-towners with guns and pitchforks, killing four of them and arresting others. The Jews of Pitigliano were saved. In gratitude the day was named a local Purim, or Purim Katan. Poems were composed and the occasion continued to be marked for several generations.[21]

Soon thereafter, the ghetto was reimposed in Pitigliano and the grandukes were back in charge, to withdraw again in 1848 and then return again. Jews, however, gradually saw their rights increased, until the ghetto was finally abolished in the 1850s. The 1841 Lorraine census of Tuscany revealed Jews engaging in a broad variety of professions, from farming to trading and crafts; the Pitigliano community at the time supported no less than five kosher butchers.[22] Once more Pitigliano was under the grand duke of Tuscany, the benevolent Leopoldo II, who gave them equal rights from 1848 on, including for some the right to vote. Jews from Tuscany took part fully in the Risorgimento and the Unification of Italy, and after, with full rights, took advantage of new educational and professional opportunities.

Giuseppe Celata, on the basis of his research into the 1825 land registry, gives the names and details of a few Jews who owned both large and mostly small farms in the area around Pitigliano. He states: "With respect to rural property, the Jews of Pitigliano . . . were non-resident owners. They maintained farms in the area, which they leased to share-croppers up until the Second World War."[23]

A beautiful piece of embroidery, a *parochet*, or Torah Ark curtain (figure 1.3), was created in Pitigliano in 1834 by four young girls, one of whom was Rachele Modigliani, the aunt, or more probably great-aunt, of the famous painter Amedeo Modigliani.[24] The girls fasted all day as they worked, in order to create the *parochet* in an atmosphere of purity and holiness. It is embroidered with gold and silver threads, as well as colored silks on a silk cloth. It portrays the Tablets of the Law surrounded by flowers, birds, and butterflies, and was designed for and used on the festival of Shavuot. It is obviously the creation of a Jewish community that was flourishing at the time.[25]

**Figure 1.3 Parochet (Ark Curtain) of Pitigliano, 1834, Embroidered by Rachele Modigliani and Friends for the Festival of Shavuot.** *Source*: Photo courtesy of the late Vivian Mann and of the Jewish Museum of New York, gift of Edda and Marcella Servi.

## EQUALITY

Though Pitigliano acquired an excellent Jewish elementary school, funded by a bequest from the siblings Giuseppe and Fortunata Consiglio (antique dealers in Florence, formerly of Pitigliano) in 1855, Jews could not pursue further education in the town. Just as the community reached its height, with a Jewish population in 1858 of 424, about 13 percent of the town's total population, many young Jewish people began to leave for the big cities, Livorno, Florence, and Rome, mainly to pursue educational opportunities. This tendency can also be seen as part of the increased mobility of Italians in general at the time. The Jews did not forget their origins, though, and many families and individuals returned over the decades for the important Jewish holidays. In the latter half of the nineteenth century, freedom and greater opportunity enabled the Jewish community to continue prospering, even though the lure of the big city was already sapping it of its young people. Jews, both the Consiglio family and others, made many important contributions to the town in the late nineteenth and early twentieth centuries.[26] Perhaps it was in the mid-nineteenth century, when the Jewish population of the town was numerically at its height, that Pitigliano came to be known as "la Piccola Gerusalemme"—the Little Jerusalem. Or perhaps it was due to the positive interactions and solidarity between Christians and Jews.

The good relations were upset by certain minor convulsions in the 1870s due to mismanagement of the funds in the Consiglio Foundation. The chief administrator was arrested, and there was apparently an attempt to replace its Jewish administrators with Christians and to remove it from affiliation with the Jewish community and its needs. It was saved by intervention from the central Jewish institutions in Rome and continued to provide education for Jews, whether wealthy or poor.[27]

Jewish-Christian cooperation and friendship continued in the later nineteenth century and early twentieth century, in which pastimes and interests were essentially shared. A well-known member of the Paggi family, Salomone Paggi, may have typified leisure-time interactions between the two groups. He was famous in all of Maremma for his appetite: he ate and drank prodigious quantities, including omelettes made of forty eggs. Paggi also excelled at the game of La Ruota, which consisted in rolling a large parmigiano cheese through the streets of Pitigliano, and then probably eating it.[28] In times of extreme drought, for example, in 1893, practicing Christians would come and pray in the synagogue for rain (Salvadori, *La Comunitá ebraica* p. 92). Another less likely version of this story tells of Jews and Christians walking in procession to pray together for rain in a small church, La Madonna delle Grazie, just outside town. Franco Paioletti, in *Pitigliano dal Risorgimento al primo Novecento* brings a number of small and large instances of such good relations. Pitigliano honored its prominent Jews, such as Angiolo Servi, the assistant rabbi, who was a proud member of the Corpo Armonico Populare, the local marching band. When he died in 1893, he was honored at his funeral by the marching band itself. Also honored a decade and a half later were the Jewish soldiers who fought or fell in World War I, such as the hero Diulio Bemporad, who had also previously seen combat in Libya in 1911 and died at the battle of the Carso, near Trieste.[29] The soldiers were welcomed home in an official ceremony organized by the Jewish Abramo Moscati, *consigliere comunale,* a member of the town council.[30] Many other Jewish names are mentioned in Paioletti's anthology of newspaper articles and documents.[31]

Ariel Paggi mentions a Jewish wedding, which took place in 1928 between the war veteran Arrigo Sadun and Anita Servi and which was attended by several dignitaries: the mayor of Pitigliano, the historian Giuseppe Bruscalupi, and the director of the hospital, Dr. Bruno Bognomini. This Sadun family by then had a business and resided in Latera, in the neighboring province of Viterbo. Other family members had also moved to nearby towns where the economy at that time was better than in Pitigliano.

An important representative of Italian culture and education since 1876, in Libya, colonized in 1911, Giannetto Paggi (who grew up in Pitigliano) received a state funeral, in 1916.[32] The local newspaper and publishing house, *La Lente* (named after the river very close to Pitigliano), was founded by Osvaldo Paggi, a Jew. Osvaldo Paggi's marriage, the first non-religious marriage in Pitigliano, caused some scandal. Rabbi Camerini, the rabbi of the time, made common cause with the bishop in condemning it. Osvaldo was greatly admired, though, and became deputy mayor. When invited, he declined to run as a candidate for the position of mayor. Osvaldo may have found Pitigliano a little too provincial, as he moved his publishing activities first to Grosseto where he was editor of *Etruria Nuova* for a few years, and later to Florence where he reestablished La Lente publishing and printing house.[33]

The Jewish sons of Pitigliano who achieved some intellectual prominence, however, seem to have done so elsewhere, finding the opportunities in southern Tuscany too limited. Another scion of Pitigliano was Rabbi Dante Lattes, a prominent Italian Jewish intellectual who founded *Israel,* one of the first Zionist periodicals of Italy. Dante Lattes left Pitigliano at a young age to study in Livorno, in the school of Elia Benamozegh, the "last Kabbalist," and was active from the 1920s, editing his journal, organizing and speaking at conferences, publishing two volumes of a work called *Sionismo* explaining Zionism to Italian Jews, and initially attempting to persuade the Mussolini government that a pro-Zionist policy would be to its advantage. He pursued a peripatetic career as a major Jewish intellectual, living in Trieste, Florence, Rome and several other Italian cities (as well as Tel Aviv and Jerusalem). He is buried in Padua near one of his mentors, Samuel David Luzzatto. Similar demographic trends were also affecting ambitious Christians of rural Italy at the time.

The photograph of the entire Jewish community at the Bagni degli Ebrei, the thermal baths designed and constructed by Jews, about three kilometers out of town, in the Valle Orientina, in about 1910 shows some of the paradoxes of the turn-of-the-century Jewish community. The baths were probably built at a time when indoor bathrooms still did not exist; Jews appreciated the scientifically approved health benefits of thermal baths. There was also a small outdoor pool, divided into two parts for women and men, where Jewish boys learned to swim. Though it has been surmised that these baths were built to serve as a *mikva*, it is unlikely to have often been used as such. Women who needed the *mikva* after nightfall would likely be reluctant to travel so far out of town.[34]

In the meantime, though, since Jews now had equal rights and the same freedom of movement as Christians, we witness a precipitous demographic decline. Rather than stay in this remote and still somewhat backward little town, Jews were emigrating to the larger centers of Livorno, Florence, and Rome for many reasons. Already in 1910 *La Settimana israelitica* reported that a total of sixty Jews remained in Pitigliano, though it is not clear whether this figure is Jewish males, or heads of families, or total Jewish population including women and children (probably the latter). The publication also suggested that the community would disappear in a few decades and advocated its merging with some other larger Jewish community in Tuscany,[35] which is what did eventually happen.

Pitigliano's remoteness was still very tangible in the early 1900s, as the projected railway line was never built. The first car arrived to great fanfare in Pitigliano in 1902, and a bus service, actually converted World War I camions, was not established until 1924.

After a succession of young rabbis at the beginning of their careers, many of whom contributed valiantly (despite a continuing risk of malaria, which one contracted) to Jewish education in the town, Pitigliano was left without a rabbi after 1924. For forty years the assistant rabbi maintained Jewish life there. Abramo Disegni, an elderly rabbi, was in residence for a few years in the later 1930s, until he and his family left for Palestine. In 1931, in a national reorganization of Jewish religious institutions that was part of the Vatican's agreement with the state, Pitigliano's Jewish Community had fallen under the jurisdiction of Livorno, which is still the case today. Jews were increasingly abandoning tradition, moreover: for example in the cemetery at least two tombstones are adorned with statues, in the Christian manner. A few cases of intermarriage with Christians, initially Jewish men marrying Christian women, began to show up.[36] I do not imply that intermarriage, at least at that time, necessarily implied assimilation to the Christian majority. One can assume that the Jewish men who married non-Jewish women, confident in their identity at that time, often had sincere intentions to maintain their personal faith, and not to assimilate, but over the decades, and in the next generation, especially with the effects of the Holocaust, such assimilation did frequently happen. Paradoxically, at the time intermarriage was one fruit of the excellent social relations that continued to prevail between the two faiths. The Paggi brothers, who founded the publishing house, La Lente, and were considered intellectual leaders of the community, justified secular marriage before the community. Secularism and intermarriage began to take a toll. We should not forget, though, that this was a time of great optimism, confidence, a sense of adventure among Jews who were mostly secure in their identity, and willing to open new though perhaps risky paths.

After the mid-1920s, there must have been a deep intellectual split between progressives and traditionalists within the community. Those Jews who considered themselves more progressive often moved away, in any case: such was the outcome with Osvaldo Paggi's family. The assistant rabbi, Azeglio Servi, labored to maintain religious services and Jewish needs such as *kashrut*.[37] His daughters Edda and Marcella Servi described how their family did not often have meat to eat, because by the time they were growing up in the 1920s and 1930s, the community had dwindled so much that it did not make sense for their father, the *shohet*, to slaughter a sheep or a cow for the few families remaining; compare this with 1841, when the community provided livelihood for five kosher butchers. Those who had moved away often returned during the 1920s and 1930s for the High Holidays and Passover and for family events such as Bar Mitzvahs when the synagogue functioned. Eventually attendance dwindled even more until there were only services for Yom Kippur. Pitigliano still served as a reference point for Jews of neighboring towns, though, as Marco Servi of Grosseto writes that in 1938 his Bar Mitzvah was celebrated in Pitigliano, his mother invited "all of Pitigliano" and the entire community attended.[38]

However, as can be seen from the picture taken at another Bar Mitzvah, two years earlier, in 1936,[39] (figure 1.4) those who remained presented the aspect of a very lively and cohesive group. The rhythms of Jewish life continued in Pitigliano. In particular, the magical excitement of descending into a sort of cave where the matza oven is located (still visible today) and baking matza in ornate designs and other baked sweets for Passover as evoked in old photographs and by Edda Servi in her cookbooks. The measure of the residual trust between Jews and Christians can be seen in her remembrance, when as a teenager she found herself having boyfriend problems. To whom did the daughter of the prominent Jewish family, pillars of tradition, turn as late as mid-1943 for advice in this delicate matter? She went to her parent's friend, the local priest, to receive some comfort.[40]

There was thus a great deal of goodwill, based on the close and usually cordial relations between Jews and non-Jews over the previous four centuries. A few of the elderly Christian inhabitants of the area still remember when there was a functioning Jewish community and many express warm memories of their Jewish neighbors. I, myself, about to give a speech at the opening of an exhibit of Jewish arts in 2002, was suddenly greeted in the street by an elderly lady wearing a large cross around her neck who most warmly said that she had fond memories of when the Jews were there and that her own mother had actually been Jewish. Vera Paggi, the author of a 2013 book on the Paggis of Pitigliano, interviewed elderly non-Jews in the area and expresses it thus:

> On other occasions I received from elderly locals testimonies of pleasant memories about some Paggi. A Paggi who was an elementary schoolteacher for example would go to their home in the evenings to teach everyone to read and write. Lilio Niccolai, born in Manciano in 1925, a historian, politician, former

**Figure 1.4   Bar Mitzvah in Pitigliano, 1936.** *Source*: Courtesy of Ariel Paggi.

mayor of Manciano, the son of modest farmers, in 1999 wrote a book about his family, *Appunti di cronaca famigliare*, in which among other things he tells how when he was a child he fell gravely ill and how the Sadun family made sure he was cared for until he got well. The Jews in Maremma are remembered with pleasure.[41]

Thus, the 1938 racial laws took most Jews in Pitigliano and in the rest of southern Tuscany as a complete surprise, a bolt from the blue.

## NOTES

1. Giuseppe Romani completed a beautiful series of twenty-one architectural etchings *of La Rocca degli Aldobrandeschi e degli Orsini in Pitigliano 1290–1865* (Pitigliano: Stampa ATLA, 1983). I am very grateful to the Romani family for providing a set of these. Browsing through them, one has a very good idea of how the fortress and the town must have grown over the centuries.

2. Many travel articles repeat and perpetuate this narrative. For example, Abby Ellin, "In Tuscany, a Jewish Heritage," *New York Times*, November 25, 2012, p. 8, which erroneously describes Pitigliano as "a tiny, medieval village." It is a small town rather than a tiny village and dates mostly from the Renaissance. Such articles written after a one day visit to Pitigliano are often accompanied by gorgeous, glossy photos of the town, and luscious pictures of its Jewish foods.

3. In *Gli Ebrei a Pitigliano: La Piccola Gerusalemme* ed. Angelo Biondi, with parallel Eng. trans. by Steven Siporin (Grotte di Castro: Tipografia Ceccarelli, 2009), Siporin more accurately renders "contea" as "earldom." Chapter 1, "Pitigliano e le comunità di confine" pp. 5–6, gives information about the early Jewish settlements in the area.

4. Angelo Biondi, "Le Comunità ebraiche nei feudi di confine e la loro confluenza in quella di Pitigliano," in *Pitigliano 'La Piccola Gerusalemme' terra della libertà e dell'accoglienza*, eds. Roberto Giusti and Giovanni Greco, pp. 27–53. (Pitigliano: Banca di Credito Cooperativo, 2009). Biondi provides invaluable data on these and other small fiefdoms around the area where Jews lived from the 1400s on; see esp. pp. 27–28. This is in contrast to the older research of Roberto G. Salvadori, in *Breve Storia degli ebrei toscani* (Florence: Le Lettere, 1995) who stated (p. 60) that De Pomis was the first Jew to find refuge in Pitigliano. In his very scholarly *La Comunità ebraica di Pitigliano dal XVI al XX secolo* (Florence: Giuntina, 1991), Salvadori had mentioned the opinions of others such as Edda Servi Machlin who maintain a much earlier origin for the community (see *Child,* p. 21), but without agreeing. In our interview with Prof. Biondi, he expanded on the earlier origin of the Jewish presence in the area, as he does in his article cited in this note. Interview by Judith Roumani and Jacques Roumani, Pitigliano, October 26, 2011.

5. "It seems to us absurd. . ." The pope may have had reasons other than theological when he issued this. Apparently Jews had been very successful in the grain trade, and associated loans to farmers, and the church resented this. Conversation with Bernard Cooperman, September 14, 2014.

6. Interview with Angelo Biondi, cit.

7. See Pietro Fanciulli, *La Contea di Pitigliano e Sorano nelle carte degli Archivi Spagnoli di Simancas e Madrid e dell'Archivio di Stato di Firenze Mediceo del Principato* (Pitigliano: ATLA, 1998), intro. by Angelo Biondi, pp. 226–231 reproduces the document listing the accusations against Orsini and the witnesses against him. Among them are Iacob ebreo and Fiammetta his wife. See also Salvadori, *La Comunità ebraica*, esp. p. 23, who says that the accusations of fraternizing with Jews and carnal relations with Jewish women were the most damning, and sealed Orsini's political fate.

8. On the contest between the municipality, backed by the Medici, and the Orsini, and other aspects of the Orsini period, see Giuseppe Celata, *The Jews of Pitigliano: Four Centuries of a Diverse Community* (Pitigliano: ATLA, 2001), pp. 7–17. This is a trans. of *Gli Ebrei a Pitigliano: I Quattro secoli di una comunità diversa* (Pitigliano: Comune de Pitigliano, 1995).

9. Interview with Angelo Biondi.

10. Celata, *Jews of Pitigliano*, p. 72. Celata calls this the "age of oppression."

11. When a smaller Jewish community was abandoned, over the centuries, the holy ark (*aron hakodesh*) was moved to a larger community with a functioning synagogue and Torah scrolls for the ark. See Rivka and Ben-Zion Dorfman, *Synagogues without Jews* (Philadelphia: Jewish Publication Society, 2000), pp. 3–5.

12. I am inspired by the anthology, Francesca Bregoli, Carlotta Ferrara degli Uberti, and Guri Schwarz, eds., *Italian Jewish Networks from the Seventeenth to*

*the Twentieth Century: Bridging Europe and the Mediterranean* (London: Palgrave Macmillan, 2018). This collection devotes no less than three chapters to Livorno.

13. See figure 1.2. This marriage document is housed in the B'nai Brith Klutznick Museum, Washington DC. For a reproduction of the ketuba drawn up between the Levi and Gallichi families, see also https://www.jipitaly.org, "Jewish Life in Pitigliano." Today it is considered decorative enough to be featured on a Hallmark greeting card.

14. The Sorano synagogue may still be visited with special permission.

15. Riccardo Pivirotto and Monica Sideri, *L'Ebreo errante: Guida ai luoghi ebraici tra arte e storia nella Maremma Collinare* (Pitigliano: Rotary International, 1997), pp. 79–110. See also Salvadori, *Breve storia degli ebrei toscani*, passim., and Biondi, "Le Comunità ebraiche nei feudi di confine," p. 36.

16. Angelo Biondi, *Gli Ebrei nel marchesato di Piancastagnaio*, introduction by Rabbi Riccardo Di Segni. "La Vicenda dell'ebreina" (pp. 70 et seq.) began when the six-year-old girl walked into a local church and supposedly said that she wanted to become Christian. Marquis Giovan Battista Andrea wanted to restore the little Sara Passigli to her family but the people's violent opposition threatened the Jewish community, involved church authorities (remarkably balanced), and eventually Grand Duke Cosimo II, though "poco incline verso gli ebrei" (hardly favorable to Jews} intervened. Brought to Florence, she was adopted by the wife of a senator, became Maria Maddalena Copponi, converted at age twenty-four, and eventually became a nun as having no dowry she could not find a match (p. 76). Biondi (p. 77) sees the church as defending the Jews in this incident.

17. Celata, *Jews of Pitigliano*, p. 81. In 1639, the bishop of Sovana had three Jewish orphans taken from their relatives, removed outside the county, and baptized. This caused the intervention of Medici Prince Giovan Carlo, in Florence, who accused the bishop of interference in civil matters, and had the children returned.

18. Anna Maria Isastia, in "Salvare o rubare le anime?" in Giusti et al., pp. 83–93, discusses the generally dismal history of Italian forced conversions of Jews, mainly women and children, from the sixteenth to the nineteenth centuries. For example, converted grandparents could kidnap their grandchildren and have them converted: one Jewish couple, after seeing their first five children lost in this way, when the wife was expecting again in 1703 fled Rome for Tuscany, and were never found by the pursuing papal police (pp. 89–90). Spurned suitors were often the source of these denunciations. The Edgardo Mortara case in the mid-nineteenth century was one of the most egregious. See David Kertzer, *The Kidnapping of Edgardo Mortara* (New York: Random House, 1997).

19. Celata, *Jews of Pitigliano*, pp. 71–72.

20. See Ferrero Pizzinelli, *Vocabolario del vernacolo pitiglianese* (Pitigliano: Editrice Laurum, 2001) with intro. by Giuseppe Celata, including a number of words with Hebrew roots, such as "sciatta," "manzarre," "Bbadonai!," "gadollu."

21. See especially Roberto G. Salvadori, *La Notte della Rivoluzione e La Notte degli Orvietani: Gli Ebrei di Pitigliano e i moti del 'Viva Maria' (1799)* (Pitigliano: Comune di Pitigliano, 1999) which reproduces six hymns in Italian in honor of the event, edited by Amedeo Spagnoletto. Also Salvadori, *1799: Gli Ebrei italiani*

*nella buffera antigiacobina* (Florence: La Guintina, 1999). Part of the information was apparently unearthed from oblivion by Eytan Kahn and Professor Salvadori searching in the archives of Pitigliano. See the website, "Pitigliano, A True Love Story," "Pitigliano 1799: Ritrovata la terza filza del Processo della Rivoluzione," www.pitiglianotoscana.com/pitigliano.html. See also Davide Mano, "Giacobini di Pitigliano nel 1799" in Giusti and Greco, eds., cit., pp. 55–81. It was not unusual for Italian towns to have their own local Purims celebrating delivery from danger. Florence celebrated the "Purim di Firenze" every June (Lecture by Rabbi Borenstein in Florence, June 9, 2018). In Rome, a similar event occurred in 1793. Giancarlo Spizzichino, *Il Mo'èd di Piombo*, (Milan: Morasha, 2008). This was commemorated in the month of Shevat, with special hymns. With thanks to Rabbi Riccardo Disegni.

22. For a highly informative presentation and analysis of the 1841 census, see Lionella Viterbo, *Le Comunità ebraiche di Siena e Pitigliano nel censimento del 1841 ed il loro rapporto con quella fiorentina* (Livorno: Belforte, 2012), passim. See also for the actual census, http://www.antenati.san.beniculturali.it/v/Archivio+di+Stato+di+Firenze/Stato+civile+della+restaurazione/Pitigliano+Universita+Israeliticaprovincia+di+Grosseto/Censimento/. Viewed courtesy of Dr. Adamati of Archivio Storico Diocesano, Pitigliano.

23. See Celata, *Jews of Pitigliano*, 96–97. Today, one Jew of Pitigliano (Ariel Paggi) owns a farm and grows olives and grapes in the countryside nearby.

24. Rachele Modigliani would have disapproved strongly of the lifestyle of her nephew, regardless of the genius of his art, which she would probably not have appreciated either. It must have been her much younger brother and brother's wife, or more probably nephew and nephew's wife, the parents of Amedeo, who in 1884 when in bankruptcy and seeing all their furniture being confiscated in Livorno, at the same time as the wife was giving birth, piled their most precious possessions into their son Amedeo's cradle, the one piece of furniture remaining to them by law. With thanks for this story to Guido Guastalla.

25. See https://thejewishmuseum.org/collection/19608-torah-ark-curtain. With thanks to the late Vivian Mann and the Jewish Museum of New York.

26. See Salvadori, *Breve storia degli ebrei toscani,* chapter 8, "La Seconda emancipazione," pp. 96–105.

27. Roberto Salvadori, *La Comunita ebraica,* pp. 92–97.

28. See Vera Paggi, *Vicolo degli azzimi: Dal Ghetto di Pitigliano al miracolo economico* (Rimini: Panozzo, 2013), p. 15. Salomone was paralyzed for the last eighteen years of his life, perhaps a result of a stroke due to eating all those eggs. He died in 1915.

29. Several other Jews from the area served in the Great War. Edda Servi has a photograph of "Uncle Angelo, wounded in the battle of Caporetto," in *Child of the Ghetto: Coming of Age in Fascist Italy*, ed. Edda Servi Machlin (Croton-on-Hudson: Giro Press, 1995), p. 65. Arrigo Sadun, Gino Bemporad, Livio Servi are all mentioned as soldiers in Ariel Paggi's interview summaries, "Famiglie coinvolte nelle vicende del periodo," unpub. ms. at that time. I am most grateful to Ariel Paggi for access to these summaries.

30. This same Abramo Moscati, adviser to the mayor and founder of Società Agricola Operaia, had protested energetically when he was not invited to the funeral of a Catholic colleague of his, in 1894.

31. Newspaper reports and vignettes give this picture, assembled by Franco Paioletti, *Pitigliano dal Risorgimento al primo Novecento* (Arcidosso: Effigi, 2011), esp. pp. 150–162.

32. See Ariel Paggi and Judith Roumani, "From Pitigliano to Tripoli via Livorno: The Educational Odyssey of Giannetto Paggi," *Sephardic Horizons*, 2.4 (Fall 2012), https://www.sephardichorizons.org/Volume2/Issue4/paggi.html

33. More details are found in Paggi, *Vicolo degli azzimi*, which includes a short article on Osvaldo Paggi by Roberto Salvadori, pp. 248–254. Though Osvaldo Paggi did not have a religious wedding, when a son was born he had him circumcised. More on this son in later chapters.

34. Edda Servi has a photo of herself and a group of other young girls in front of a small donkey carriage which is to take the family to what she calls the "mikva," and a short chapter reminiscing about family picnics (*Child,* pp. 60–61). When I first visited, in 1999, the baths were not in use and had not yet been renovated. There was a dingy building containing small tiled rooms, each with an individual bathtub, just as Servi described them. Outside was a small open pool. A simple hotel stood nearby. Today, the building has been renovated as a spa and the entire interior consists of one large circular pool, with stone steps, underwater lighting, and little fountains. The hotel has also been renovated, and sends out a Christmas greeting card with the picture of the Jewish community's visit from 1910 as a background. See https://www.flickr.com/photos/jipitaly/with/5985498167/.

35. Paioletti, *Pitigliano dal Risorgimento al primo Novecento*, esp. pp. 150–162.

36. Salvadori, *Comunità,* pp. 92–93.

37. Edda Servi Machlin, *Child,* describes her father's heroic efforts, as does her sister, Marcella, in our interviews.

38. These are his words, but I am not sure whether he meant that non-Jews too were invited and attended: probably he did not. He turned thirteen in 1938, and he tells us that his Bar Mitzvah was the last one to be celebrated in Pitigliano. Video interview with Marco Servi, recorded for the USC Shoah Foundation in Southern California, accessed via USHMM.

39. http://www.pitigliano-toscana.com/italobarmitzva.html. Italo Servi's Bar Mitzvah, with most of the guests in the picture identified. This picture is also included in Ariel Paggi, *Un Bambino nella tempestá* (Livorno: Belforte, 2009), pp. 24–25, and is reproduced herein with permission of Ariel Paggi.

40. *Child,* pp. 129–130: "I felt that my little world of make-believe romance was crumbling too suddenly . . . . Don Omero, our good friend Don Omero Martini was a priest; perhaps he would be able to help me. The next day I went in tears to talk out my desperation with . . . a Catholic priest! . . . As I walked home still in tears, I had to admit to myself that I was feeling a lot better."

41. In altre occasioni ebbi da anziani contadini testimonianze di ricordi grati nei confronti di qualche Paggi. Una Paggi maestra elementare ad esempio andava la sera a casa loro per insegnare a tutti quanti a leggere e scrivere. Lilio Niccolai nato a

Manciano nel 1925, storico locale, politico, ex sindaco di Manciano, figlio di modesti agricoltori, nel 1999 scrisse un libro sulla sua famiglia *Appunti di cronaca famigliare*, dove fra l'altro racconta come da bambino si ammalò gravemente e di come la famiglia Sadun si occupò di farlo curare. Gli ebrei in Maremma sono ricordati con piacere.

See Paggi, *Vicolo degli Azzimi*, p. 15. See also the short film directed by Naor Meningher, *Our Hebrews*, 2016, which consists largely of interviews and reminiscences by the elderly Christian townspeople of Pitigliano.

*Chapter 2*

# A Bolt from the Blue?

## *Fascist Racial Laws of 1938 and Their Effects in Southern Tuscany*

### RISE OF FASCISM AND ANTISEMITISM

In order to begin to understand the 1938 racial laws and their effects, we have to look outside southern Tuscany to the national stage. We also have to revisit the rise of Fascism twenty years earlier. Mussolini's dictatorship and the Fascist party had been in power since the early twenties. They set in place not only a government bureaucracy and army to do his bidding but also a whole media industry and educational system. The strong-arm excesses and threats over these years, the propaganda machine and program of "fascitizzazione," not to mention the charm that we are told Mussolini possessed, seem to have led many Italians to temporarily suspend their critical faculties with regard to Fascism. Those whose ambitions were strong, who exist in any society, took advantage of opportunities for advancement at all levels within the party, the squads, the government, and local bureaucracies. The Catholic church was also pleased with Mussolini's religious conservatism and inclusion of church functionaries in many aspects of Fascism, such as Fascist ceremonies. Many factors converged to make Italians and even the mainly middle-class Jewish Italians comfortable with the Fascist government, at least for a while.

Despite his personal antisemitism, Mussolini did not conceive of an antisemitic policy until 1936 or 1937. Mussolini's own racist leanings did not necessarily imply persecution of Jews; the government's policy toward Jews could have continued as it had been since the 1920s. There was, indeed, a "turn" toward antisemitism in public policy around 1936. The reasons for this turn are partly linked with Italy's acquisition of an empire; it started with the occupation of Libya in 1911, then was joined by other colonies such as Ethiopia, after 1936. Jews were viewed favorably at the onset of the Italian colonization of Libya which was helped initially by the efforts of Giannetto

Paggi, a Jew born in Pitigliano and invited by the Jewish community of Tripoli in 1876 to run an Italian-language school. Paggi went on to found the Italian school system in Libya and received state honors at his funeral in 1916 for his service to Italy. But Italian Jews were not in favor of the invasion of Ethiopia in 1936, and Mussolini held this against them.

Policies came into being to prevent inter-racial relations, including with Jews. In Libya, there had been a policy in the 1920s and early 1930s to "civilize" Libyan Jews in order for them to gain Italian citizenship, as the French had done with the Algerian Jews since the 1870 Crémieux Decree. But Italo Balbo, governor of Libya, encountered resistance from the traditional Libyan Jews from 1934 on. Abetted by the local rabbis and by Rabbi Gustavo Castelbolognese, the Italian chief rabbi in Libya, the rank and file rather than the Italianized elite resisted imposed changes to their religious observance. Balbo alternated harsh and friendly approaches, but neither worked. Starting in 1935, marriage customs and school attendance on the Sabbath had become particular bones of contention.[1] Although some were severely punished in 1938 with floggings, the Jews of Tripoli refused to open their shops on the Sabbath. Perhaps the issues with Jews in the colonies during this period particularly annoyed Mussolini, upsetting the delicate relations that Italian Jews were trying to maintain with him. They also possibly hastened the arrival of the antisemitic laws in 1938.[2] This could be one of many other causes for the laws, though, none of which Italian Jews could have controlled.

There is more than one form of antisemitism, with differences of degree, of course, even if their effects are similar. Aaron Gillette (2002) highlights the distinction between racism imposed by Mussolini and that of Hitler. He sharpens the analysis of Mussolini's rationale for adopting racism, as characterized by earlier scholars such as De Felice (pp. 51–104):

> Like the Germans, Mussolini considered non-European peoples inferior to whites. But because the spiritual element was so important to Mussolini's racism, he outrightly rejected National Socialist racism, which was based on the importance of physical uniformity. Unlike National Socialism, Italian fascism was imbued with philosophical idealism."[3]

Following the 1938 racial laws, Jews began to be removed from almost all aspects of Italian national life. Ironically, "La Sarfatti," Margherita Sarfatti, Mussolini's sophisticated Jewish mistress of earlier years, had played a large role in fomenting his ambitions and giving him an aura of culture. Mussolini had underwritten Hitler's aspirations for some time, but after his visit to Germany in September 1937, his admiration for the Germans' "discipline, hardiness and military prowess" (Gillette, p. 56) increased. His aim was to create the new Fascist Man, but he grew frustrated by the Italians' resistance to greatness. He turned to racism as a means to create a race of masters out of a race of slaves in 1938 after finding eugenics to be too slow a process for him (Gillette, p. 54). As always, though, in times of uncertainty, demagogues turn to antisemitism as a sure way to rally their loyal followers. Germany's Nuremberg Laws, thus, found their equally harsh equivalent in Italy. Nevertheless, differences still remained between Germany's Aryanism and Mussolini's application of "Romanità."

Mussolini insisted on calling his policy toward Jews separation rather than persecution. Separation sounds something like apartheid to modern ears, and is bad enough, of course; among other applications of Mussolini's separation was that Jews were no longer to be seen in the education system. Thus, students were expelled from the elementary schools all the way through the university programs. Jewish teachers and professors throughout the system were dismissed. In addition, army officers and soldiers were discharged; Jewish employees of government and large enterprises were fired. Jewish businesses and shops were closed, and their equipment and goods confiscated; eventually bank accounts were frozen and emptied, insurance policies canceled. Apartments and homes were toward the end confiscated. Ration cards, or the right to buy food, were canceled. Jews deprived of their livelihoods, their education, and eventually their assets and homes certainly experienced it as persecution. By 1943, when the Nazis occupied central and northern Italy, the economic pressure and social discrimination became a threat to Jews' very lives. Eventually, all Jews, whether foreign or Italian, even those who were formerly exempted by the regime, were officially to be rounded up, placed in camps, and subjected to deportation to the death camps in central Europe. The last decision was freely arrived at by Mussolini's Italian Socialist government in late 1943.

## EFFECTS OF FASCISM

How did the Italians, with their recent history of the Risorgimento, their granting of equal rights to religious minorities, their reputation for humanism and tolerance, succumb to the vainglorious designs and narrow ambition of such a one as Mussolini, only to let him lead the country to disaster? How were Italians seduced by the appeal of Fascism? Why did two popes, Pius XI and Pius XII, fail to adequately defend the Jews in Europe and in Italy? What were the manifestations and repercussions on a local level in southern Tuscany of these larger phenomena, and how did local issues impinge on Jews living there, up to and including the passing of the racial laws in 1938 and through the terrors of World War II?

The answers to the first questions will be left to far more skilled historians.[4] Others will be addressed especially as they affected southern Tuscany and provide what will necessarily be some schematic and brief answers, in an effort to link the currents of national history with their local expressions.

It is necessary to return to the beginnings of the "Fascist Revolution" to understand the roots of events in 1938 and 1943. From 1919 onward, young men who were discontented at not standing out during World War I or who were anti-communist and anti-socialist were seeking some movement that would engage them and express their frustrations. Also, like the Germans, the Italians were disappointed at the outcome of the postwar peace treaty; they felt their country had been short-changed. In 1921, Italian socialists achieved a great victory, but it provoked a backlash among these disaffected young, as well as among the landowners and aristocrats who felt that their interests were threatened by the new rights of the landless peasants. From 1920 onwards, the landowners and aristocrats started to form an alliance against the peasants, mostly tenant farmers whose relations with the landlords was one of *mezzadria* or sharecropping, a relationship usually tipped heavily in favor of the landlords, but that the latter now perceived to be in jeopardy. The Tuscan landowners and aristocrats devised a new organization in opposition to the socialist unions, the Tuscan Agrarian Association (AAT), which was actually closely linked to the *fasci* or supposed unions of the Fascist party. The latter were directed at protecting the interests of the landowners rather than the farmers. The Fascist *squadri* (squads) attacked, threatened, beat up, and murdered prominent socialists and those who wished to claim their rights. They strongly discouraged and intimidated the majority and rapidly acquired new adherents. This rule of thugs was particularly obvious in Tuscany.

Its cruel logic eventually led some of the more idealistic Fascists who actually believed in Mussolini's professed ideals, of patriotism and working for a strong Italy made up of the new Fascist race, to abhor these methods. But Mussolini and the majority of the party pressed on. Italy's previous weaknesses and vices were all to be abolished in the new "ethical" state that by 1925 Mussolini was imposing on Italians. It was to be a totalitarian state with his motto, "Everything in the state, nothing outside the state, nothing against the state."[5] By 1927, Mussolini was reining in the Fascist squads which were constituting bad publicity; soon after, he began curtailing the Mafia in the South. The army, the police, and almost all other institutions were already fully obedient to Fascism.

The Fascist state's so-called ethics, a Nietzschean, power-driven form, constituted an extreme form of Italian nationalism and patriotism, requiring sacrifices from ordinary people but dispensing privileges and glory to the elite. These "ethics" were imposed on Italians through a complex bureaucracy and through mass media that made anything other than conformity very difficult. Anti-Fascist writers, from Benedetto Croce to Alberto Moravia, were blacklisted and could not find publishers for their works. Opposing journals and newspapers were closed down. The vast bureaucracy necessitated a building spree to provide national and local government office space. The emphasis on education required that new schools be built. Italy's acquisition of an empire provided many new opportunities for construction in the colonies, including administrative buildings, barracks, hospitals, roads, schools and hotels for those touring the pacified colonies. Thus, the modernist aesthetic of Fascism expressed itself preeminently in architecture.[6] Literature, film, radio, other mass media, and the education of young people were all enlisted in an effort to create a Fascist culture. Naturally, funds, opportunities, and awards flowed in the direction of those loyal to the Fascist regime, while opponents saw their work suppressed. Even when the books of writers opposing Fascism could get published, booksellers simply refused to stock them, on orders from above.

Two Italian intellectuals stand out among many for how Fascism and antisemitism intertwined and synthesized with Catholicism in a sympathetic constellation of views. Padre Agostino Gemelli, a leading educator from the 1920s to the 1950s, was chancellor of the Catholic University of the Sacred Heart of Milan. A prestigious annual prize is still awarded in his name. His anti-Jewish views expressed in annual speeches and publications must have influenced hundreds of students over decades. Giovanni Papini was an avant-garde Futurist writer who, despite presenting himself as an original, individualistic, freethinker who went against the grain, held antisemitic views in line with Fascism and the age-old ideology of the church. He signed the 1938 Manifesto on Race and achieved high cultural positions under Fascism. He also must have had untold influence on ordinary Italians over the Fascist period.

Opposing writers who were critical and anti-Fascist tried to convey the process by which Fascism distorted the psyche. Alberto Moravia's novel, *Il Conformista* (The Conformist), which later gave rise to Bernardo Bertolucci's film of the same title, presents the type of the Italian Fascist conformist developed to the ultimate. The main character, Marcello, is hardly ever sincere in his emotions: he cannot love his new wife because he seems almost incapable of feeling love. Ambition and the underlying urge for conformity push him to become an undercover state operative who collaborates in murder. His first assignment is combined with his honeymoon. He appears to feel nothing in the way of idealism, and cynicism and hypocrisy permeate his every action and emotion. Yet he yearns for an authenticity that evades him. Underneath Marcello's melancholy is a deep fear of being seen to be different, compounded by his sexual orientation, which was in no way tolerated under Fascism. Moravia presents Marcello's meditations after the murder:

> What was needed for him was the complete success of that government, that social system, that nation; and not merely an external success but an intimate, essential success as well. Only in that way could what was normally considered an ordinary crime become, instead, a positive step in a necessary direction. In other words, there must be brought about, thanks to forces which did not depend on him, a complete transformation of values: injustice must become justice; treachery, heroism; death, life. (p. 324)

Obviously, this is how Moravia saw the masses of Italians who conformed and collaborated with the Fascist state and the deforming values it imposed on them.

Moravia's novel could not be published during the Fascist era, when the author had to publish under pseudonyms and eventually went into hiding. Perhaps its eventual publication in 1951 helped previously conforming Italians glimpse at how Fascism had deformed their society and psyches.[7] Another, less renowned writer, Paola Masino, a few years later presented a similar portrait of a housewife driven to her death by the process of trying to be the perfect Fascist housewife and lady.[8] The Fascist colonial enterprise and its distorting psychological effects on both colonized and colonizers are indicted in Alessandro Spina's lengthy, long-delayed novel, *The Confines of the Shadow,* published in 2006.[9] Thus, fiction can cut through the vainglorious illusions of those who benefited from being the favored elites of Fascism to portray its psychological effects on the dispossessed whom it touched, marginalized, and victimized: homosexuals, women, the colonized, blacks, and, of course, Jews.

## FASCISM, THE MEDIA, AND THE ARTS

Because of Fascism's stress on youth, much emphasis and many resources were poured into the Fascist student organizations, the Gruppi universitari fascisti—Fascist Student Groups (GUF), and many other groups engaged in zealous Fascist activity. From the government's point of view, however, because student organizers were often unreliable and they often used their meetings to present films or speakers who did not follow the Fascist line, the authorities were only partially successful. In late 1938, a Fascist student-oriented newspaper from Rome, *Roma Fascista,* published out of Palazzo Braschi, the Interior Ministry, called for the expulsion of Jews from the party (headline: "I Giudei fuori dal Partito"). On the same front page the appearance of Black Africans freely enjoying the elegant cafes of Via Veneto ("I negri a Via Veneto") was lamented.[10] These student organizations held prestigious annual debate matches to which talented young intellectuals were drawn.

The government's efforts to establish and control a Fascist cinema were more successful than media efforts for youth. The film industry was always dependent on large amounts of funding, thus more controllable by the government. Studios were set up, equipment imported from America, and a number of films were produced, with the emphasis on escapism and entertainment.[11] Certainly the Fascist cinema was not aimed at provoking deep thinking.

The media industry in Tuscany was especially zealous for Fascism:

> The ultraracists of *Il Tevere, Quadrivio,* and *Il Giornalissimo* [Rome newspapers], and many journalists who dreamed of making the transition from their provincial papers where they starved, to the big national dailies, were hard at work to show their zeal in every possible way, loudly demanding harsher measures that were obviously inspired by those enacted in Germany. . . . The assembly of journalists of Tuscany was up to the standard, and . . . on October 23 [1938] it voted a position paper demanding the exclusion of "all those belonging to the Jewish race, without consideration of any type of discrimination" from the lists of their profession.[12]

One local Fascist from Tuscany who rose to national prominence in the media industry was Ferdinando Pierazzi, a landowner from Civitella Paganico who became Mussolini's undersecretary in the Ministry of Communication (1929–1932). In 1923, he had founded *La Maremma*, the local weekly that effectively spread the Fascist message in the province.[13]

Some nuances are evident in the Italian experience of Fascism. The pioneering historian Renzo De Felice pointed out that though Italo Balbo was responsible for harsh measures against Sabbath-observant Libyan Jews, he counted Jews among his friends (perhaps not exactly friends, but persons to whom he was favorably inclined), and resisted applying the full gamut of racial laws in Libya. He went out of his way at a Fascist party convention in Tripoli to praise Umberto Di Segni, a Jewish war veteran from World War I, asking him to raise first one arm, which he did, and then the other one. He could not raise the second arm as he had lost it in the war.[14] Balbo gave the Jewish architect a number of commissions for prestigious buildings. Even after the racial laws came into effect, he managed to find the architect smaller assignments. An irony of history is that the Giado police station, where hundreds of Libyan Jews lost their lives in a concentration camp late in the war at the hands of Italian police, had been designed a decade earlier by Umberto Di Segni.

Middle-class Italian Jewish families were likely members of the Fascist party until they were finally expelled. The ironies do not stop here. A perusal of the winners of debate prizes in the GUF Fascist student organization reveals the names of many who would become the postwar icons of left-wing and progressive Italian culture; Alberto Moravia himself was a prizewinner. The tentacles of the Fascist party system embraced the most unexpected figures. Ignazio Silone, author of *Pane e Vino* (Bread and Wine) (1936, revised 1955), turns out to have been a Fascist collaborator in France. This novel celebrates the best of the Italian spirit and searingly shows how its saintly main character returns to Italy from exile disguised as a priest to stir an idealistic socialist movement among the peasants against Fascist brutality and oppression.[15]

## ANTISEMITISM

The propaganda system of Fascism was set up most efficiently. When Mussolini finally embraced an antisemitic policy, which he had previously disdained, in 1936–1938, the whole machinery of the mass media and the education system, as well as cultural institutions, sprang into action to make his policies into reality, a reality that turned out to be beyond the nightmares of the Jews. Some Jews who were loyal Fascists continued working for the regime.[16] The majority of Jews, in most cases, were slow to react, hamstrung by misplaced priorities and over-optimistic misunderstandings of the situation, thus leading to inappropriate and ineffective reactions. This was true nationally, and was especially the case in southern Tuscany, a largely rural area whose Jews were even less in touch with national realities than were city Jews.

The largely rural province of Grosseto had a weak center in its provincial capital, as well as many problems of feuding landowning cliques and corruption. But Fascism achieved and kept a firm hold there. Jewish influence in "La Piccola Gerusalemme," as Pitigliano was known, turned out to be not so strong after all. Jews had been largely marginal, not actual power-holders. For example, Abramo Moscati was an adviser to the mayor but no Jew ever ran for mayor (Osvaldo Paggi declined to do so). In other Italian cities, the removal of the Jewish mayor of Ferrara in 1938 must have been extremely traumatic. In Livorno, Jews had been predominant in the printing, olive oil, and coral industries and had constructed one of the largest synagogues in Europe, but Jewish businesses, such as the Belforte publishing house, were handed over to Christians by the Fascists as elsewhere. The enormous synagogue there became a liability as the Jewish population left the city. From its height in the mid-nineteenth century, Jewish influence in Pitigliano had already been ebbing when Jews started leaving for larger cities. Political power in the town became a matter of internal feuding between landowners with similar Fascist tendencies. When Jews were removed from party membership in 1938, any previous influence, good relations, and philanthropy in the town of Pitigliano became irrelevant.[17]

Many decades later, Jewish survivors from the area mention in a bemused way how other Jews in the community, and often their own parents, had joined the Fascist party out of Italian patriotism or as a passport to a job and good standing in society. The Jews in the province of Grosseto did as did city Jews. Children belonged to the "Lupi" or carried the "tessera di Balilla," membership cards in the various Fascist youth organizations. The uniforms of the movement also hung in their closets. Like other children, they enjoyed the marching, the parades, the gymnastics, and making the "saluto romano" (Fascist salute); and their parents approved. Their expulsion from the Fascist youth organizations was all the more painful for Jewish children because of their lack of understanding.

One of the few local Jews who refused invitations to join the Fascist party was Azeglio Servi, the acting rabbi of Pitigliano. His close relatives included the well-known proponent of Zionism, Dante Lattes, a national figure whose sharper views may have permeated to Azeglio, who felt responsible for the welfare of local Jews. Azeglio, according to his children Edda and Gino, was pressured by his non-Jewish friends to join the Fascist party but consistently refused to. However, he had been proud to be included in a group photograph together with Marshall Badoglio, a member of the Fascist cabinet, at Fiuggi (spa town south of Rome). Servi and Lattes shared a grandmother in common, and thus Servi might have had some intuition of Fascism's dangers.[18]

## THE RACIAL LAWS

Despite all this Fascist activity, Michele Sarfatti emphasizes how profound in his view was the break with the Italy of the past that occurred with the racial laws of 1938.

Italy broke with its Risorgimento values which since the mid-nineteenth century had included Jews in the nation. For five years, from 1938 to 1943, Italy ceased to be the nation that it had been, Sarfatti maintains, until with the activation of the Resistance in 1943, and its inclusion of Jews in the Resistance, it began painfully to reconstitute and reintegrate itself. Other historians might not agree with Sarfatti's argument, seeing a basic continuity and only special conditions that brought out Fascism, racism, and antisemitism that had been latent. Sarfatti continues:

> The Fascist legislation did not go as far as general revocation of citizenship. However, since the legislation totally excluded all Jews from the armed forces, . . . and given that such participation constituted for male citizens the incarnation of citizenship itself, they were in practice excluded from the nation, and thereby the legislation announced the end of the historical-national story that the Risorgimento had launched.[19]

Though Sarfatti states that Italy was breaking with its traditions, he does perceive a progression in the destruction of Jewish rights during three phases of Fascism. The three periods he perceives are 1922–1936, "The Attack on Jewish Equality"; 1936–1943, "The Attack on Jewish Rights," occasioned by the conquest of Ethiopia, leading up to and including the racial laws and outright persecution; and 1943–1945, the ultimate "Assault on Jewish Lives," in which deportations to the death camps took place.[20]

## SOUTHERN TUSCANY IN THE FASCIST PERIOD

Official figures in the province of Grosseto toed the Fascist line assiduously, whether because of their proximity to Rome or their provincialism. The problems of Maremma have been compared to those of the South and Sicily in terms of underdevelopment. The area of Bassa Maremma, Lower Maremma, had been a region of marshes since late antiquity. It was subject to malaria and plagues and, historically, was sparsely populated. During the Fascist period, the region benefited from a concentrated reclamation and development effort, *bonifica*. Perhaps the time was ripe and any government then would have achieved reclamation, possibly with less corruption, as Luciana Rocchi postulates. Its reputation as a haven of bandits receded into history. Farmland was created, and villages and farms were built. Grosseto, the provincial capital, benefited from a building spree that produced several impressive official buildings. Because of the population growth, the Catholic church needed bigger facilities, and Monsignor Paolo Galeazzi, the bishop of Grosseto, received support from the government and the Vatican to build numerous churches and other facilities in the area. He was also apparently closely connected to a high official in Rome, the foreign minister Galeazzo Ciano, who was also Mussolini's son-in-law. Thus by the 1940s both the prefect and the bishop of Grosseto strongly supported the Fascist regime in the area, the one officially and the other informally.

In the early 1920s, Grosseto had been considered "the traditional place of punishment and exile for state officials who had fallen into disfavour" (Snowden, p. 196). Thus, officials, perhaps rather cynical, were not likely to crack down very assiduously on lawlessness. Grosseto seems to have had a series of Fascist prefects in the 1920s, each serving for a short period, such as Domenico Soprano and Federico Miglio.[21] It had previously been a largely socialist town, until one of the largest Fascist "actions," in June 1921, violently overwhelmed any opposition to Fascism there. The town was overrun by a thousand *squadristi* (squad members), many from Siena, and the violence claimed fifty-five lives, while Prefect Boragno looked away (Snowden, p. 201). Another "action" later in 1921 in the small town of Roccastrada, north of Grosseto, a holdout nest of socialists, claimed ten lives. In both cases, the carabinieri were complaisant, failing to stop the violence.[22] Inspector-General Paollela was very frustrated because of the collusion between the police and the violent Fascist squads. He deplored the passivity of the carabinieri and of the magistrates: the first refused to arrest Fascists and the second refused to prosecute them. After these and other incidents, the local people sank into willing or unwilling conformity with Fascism,[23] a situation that seems to have prevailed for over two decades until the Resistance became active after the German takeover in 1943. From then on, a courageous local Resistance, based partly in some of the unused mines in the north of the province, was operating in the hills and marshes of Maremma.[24]

## EFFECTS OF FASCIST ANTISEMITISM

The intensification of antisemitism in 1937, instigated by Mussolini, constitutes one of the low points in modern Italian history.[25] Italy's treatment of its colonized populations in Africa a few years earlier had been another low point. Fabio Levi writes that the extent of Italian antisemitic legislation has often been underestimated by scholars comparing it to that of other countries, especially Nazi Germany and its 1935 Nuremberg Laws. He writes that "The mark of shame imposed by the law . . . inevitably introduced reciprocal suspicion, fear or at least embarrassment into many personal relationships between Jews and non-Jews . . . what had been a history of growing integration and assimilation was rudely interrupted, and a trajectory in the opposite direction started." After the war, little was done to "re-forge those relations that the Fascist state had brutally cut,"[26] an aspect that will be considered in our last chapter. Ana Bravo emphasizes that Jews suffering from persecution had little chance in Italy "of being helped by any wider social awareness of the constitutional violation that these discriminatory laws represented, or any feeling of duty to defend people who were Italian citizens."[27] Michele Sarfatti, attempting to plumb the depths of anguish caused among Jews, quotes Paolo D'Ancona, a university professor fired at the time, writing in May 1939:

> I have suddenly found myself cut off from all my activities as a citizen and as a scholar; expelled from the army, from my university chair, through my books from the schools [meaning that his books were banned], I am experiencing the destruction of everything that has made up my very reason for existing.[28]

Several shocking suicides of prominent Jews were perhaps not only signs of personal despair, but above all desperate attempts to inscribe the moral deformity and injustice of Fascism on the public consciousness by writing in the victims' own blood.[29] The Fascist elite responded to and suppressed these statements with total cynicism.

Turning to fiction once again, for fiction can arouse our stultified imaginations to empathize with the plight of Italian Jews at that time, Lia Levi's novel *L'Albergo della Magnolia* [Magnolia Inn],[30] helps us to plumb their pain. It tells a poignant story of a young assimilated Jewish high school teacher in Rome who intermarries with the daughter of a zealous Fascist. Although the young man has made concessions to the family's "values" at every point, and the couple already have a son, the Fascist family gradually obliterates him. This is accomplished first through divorce, then by pressuring him to give up his paternal rights after his former wife marries her cousin who then adopts the Jewish protagonist's son. All of this is gradually accomplished in a stifling atmosphere of moral superiority, as the jobless, family-less protagonist goes into hiding. His own family is deported to Auschwitz and he loses his friends and his son. Barely surviving, he eventually moves to Israel, alone and grieving. After so much compromise and humiliation, he is a psychological disaster. The book ends as he leans out of his tiny Tel Aviv balcony to catch a glimpse of the Mediterranean Sea, on the other side of which he knows his son is growing up unaware that his father exists.

## POPE PIUS XI AND FASCISM

If some provincial bishops were fellow-travelers of Fascism and the church was generally pleased with Fascism's upholding of public morals and enlistment of church officials in its pageantry, Pope Pius XI had some doubts about Fascism, so that Mussolini was constantly frustrated with that particular pope's independent thinking.

Though this pope himself had previously made antisemitic statements about the "swarming" Jews of Poland, he distinguished between Polish and Italian Jews.[31] He tried to warn the Italians against the Nazis and called the swastika "the cross that is the enemy of the Cross of Christ."[32] To the displeasure of the duce, the ailing pope opposed the racial laws of 1938 in one particular aspect. While he approved of the separation of Jews from Christians in Italian society, in education and the workplace, his vehement opposition was to Mussolini's insistence that converted Jews should also be subject to the racial laws. The pope considered that a Jew who had converted to Christianity should be "discriminated," or distinguished, from other Jews, and allowed to marry someone Christian since birth. He supported the 1929 Vatican-Italy Lateran Accords, which contained this provision. By 1938, however, Mussolini had already begun to think in purely racial categories and believed that so-called Aryans and Jews should never mix, even if the Jew had abjured Judaism. This shows his transition from spiritual/Mediterranean racism, which accepted that a change of faith signaled the ability to join the master race, to, in Gillette's terms, a Germanic, biological form of Aryanism. Thus, Fascist law forbade such marriages. The duce's conclusion was supported by numerous scientists. It was also backed by the entire machinery of the racist press, which consisted not only of the pseudo-scientific magazine, *La Difesa della Razza*, but of many national and provincial newspapers, student newspapers, and other media, such as radio.

The pope lost his struggle with Mussolini, not only because of all the secular and state institutions arrayed behind Mussolini's racism but also due to his failing health and because the pope's personal efforts were constantly subverted by his own Vatican staff. He could no longer control what was published in the Vatican-backed newspaper, *L'Osservatore romano*, and his statements were often suppressed, especially by his secretary Eugenio Pacelli, who succeeded him as pope. Pius XI prepared carefully to issue *Humani Generis Unitas* "On The Unity of the Human Race," an encyclical against racism, as well as an extremely important speech on the subject to a large convention of bishops. But the encyclical, known as the "Hidden Encyclical," prepared for the pope by John Lafarge and two other American Jesuits, was never quite completed; it was sent unfinished to the Vatican archives. As for the speech, Pius XI died two days before he was to deliver it, in February 1939. The speech had already been printed in hundreds of copies, ready to distribute to the assembled bishops. But as one of Pacelli's first acts after Pius XI's death, all the copies were destroyed. Any hope of a pope who would oppose racism died with Pius XI (Kertzer, *Pope and Mussolini* pp. 169–171). The next pope, Pius XII (Pacelli himself), was a supporter of Mussolini and tended to share his views.

## THE RACIAL LAWS AND THE JEWS

Mussolini's racial laws, in his own eyes, expressed a policy whose time had come. In the series of laws drafted and passed by the national assembly between September and November 1938, and signed by the king, Jews were progressively excluded from economic life, social life, and national life.[33] Jews were demoted by stages until they became an alien element, accused of being the enemy within. In addition, from being a de-facto place of refuge for foreign Jews fleeing war and antisemitism, Italy first froze Jewish immigration, then actively encouraged both foreign and Italian Jews to emigrate, until by 1943 it worked for the arrest and deportation of all Jews in Italy to the Nazi death camps, thereby collaborating in the Holocaust.

Jews at all levels of society felt abandoned by their peers. The campaign actually began with a declaration by a group of scientists handpicked by Mussolini affirming the inferiority of the Jewish race and the superiority of the Italian Aryan race. This pseudo-science was a fig leaf for Mussolini's desire to eject Jews from Italian society. It was somehow justified as part of a policy that had to be imposed because Italy now had an empire outside Europe (Libya, Ethiopia, Eritrea, Rhodes) and, therefore, needed to control the legal and social status of subject races. Despite Italian Jews' previously excellent record of integration into society since the mid-nineteenth century and their enthusiastic Italian patriotism, not to mention their residence in Italy for 2,000 years, it was suddenly remembered that Jews possessed all sorts of negative traits. This was no doubt a continuation of the Catholic Church's age-old condemnations of Jews.[34] Very few Christians, when Jewish professors were about to be dismissed, refused to fill in the form defining one's race. This challenge to academics had had a precedent in October 1931, when the government required that all professors swear an oath of allegiance to the regime. Out of 1,250 professors, twelve refused. Francesco Ruffini, an eminent Christian scientist, and his son, Edoardo, were among the twelve.[35] Matard-Bonucci states that the Fascist, anti-Jewish measures went further than those of the Germans or of the Vichy government in excluding Jews (p. 28).

De Felice analyzes how the Jewish community reacted. Jewish response ran the gamut from courageous statements by Dante Lattes,[36] through initial panic and dismay, to craven efforts to prove Italian Jews' loyalty to Fascism and Jewish rejection of ethnic particularism.

## THE RACIAL LAWS AND JEWS IN THE PROVINCE OF GROSSETO

For Jews who were aware of national trends and certain danger signs, these events were not exactly a bolt from the blue, but for most of those living in the province of Grosseto, they came as an extreme and unanticipated shock. For Jews of Pitigliano there was sudden exclusion from the education system.

Next came the social stigma and exclusion from friendships, as recalled by those who were children at the time. Adults were concerned, we surmise, about their businesses and professional lives, the confiscation of bank accounts, the boycotting of businesses. "Negozio ariano" (Aryan Business) signs were springing up around Pitigliano's town center.[37] Finding enough for their families to eat, social exclusion, and ultimately, by 1943, escaping arrest, were of foremost importance to the Jews.

Nevertheless, as in the rest of Italy, the physical deprivations and persecutions probably came second to an acute sense of being stripped of a hard-won identity: the status of Italian citizen, of which many, perhaps most, Italian Jews were particularly proud. The idealism of the late nineteenth and early twentieth century had led to their desire to participate fully as Italians in the new national order.

Their belonging to the new order had often been bought with Jewish blood loyally shed in the Great War. The many appeals in the province of Grosseto from 1938 on for "discrimination," exemption from some of the new racist legal strictures, express a poignant trust in the Fascist state's acceptance of their sacrifice in shedding much of their outwardly Jewish identity, their wartime sacrifices for Italy, and loyalty to Fascism.

It is probable that the number of suicides of Italian Jews could be attributed not only to loss of professional identity and livelihood but also to this stripping of their Italian identity, which was too much to bear. Vera Paggi reproduces in full a chapter-long letter of appeal that Mario Paggi, son of Osvaldo Paggi, submitted in 1938 to the ministry in charge of demography and race, Demorazza. He makes an eloquent case for "discrimination." He writes to the minister that his earliest teacher, had been a priest, as an expression of his father's universalist principles, after which he attended state school in Florence. Mario fought bravely in the Great War, had been a prisoner of war for three years, and received a commendation before being demobilized in 1919. In university, he used his skills as an orator and journalist to promote Fascism, which he viewed as a movement of national renewal. As a lawyer in Florence, he successfully defended Fascist activists in court:

> On many occasions I had the opportunity to express my opinion as an Italian who firmly believes in the renaissance that Benito Mussolini has desired and has brought about.[38]

He had not, however, officially joined the party until 1932. In a particularly revelatory passage, Mario Paggi describes his relationship to Judaism:

> The failure to receive a Jewish religious education had determined in us children the ignorance of the existence of a Jewish problem and meant that our

spiritual and moral lives were free from any mental reservation. We perceived Italianism as an indispensable element of civilization in the world; the country, the environment and traditions formed and shaped the character and the style of our life. . . . .Wrong was he who . . . [thought he foresaw] a tragedy, who did not know, especially now, how to feel always and deeply Italian, confident and serene.

Mario Paggi's appeal on behalf of himself and his mother, and attempt to show that he was an Italian person of the Fascist faith, were to little avail. He was interned in the Pozzoli camp in Aquila, on the initiative of the prefect of Florence. In early 1940, he was baptized and released, though, on the initiative of a Jesuit, Alfonso Martin, as well as with the intercession of the Vatican. He and his mother survived the later years of the war in hiding in Florence (Vera Paggi, p. 240).

The experience of Manlio Paggi, who remained in Pitigliano, is in stark contrast. His son, Ariel, tells how his father had been arrested in 1940 and sent into internal exile ("confino") in the south of Italy, a common treatment for political undesirables. Two other Jews of Pitigliano received the same sentence at the same time. Ariel's mother took her two young sons and dragged them southward in an arduous two-day train and bus journey, via Naples, involving a hotel swarming with bedbugs, as Ariel remembers, to join the father in exile at Tricarico. There, they fortunately found that the head of police was of Pitiglianese origin and was willing to do whatever he could to ease their lives.

Manlio was a mathematics teacher, but had lost his job because of the racial laws. Ariel says his father had been arrested for allegedly sending signals to enemy airplanes while walking along the highway. He was also arrested for being a Jew and a Zionist in addition to knowing foreign languages. He, therefore, constituted a security risk. Michele Sarfatti writes that Manlio Paggi was arrested on the prefect's initiative after making some rather rash statements:

The prefect of Grosseto asked for and obtained the internment of a Jew from Pitigliano with "an immense faith in the rebirth of the Jewish state and in the affirmation of Israelite civilization, which, in the end, he says, will have to avenge all the injuries suffered during these two thousand years."[39]

We can certainly understand Manlio's frustration. It took courage to say such things in the Fascist state in 1940. The family did not return to Pitigliano until September of 1941. Two people might have influenced Manlio Paggi's Zionism. Dante Lattes, the leader of Italian Zionism, had a family connection with Pitigliano through his close relationship with the family of Azeglio

Servi. No doubt some of his publications would have reached other families in Pitigliano, such as the Paggis. The elderly Rabbi Abramo Disegni, who spent a few years in Pitigliano before he and his family attempted to leave for Palestine, was a close friend of the Paggis. He was very pessimistic about the future of Judaism in Italy. Rabbi Disegni died in Bologna as he began his trip, but his wife and children continued to Palestine.

The injustice and cruelty of Fascist policy on a local level can be seen in the treatment meted out to Temistocle Sadun, a Jew from Pitigliano. He was an engineer who brought electricity to Pitigliano and surrounding towns, at his own expense. He also designed a new mayor's office, which was completed in 1939. At the inauguration ceremony in 1939, he stood discreetly on the side, and was not even named.

> For the inauguration of the new municipal headquarters, the federal secretary of the Province of Grosseto, comrade Elia Giorgetti, founder of the fascio of Scansano, attended, and gave a speech in which he was careful to avoid naming the engineer. The gerarch, referring to the planner, seems to have said "the person who shall not be named," while Temistocle Sadun listened in silence, on the side. Shortly after, the man who had contributed more than anyone else to modernizing the area of the Fiora hills moved to Rome, and never came back.[40]

Though "provincial" and less well informed than city Jews, the Jews of the province of Grosseto used all their powers of intellect, their networks of connections with non-Jews, and their powers of persuasion and will to survive, in their attempts to deal with persecution and in their search for refuge.[41] In southern Tuscany, unlike many other places in central and northern Italy, an area that did not even have a rabbi and whose once-flourishing community was now considered an annex of the Jewish community of distant Livorno, there was only local leadership, and no succor from any organized Jewish entities.[42] The Jews of Pitigliano and the rest of Grosseto Province had to rely on their own resources, ingenuity, and connections.

On a provincial level, the majority of non-Jewish Italians in the towns in southern Tuscany, many of them convinced Fascists, withdrew and treated Jews as pariahs, although a few compassionate individuals often helped in some small way, out of long-term friendship or sympathy. Many courageous small farmers did risk their lives to shelter Jews. Self-preservation is the way of reason, sticking one's neck out and becoming a hero is impossible to explain. Naturally, little was permanent, every refuge was precarious, as the situation evolved from bad to catastrophic and as the Nazis, abetted by the local Fascists, invaded and occupied southern Tuscany, in 1943 and 1944, initiating even more active persecution and the "hunt for Jews."

## NOTES

1. After the imposition of the racial laws in 1938, Balbo took into account the importance of Jews in the Libyan economy and tried to mitigate the effects of the laws there. See Renzo De Felice, *Ebrei in un paese arabo: Gli ebrei nella Libia contemporanea* (Bologna: Il Mulino, 1978), trans. Judith Roumani, *Jews in an Arab Land* (Austin: Texas University Press, 1985).

2. On these events, see esp. Maurice M. Roumani, *The Jews of Libya: Coexistence, Persecution, Resettlement* (Brighton: Sussex Academic Press, 2008), pp. 20–27.

3. Aaron Gillette, *Racial Theories in Fascist Italy* (London and New York: Routledge, 2002), p. 51. As for Renzo De Felice, he has been roundly criticized for failing to recognize that Mussolini was a racist and antisemite. See Massimo Lomonaco, "Gli ebrei: Sul non razzismo del Duce, De Felice sbagliò." www.StoriaXXIsecolo.it. January 16, 2002 (on the views of Michele Sarfatti and Liliana Picciotto).

4. Some of these are: Ruth Ben-Ghiat, *Fascist Modernities: Italy, 1922-1945* (Berkeley: University of California Press, 2002); Michele Sarfatti, *Le Leggi antiebraiche spiegate agli italiani di oggi* (Turin: Einaudi, 2002); R. J. B. Bosworth, *Mussolini's Italy: Life under the Dictatorship, 1915-1945* (New York: Penguin Press, 2006); Marie-Anne Matard-Bonucci, *L'Italie fasciste et la persecution des juifs* (Paris: Quadrige, 2007, Presses universitaires de France, 2012); David I. Kertzer, *The Pope and Mussolini: The Secret History of Pius XI and the Rise of Fascism in Europe* (New York: Random House, 2014); Michael Livingston, *The Fascists and the Jews of Italy: Mussolini's Race Laws, 1938–1943* (Cambridge: Cambridge University Press, 2014).

5. In fact the word "totalitarianism" originated in Italy and originally had a positive connotation. See Christopher Duggan, *The Force of Destiny: A History of Italy since 1796* (Boston: Houghton Mifflin, 2008), chapter entitled "The Fascist Ethical State," esp. pp. 449–453. An example of Fascism's doctrinal/philosophical pretensions is Renzo Sertoli Salis, "Nazionalità e razza nell'ordine nuovo," *Dottrina fascista* 6 (February–March 1942), offprint from a journal published by the Scuola di mistica fascista Sandro Italico Mussolini, quoting from Hitler and Mussolini's writings.

6. See Ben-Ghiat, for details of Fascist policies mentioned here. Also Matard-Bonucci, *L'Italie fasciste et la persecution des juifs*, pp. 3–9. A major contribution to Fascist architecture in the colonies was made by the Jewish architect, Umberto Di Segni, who left his mark via many official buildings in Libya and worked closely with Italo Balbo. After 1938, though, he could only work anonymously. See Jack Arbib, *L'Ombra e la luce: Note su Umberto Di Segni, architetto* (Nola: Il Laboratoio, 2010).

7. See Alberto Moravia, *The Conformist*, with introduction by Tim Parks (London: Prion, 1999), p. 324. There is neither a hint of antisemitism on the part of the conformist nor a mention of Jews in the novel. But the person whose murder he is complicit in, his former professor Quaddri, definitely resembles the Fascist, antisemitic depiction of the Jew: ugly, misshapen, hunchbacked, and a scholar surrounded by piles of old books.

8. Paola Masino, *Nascita e morte della massaia* (Birth and death of the housewife; Milan 1945, rpt. 1982) discussed in Ben-Ghiat, *Fascist Modernities,* pp. 162–165.

9. Alessandro Spina, *I Confini dell'ombra* (2006), *The Confines of the Shadow* (London: DARF, 2015). Spina began writing this vast novel in the 1960s. Its publication delayed into the following century shows the deep and long-lasting discomfort that Fascism and Italian colonialism left.

10. See *Roma Fascista* (Nov. 5, 1938), p. 1. With thanks to Rachel Simon of Princeton University Library.

11. Ben-Ghiat, *Fascist Modernities,* pp. 70–88, discusses several of these films, as does Giorgio Bertellini in the volume, ed. Patrizia Palumbo, *A Place in the Sun: Africa in Italian Colonial Culture from Post-Unification to the Present* (Berkeley: University of California Press, 2003), pp. 253–278.

12. De Felice, *The Jews in Fascist Italy,* pp. 256–258. The author goes on to describe the situation as a series of "moral miseries."

13. Galimi, *Il Fascismo a Grosseto: Figure e articolazione del potere in provincia* (1922-1938) (Grosseto: ISGREC and Effigi, 2018) p. 143 (chapter by Marco Grilli).

14. De Felice, *Ebrei in un paese arabo*, p. 262.

15. This aspect of the famous left-wing novelist emerges from Fraser Ottanelli, "Fascist Informant and Italian American Labor Leader: The Paradox of Vanni Buscemi Montana," *The Italian American Review* 7.1 (Spring/Summer 1999), pp. 108–109 and 114–115. Siloni himself recruited Boscemi as collaborator in about 1924, and they remained friends over the years. It is a supreme irony that Siloni found it necessary to do this in order to survive.

16. See the story of Ettore Ovazza, founder of a Jewish Fascist movement, recounted by Alexander Stille, in *Benevolence and Betrayal: Five Italian Jewish Families under Fascism* (New York: Summit Books, 1991), pp. 17–90. Stille writes, "In Italy, Jewish fascism was a real ideological movement. . . . In 1938, at the beginning of the racial laws, more than 10,000 Jews—about one out of three Jewish adults—were members of the Fascist Party" (p. 22). Patriotism, for Jews like Ovazza, was almost a religion, and patriotism meant Fascism.

17. See Valeria Galimi et al., *Il Fascismo a Grosseto*, a highly informative text details these local trends in the province. Galimi states though that the "Jewish question" in Pitigliano or the province was not a major one for the Fascists. See pp. 141–143, 207–214, 295.

18. See interviews with Marco Servi of Grosseto and Eugenia Servi of Pitigliano. The photo of Azeglio is undated, and included in his daughter Edda Servi Machlin's memoir, *Child of the Ghetto,* p. 106. On Dante Lattes and antisemitism, see Renzo De Felice, *Jews in Fascist Italy*, pp. 75–77. De Felice states that initially in the 1920s "the Jewish organizations were careful to praise any measures taken by the government and the Fascist Party in favor of the Jews that brought about a relaxation of tensions, and to show themselves to be, while avoiding excessive conformity, "good Italians." At the same time, however, any evidence of antisemitic attitudes was quickly and resolutely pointed out and disapproved of" (p. 75). By the late 1930s, though, Zionist activity became more and more difficult, and such protests became impossible, until the Zionist periodical *Israel* was finally shut down.

19. "Il legislatore fascista non giunse alla revoca generalizzata della cittadinanza. Tuttavía, poiché egli escluse definitivamente tutti i perseguitati dalle Forze Armate . . . e dato che tale participazione costituiva per il citaddini maschi l'incarnazione della cittadinanza stessa, egli li excluse di fatto dalla nazione, proclamando quindi la cessazione della vicenda storico-nazionale avviatasi col Risorgimento." See "La Vera morte della patria," *La Repubblica*, January 20, 2002, p. 27 (extract from his book, *Le Leggi antiebraiche spiegate agli italiani di oggi*, Turin: Einaudi, 2001).

20. Michele Sarfatti, *The Jews in Mussolini's Italy: From Equality to Persecution*, trans. John and Anne Tedeschi (Madison: University of Wisconsin Press, 2006), pp. 42–213.

21. See Alberto Cifelli, *I Prefetti del regno nel ventennio fascista* (Rome: Scuola Superiore dell'Amministrazione dell'interno, 1999), pp. 176, 261–262.

22. Frank Snowden, *The Fascist Revolution in Tuscany, 1919–1922* (Cambridge: Cambridge Univ. Press, 1989), p. 203. Rino Daus, a Fascist *squadrista* from Siena, was killed by socialists in the action in Grosseto and, thus, provided Siena with a Fascist martyr. All the local Sienese officials as well as 10,000 people, attended his funeral. The Siena stadium was renamed after him. Paollela writes that after the violence, the party headquarters (la sede del Fascio) reopened in Grosseto and four hundred people joined up immediately, as well as many more all over the province. The message was that Fascist violence paid.

23. A similar situation existed in Perugia, the capital of the neighboring province of Umbria, where the bishop was enthusiastically pro-Fascist.

24. Today, Grosseto is proud of its anti-Nazi and anti-Fascist record. An excellent bibliographical article on the subject is Ilaria Cansetti, "Bibliografia sulla Resistenza in Provincia di Grosseto," *Grosseto contemporanea* (2012/04/19) (online).

25. The 1938 developments, a series of Decree-Laws and a Royal Decree, are first described in Renzo De Felice's *The Jews in Fascist Italy* (1961, 1987), as well as later by a new generation of historians like Marie-Anne Matard-Bonucci, Michele Sarfatti, Giorgio Israel. See also Shira Klein (2018) and Simon Levis Sullam (2018) on Fascist antisemitism and persecution of Jews. See especially Sarfatti, *Leggi antiebraiche* which has a useful timeline and reproduces the texts of many of the antisemitic Decree-Laws, pp. 60–87. The first was the Regio Decreto [Royal Decree] of November 17, 1938, No. 1728. They were officially called "Le Leggi per la Difesa della Razza."

26. Fabio Levi, "Social Aspects of Italian Anti-Jewish Legislation," in *The Jews of Italy: Memory and Identity*, eds. Barbara Garvin and Bernard Cooperman (College Park, MD: University Press of Maryland, 2000), pp. 404 and 408.

27. Ana Bravo, "Social Perception of the *Shoah* in Italy," p. 383 in ibid. She believes that the myth of "italiani, brava gente," has prevented Italians from fully coming to terms with the antisemitism inherent in the racial laws, and traceable to an endemic, unacknowledged traditional antisemitism that could have been eradicated if Italians had afterwards been able to come to terms with/confront the Fascist period fully (p. 384 et seq.). See also the similar conclusions in a recent study, Shira Klein, *Italy's Jews from Emancipation to Fascism* (Cambridge and New York: Cambridge Univ. Press, 2018), esp. pp. 204–235. David Kertzer frequently points out the link

between the church's traditional anti-Judaism and the modern Fascist version of antisemitism.

28. A me è stata improvvisamente troncata ogni attività di cittadino e di studioso; espulso dall'esercito, dalla cattedra, attraverso i miei libri dalla scuola, assisto alla distruzione di quanto formava la ragione stessa della mia vita (Sarfatti, *Leggi antiebraiche*, 2002, p. i).

29. De Felice *Jews in Fascist Itay* discusses two well-known Jewish suicides of the time (pp. 324–325).

30. (Rome: Edizioni e/o, 2001, 2004, 2006). The numerous editions of this novel underline that many found it embodied the psychological essence of Fascist antisemitism and persecution of Jews.

31. Kertzer, *Pope and Mussolini*, p. 186.

32. Ibid., p. 156.

33. Livingston, *Fascists and the Jews of Italy*, see esp. p. 17 for a summary.

34. See David Kertzer, *The Popes against the Jews* (New York: Vintage Books, 2002).

35. See Matard-Bonucci, *L'Italie fasciste et la persecution des juifs*, pp. 27–28. "Le 19 août, une circulaire ordonna le recensement de tous les intellectuels juifs membres des sociétés savantes. . . . Rares furent ceux, à l'instar de Croce, qui refusèrent de remplir la fiche d'appartenance." (On August 19, [1938], a circular ordered that a census be taken of all Jewish intellectuals who were members of learned societies, It was the rare few who, like Benedetto Croce, refused to fill in the form stating their identity.) On the 1931 demand, see Giorgio Boatti, *Preferirei di no: Le storie dei dodici professori che si opposero a Mussolini* (Turin: Einaudi, 2001).

36. See Renzo De Felice, *Jews in Fascist Italy*, p. 321, for Dante Lattes' dignified response.

37. A case was brought against one shopkeeper who put up the Aryan sign, because his wife was Jewish and so his business did not qualify. Franco Dominici, "La persecuzione degli ebrei a Pitigliano." March 22, 2017, *Il Corriere del Tufo* (http://www.nctufo.it/corriere/rubriche/pillole-di-storia/).

38. "In molte occasioni ebbi a manifestare il mio pensiero di italiano credente fermamente nella rinascita voluta e attuata da Benito Mussolini" (Vera Paggi, p. 246).

"Il non aver avuto educazione religiosa ebraica determinò, in noi figli, che ignorassimo l'esistenza di un problema ebraico e che la nostra vita spirituale e morale fosse libera da ogni riserva mentale. Abbiamo sentito l'italianità, come elemento indispensabile di civiltà nel mondo; la terra, l'ambiente, le tradizioni hanno formato, plasmato il carattere, la tendenza, la vita nostra. . . . Chi ha creduto di vedere la tragedia, chi non ha saputo, sopratutto in questo momento, sentirsi sempre e profondamente italiano, fiducioso e sereno, ha errato." (Vera Paggi, p. 242). Translation of second passage is from Robert Aleksandr Maryks, *Pouring Jewish Water into Fascist Wine.* Vol. 1, *Untold Stories of (Catholic) Jews from the Archive of Mussolini's Jesuit Pietro Tacchi Venturi* (Leiden: Brill, 2012), p. 200, slightly adjusted.

39. Paggi, *Bambino*, p. 33, writes he has consulted documents in the Archivio Centrale dello Stato, and Sarfatti lists a number of official state archival sources. Sarfatti, *Jews in Mussolini's Italy*, pp. 146–147, and note 263 on p. 348. Paggi writes

that while documents in the Central State Archives in Rome survived, "In Grosseto there are no documents because as soon as the front passed, all the compromising documents relating to the Jews of the province disappeared from the provincial archive of the police and the prefect's office." "A Grosseto infatti non esiste alcun documento perché dall'Archivio Provinciale della Questura e della Prefettura, appena passato il fronte, sparirono tutti i documenti compromettenti che riguardavano gli ebrei della Provincia" (*Bambino*, pp. 33–34). However, my visit in 2014 to these archives did reveal a few documents.

40. Franco Dominici, "Temistocle Sadun: Luci e Ombre" *Il Corriere del Tufo*. March 16, 2017. Pillole di storia (http://www.nctufo.it/corriere/rubrniche/pillole-di-storia/).

"Per l'inaugurazione della nuova sede municipale, giunse appositamente il segretario federale della provincia di Grosseto, il camerata Elia Giorgetti, fondatore del fascio di Scansano, che pronunci un discorso guardandosi bene dal nominare l'ingegnere. Infatti, il gerarca, riferendosi al progettista, sembra abbia detto 'persona di cui non si fa nome,' mentre Temistocle Sadun assisteva in silenzio, in disparte. Qualche tempo dopo, l'uomo che aveva contribuito più di ogni altro alla modernizzazione del territorio delle colline del Fiora, si trasferì a Roma e non fece più ritorno." Another article ("La Persecuzione degli Ebrei") by Franco Dominici also names Pitigliano Jews who were thrown out of the Fascist party in 1938, among them Tranquillo Servi, Abramo Moscati, Livio Servi, and Sadun himself. *Il Corriere del Tufo*. http://www.nctufo.it/corriere/rubriche/pillole-di-storia/

41. Following the initial dismay, De Felice writes, "Italian Jewry found the moral strength that allowed it to overcome the harsh trials of the years to come" (p. 323). Italian Jewry found the right individuals "to guide it through this trial and ensure its survival as an organized entity" (*Jews in Fascist Italy*, 1961; 1991, pp. 324).

42. None of the international Jewish organizations appear to have come to the assistance of the Jews of southern Tuscany. The issue will be discussed again later. Though part of the international networks on which Italian Jews might theoretically draw, the organizations had not been asked, were not aware of any need, neither were they equipped, to rescue Jews in this part of central Italy. See esp. Francesca Bregoli et al., eds. *Italian Jewish Networks*.

*Chapter 3*

# Town versus Country, Conformity versus Defiance

## *Contrasting Behaviors Involving Jews*

### A BAT MIZVAH RITE OF PASSAGE

Edda Servi remembered the day of her Bat Mitzvah on Shavuot, 1938, as not only one of her most joyful but also as one of her greatest disappointments. She was not the kind of person who would call it a humiliation. Dressed in a beautiful long white silk dress made for her by a trusted Christian dressmaker, she single-handedly led the service in the synagogue, reading the Torah and chanting all the prayers, as women and men clustered behind her. Some Italian synagogues in those days were adopting liberal practices similar to the Reform movement of that time in America. Due no doubt to the influence of her liberal father, the acting rabbi in Pitigliano, she was allowed to do all this. The Torah Ark was probably adorned with the beautifully embroidered curtain for Shavuot already discussed. Afterwards, together with Jewish friends, Edda paraded happily and proudly through the town, showing off her new dress and hoping for accolades. However, since this was just at the time of increasing racial discrimination against Jews, June 1938, actually shortly before institution of the racial laws that fall, she met with only incomprehension and cold stares from the local population and returned home quickly, chastened by the sudden realization that her specially made dress imitated the non-Jewish custom of a first communion dress. In a Fascist-run town (figure 3.1), such display by a Jew was viewed harshly. An experience like this, at a tender age, can mark a person for life, and Edda in later years referred often to this disappointment and how it eventually reinforced her commitment to her Jewish identity as a "child of the ghetto."[1]

**Figure 3.1** **Pitigliano Street.** *Source*: Photo by Judith Roumani, 2018.

## FASCISM AND THE TOWNS AROUND THE PROVINCE

Pitigliano and its surrounding area of small towns (Sorano, Sovana) had acquired a reputation over the centuries of constituting "cities of refuge" for Jews.[2] A turning point in this history of good relations between Christians and Jews was the Fascist period and, in particular, the war period, from 1938 to 1944.[3] For a long time, Fascism had held a firm grip on the political order in Tuscany. The province of Grosseto or at least its main town was well known for Fascist enthusiasm on the part of its leaders. There were 350 party members in the town of Grosseto in 1922. In tiny Sorano, one of the three cities of refuge including Pitigliano, there were 250 party members in 1922, while Pitigliano at the time had a more moderate 60 members.[4] The regional press, such as the newspaper *La Maremma*, endorsed and disseminated the official antisemitic doctrine spread by the national publication *Difesa della razza*,[5] whereby Italian Jews were gradually transformed from their status as Italian citizens of a different faith, ultimately into enemy aliens. *La Maremma*, following the line of the Agraria, contrasted the peasants' "fidelity to the earth" in the region, with Jewish rootless "nomadism" (ibid.) as Fascism imitated the German Romantic elevation of folk-culture into the essence of the *Volk*. The fact that Jews had lived in the province for 400 or 500 years was ignored.

A key Fascist official in Grosseto was Dino Andriani, who was simultaneously secretary of the Grosseto *Fascio*, secretary of the Grosseto branch of the Agraria, and head of the Camara Italiana del Lavoro, the organization overseeing the Fascist unions (Snowden, p. 64). Separation of powers was obviously not a characteristic of local Fascist government. Grosseto only had three or four Italian Jewish families before the war, and therefore very little for the local Fascists to defend themselves against in their defense of the race ("difesa della razza"). By 1943, the new prefect of Grosseto (installed in October), in charge of the entire province, was so eager to prove his zeal, at the same time as depriving Jews of their property, financial assets, and businesses, that during the third week of November 1943, he set up an internment camp (campo di concentramento) for all Jews in the province. He was actually criticized by the Ministry of the Interior in Rome for doing this prior to receiving proper authorization.[6]

Other than among the Fascist officials, however, antisemitism was more muted among ordinary citizens of the town of Grosseto. Apart from the dramatic exclusion from public schools, the few Jews complained of being excluded step by step from social life.[7] Marco Servi, the son of Alessandro and Linda Servi of Grosseto, tells of how, though his father was anti-Fascist, he himself like the other boys in Grosseto, was an enthusiastic member of the local Fascist youth group, the Balilla organization. They had uniforms, camping trips, and para-military training, which the Jewish boy participated in until he was expelled in 1938. The racial laws took the family by surprise. He remembers that his sister, attending a party with other young people, was publicly asked, in a most embarrassing way, to leave on the grounds that she was Jewish.[8]

Rocchi discusses several antisemitic complaints in 1943–1944, large and small, around the province. Stanislao Battistelli, the bishop of Pitigliano, reproved his parishioners for fraternizing with Jews (though we shall learn more about this bishop), and the mayor of the seaside village of Monte Argentario complained about a Jewish summer camp that he wished to see closed down, both letters being in the archives of letters written to the prefect of Grosseto in 1943–1944.[9] The author of an article discussing positively the good relations between Christians and Jews in Pitigliano, after being called in and reprimanded by the prefect of Grosseto, changed his tune in an abjectly apologetic letter and called the good relations "morbid desire" on the part of the Jews which had also infected the Christians.[10]

## FASCISM IN PITIGLIANO

With regard to Pitigliano, Edda Servi also tells of a literal slap on the face her Uncle Guido received on trying to greet an old acquaintance in the Piazza del Duomo, one of the main squares, of hostility and isolation in both social and commercial relations with townspeople, and the uncomprehending anguish the Jews suffered. The slap in the face in the town piazza was one of the common Fascist means of publicly expressing scorn toward someone considered racially inferior. It aimed to reorient previously friendly relations, through force, toward a new relationship of superior and inferior, based on fear.[11] This same unprovoked hostility or hatred was experienced as "un male oscuro" (an obscure evil, an obscure pain) by Eugenia Servi, a cousin of Edda Servi.[12] Gino Servi, Edda's elder brother, told of the discomfort that the progressive boycott of Jews caused him vis-à-vis his former friends, without even involving violence. His former friends would for example to his acute embarrassment move away from him if he tried to sit near them in the cinema.[13]

Ariel Paggi writes that his mother lost all of her supposed friends among the ladies of the landowning class and bourgeoisie under the racial laws.

> One of the first consequences of the racial laws was that my mother lost her so-called friends, that is the relations with ladies of the same class: the high-class families, one might say, with whom she had been accustomed to take walks or exchange visits, distanced themselves from her.[14]

Dante Spicci, the mayor of Pitigliano himself, was an ultra-Fascist, but as we have seen local politics consisted of in-fighting between cliques, the members of which were all pro-Fascist. In the Paggi family's experience, as in the experience of other Jews, the Jews were being progressively deprived of their jobs, their ration cards, their schooling, their non-Jewish domestic help, their radios, their homes, their businesses, and their assets in banks, by the new laws.

The Paggi family, and the other Jewish families, became very worried following the Armistice in September 1943, when German troops began to enter Tuscany. One ex-seminarian pointed out the seven-year-old Ariel Paggi to a German trooper and said, "Quello ebreo. Ebrei kaput" (He's a Jew. Jews *kaput*.) (*Bambino*, p. 45). Nothing happened, but the incident left a nasty taste. Luciana Rocchi, in Collotti, gives a list of thirty-eight Jews who were deported from southern Tuscany, and their fates.[15] In all cases, they were turned in by Italians, not by Germans, and almost all died at Auschwitz.[16] One assumes the Jews were turned in by Fascists who were not necessarily in official positions, since almost everyone was a party member, or by police, perhaps acting on a tip from the anonymous letters that were very much in vogue in those times. The prefect of Grosseto made appeals for the anonymous letter writers to give their names, but they did not. The Jews were arrested in many villages and small towns around the province, often on the suggestion of the informers, who were not lacking.

## UNPREDICTABILITY OF POLICE AND MILITIA

The carabinieri police in Pitigliano, according to Ariel Paggi, were not convinced Fascists: "The carabinieri in Pitigliano were not of Fascist inclination and thus did not force the situation" ("I carabinieri, a Pitigliano, non erano di sentimenti fascisti e quindi non forzavano la situazione. . .") (*Bambino*, p. 62). Elsewhere he adds that after June 1943, the carabinieri of Pitigliano were secretly pro-Badoglio, that is, for the anti-Mussolini government of southern Italy, which had switched sides in the war. However, whatever their secret feelings, it was still their official job to arrest Jews who had not presented themselves for internment. They searched the countryside and entered farms that were close to the highway; however, it seems that they did not search with much enthusiasm, often sticking to the center of the road where Jews were usually not to be found. The local carabinieri did, however, arrest the Jews of Pitigliano. Edda Servi tells of an encounter literally on a road with a local Fascist, not a member of the carabinieri, who did not denounce them to his companion.

> As we got nearer, we recognized one of the men as being someone a few years older than Lello from Pitigliano. His older brother was known to have killed partisans, and was a big shot in the new Fascist Republic. His younger brother, Lello's age, was fighting against the Allies. This one had been a barber all his life, and now he was serving in the militia, searching for the outlaws.

He pretended to believe their story that her brother, Lello, was a soldier on leave visiting his girlfriend, thus giving them an alibi, and even an indirect warning. Lello reciprocated with a warning about the dangers of partisans in the area (*Child*, p. 210–11). This incident further illustrates the unpredictability of the local situation.

## HOW THE JEWS OF PITIGLIANO DECIDED TO LEAVE

Elena Servi remembers how townspeople urged her family to flee because the Germans were coming. They were urged either to hand themselves over and be taken to the concentration camp at Roccatederighi or to leave. It is possible that both non-Jews and Jews saw the camp as a sort of temporary refuge, but

Elena's statement about her mother, below, shows that some Jews did make a connection between this camp and the Germans' murderous actions, probably in light of what the Jews of Pitigliano feared or suspected already about the fate of their Roman relatives:

> My family, thank God, and thanks to the people who protected us, was saved because we did not go to the camp. My mother was so scared of the Germans, she refused to go to Roccatederighi. They [local Christians] tried to persuade us to leave, "Ma che fai, Lidia? Andate via, andate via dei Tedeschi." (What are you doing, Lidia? Go away, go away from the Germans.) So we fled, on foot. The snow was up to here! [indicates about twelve inches]. We were walking through the snow, it was a terrible winter in 1943-1944.

Elena attributes the family's departure to a warning received from a local Fascist official in the town:

> My father was very well liked in Pitigliano. We had been warned, one night someone knocked on the door. If you look up in the square of the Albergo Guastini, you can see our apartment. The person at the door was the sister of a policeman, and she had come to warn us. The policeman was the guard for an important political figure. That is, the political figure had asked the guard, and the guard had asked his sister, to come to us. The message was that that very evening the Germans were coming to Pitigliano, and no one knew what could happen. (Interview, 2011)[17]

By contrast, Edda Servi specifically writes that no one native to Pitigliano alerted her family to the dangers when it was time to flee (*Child,* p. 145). The family of Azeglio Servi, father of Edda and Marcella, had heard about what happened in Rome in the following way, as Marcella related:

> By October, the Jews of Rome were all taken. The news reached Pitigliano eventually, we didn't have any television or radio, the news didn't travel fast. There was an outstanding number of *pitiglianesi* who were concierges in Rome, because their children were in higher education there. They had housing and a bit of money and they could keep their children. So the news of this "clearing" of the Italian Jews in Rome came back to us, we heard that, I don't know how fast, and that they were doing the same all over Italy.[18]

The person who alerted the family on the night of November 27, 1943, when the danger was imminent, was a mysterious upstairs neighbor who had arrived after the war had started. She was the elegant Signora Maddalena, the wife of a Fascist colonel who had sought refuge from the bombings in the big cities for his family in Pitigliano, and who now said, "Do not waste one minute. Gather the few things you can carry with you and run into the woods. At any moment the fascists may be here to get you and hand you over to the Germans" (*Child,* pp. 153–54).

Pitigliano's doctor, called in to visit Ariel's older brother who had the flu, had warned the Paggis that the Germans had asked for a list of Jewish names. On hearing this, the family consulted with two trusted non-Jews of the town: the lawyer Focacci, an elderly anti-Fascist, and Marina Felici, daughter of an intermarried Jewish woman, who had useful sources of information. There were definitely a few who privately could be trusted to help Jews, even in the town. Out in the piazza, in bars and other public places, Fascist informers were ready to report subversives to the authorities. The majority were no doubt cowed by the pervasiveness of Fascism.

Marina Felice confidentially advised the Paggis to hide in the countryside. Ariel's *babbo* (dad) was a former high school teacher who recently had been tutoring the local farmers' children, so he contacted several families who were his clients or friends. Some of these names now figure in the annals of Yad Vashem as Righteous Gentiles: Pellegrini, Dainelli, Felici, and about two dozen other courageous families.

## DANGERS IN THE COUNTRYSIDE FOR FARMERS AND FUGITIVES

It is not always easy to correlate the various accounts by Jews who were in hiding. Memory lapses have also intervened over the years, as well as, perhaps, some deliberate confusion. The dangers that faced those *contadini* (peasant farmers, some landowning and some sharecroppers) who protected Jews were real and worried them greatly. Ariel Paggi relates how the farmers protecting his family and others wanted to hide the Jewish adults more completely and in particular wanted to break up the families. Small children could more easily blend in with a farmer's family, while adults were more difficult to hide. It was a question of strained resources as well as danger. There was a mistaken belief that the Nazis would show more mercy to women than to men; at one time some farmers suggested that the Jewish women turn themselves in. Ariel Paggi tells us that this suggestion was scotched by Marina Felici who lived in the town and told the farmers sometime in late 1943 or early 1944 she had heard that the Allies had landed at Ancona and would be there liberating the region in about a week (which was not true). No Jews were turned in at that time.

The farmers heard that a farm that had harbored fugitives had been burned down by the Nazis with the inhabitants inside; the first part was true, the second not. Marcella Servi tells about this incident in more detail, which did not involve Nazis but rather Fascist militia. When she was living on a farm, she did not specify where, escaped Allied prisoners, including one who was Jewish, were hiding in a nearby cave. She went with the farmer's daughter to bring them food and wanted to linger and talk to them. Her brother, who sensed danger, had to drag her away by her hair, and they fled the farm. Very soon the militia came and arrested the fugitives. They were all shot, the farmer was killed, the wife and daughter raped, and the farm burned down, but the farmer's wife and daughter survived.[19]

> Many, many years later, his widow had moved near Grosseto, and we went to visit her there. She told us that they never succeeded in bringing her husband's murderers to justice. Usually it took some time after a tip-off for the carabinieri [*sic*, more likely the militia, or perhaps both] to arrive and locate fugitives, but this time they had arrived very fast. We suspected it was because the local priest, unusually for the time, had a phone, and had tipped them off.[20]

The Servi teenagers, Lello, Gino, Edda and Marcella, had to be constantly on the move, possibly not only because they were Jews but because they were suspected of being in touch with the partisans. They depended on finding yet another farmer willing to take the risk of sheltering or feeding them for a while. Jewish families, such as Elena's usually managed to find more permanent hiding places, even though both Elena's and Ariel's families had to move several times.

The semi-wild, wooded, and marshy countryside of Maremma, the home of bandits and wild horses until the late nineteenth century, was excellent to hide in. As time passed it also harbored several other fugitive groups, such as the Resistance, deserters/draft evaders, and enemy fighters including downed pilots and escaped prisoners of war. Thus Fascists, carabinieri, and German soldiers could appear at any time, demanding food or searching for someone. The farmers not only sheltered but also fed many people; their resources were stretched beyond their limits. Marcella Servi relates that the young people of the *macchia* (the Resistance, as in the French *le Maquis*, also means forest or bush) were welcomed at harvest time or times when more hands were needed, as many of these farming families did not have their sons around to help any more. They had often been drafted and sent off to the front, were in hiding from the draft, or, themselves, had joined the Resistance. In fact, it was not safe for young men of draft age to show themselves unless they were Fascists. The tenant farmers were under severe pressure. The system of *mezzadria* had been disintegrating over the early decades of the century, but by the 1930s and 1940s something similar to the original *mezzadria* had been reinstated. A few farmers, such as the Pellegrini family, owned their own *poderi* (farms),[21] but most were highly indebted tenants, subsisting on pieces of land that were again being subdivided, and were sometimes too small to support a family and to pay what they owed to the landlord. The countryside was pacified, but the same old problems remained.[22] The farmers thus were inclined to sympathize with anyone fighting Fascism, but at the same time were concerned for their own safety.

## NETWORKS OF SOLIDARITY

In the case of the Paggi family, we see a network of relationships being activated. The Felici family had sold the farm to the family of Stefano Perugini (figure 3.2). The Felici family seems to have occupied an intermediate position, in several senses: it is not clear whether they were small landowners who had sold the farm to their long term tenant, or were originally farmers themselves who had risen socially. In addition, since the mother was a Jewish woman who intermarried, they fell between the Christians and the Jews in terms of origins, a fact no doubt well concealed during the Fascist period. Thus, they had contacted the new owners and asked them to hide the Paggi family, who needed a more secluded hiding place (*Bambino*, p. 50).

As we already mentioned, a very few Jews of Pitigliano owned rural land. Ariel Paggi mentions several times that his Aunt Adele owned a farm,

**Figure 3.2 The Perugini Farm, One of the Farms on which the Paggi Family Hid.**
*Source*: Courtesy of Ariel Paggi, 2009.

perhaps the same one that Ariel owns today, and could survive and help her extended family with produce that the *mezzadro* tenant farmer provided. Since we do not know of any Jews actually working the land then, if they had the means to buy a piece of land, however small, they would have installed a tenant farming family on it. It was only very occasionally that Jews rose to the economic position of small landowners. Usually, the Jews were generally fairly poor craftsmen or small shopkeepers in the town. Their relations with the peasant farmers, the *mezzadri*, were as intermediaries—as salesmen, accountants, scribes, or teachers. Marcella Servi emphasizes that her father Azeglio, though he was a part-time salesman and a part-time acting rabbi, also worked as an accountant on behalf of the farmers. He was always on the side of and favored the farmers, rather than the landowners. For this he received payment in kind: a few eggs or a chicken. She also tells about a peasant woman whose husband, years before, had left for America. He had sent tickets for his wife and children to sail from Livorno to America. Marcella's father also played the role of scribe in their exchange of letters. The poor woman came to him in a panic: she had never left the area of Pitigliano. How was she to make the difficult journey to Livorno to catch the boat to America? In the end, since he wanted to visit a friend anyway, Azeglio accompanied her to Livorno. On that occasion he was introduced to his future wife, the sister of the friend's wife, who was then visiting from Rome. Thus, Jews like Azeglio Servi rendered all sorts of small services and incurred long-standing debts of gratitude. Elena Servi in her video interview mentions that her own father was a part-time salesman who sold fabrics to the small farmers on credit. He would wait until the next harvest time to get paid.

The suppressed resentment against the Fascists who had beaten them down and gratitude to Jews who had helped them in small ways, as well as perhaps their independent thinking, sense of justice, and courage, all combined to make some of the country people amenable to hiding the Jews. Today, the children and grandchildren are intensely proud of their parents' efforts. Ceremonies have been organized in Pitigliano, at which Elena Servi, on behalf of the Jews who were sheltered, presented certificates of recognition to the families. Some have been inscribed in the annals of Yad Vashem, but not all, because the institution's rules are very stringent in requiring eyewitness accounts, and the process was often started very late, after the main eyewitnesses had passed away.[23] There is a list of nineteen families that helped shelter Elena Servi's and Ariel Paggi's families in one way or another, and are acknowledged by Yad Vashem.

Ariel Paggi's Aunt Adele's tenant farmer was Agostino Guazzerotti. He and his family helped the Paggis not only by providing food but also by transporting many household items from Pitigliano to the farm via a string of other intermediaries, such as Gilberto Palombi, a neighboring farmer. When

Jews were deprived of their properties, in January 1944, a new institution, the EGELI, took ownership. The Guazzerottis were supposed to take orders from the EGELI, but they were generally left alone. Once another neighbor saw Agostino's thirteen-year-old son Piero transporting packages and reported it to the Fascists. The Guazzerottis, father and son, were then accosted by a group of two local Fascists, a fellow-Fascist from Manciano, and a German officer. When our interlocutors say "Fascist" they could be referring to several types of people.[24] In this instance, it seems to mean those who are sometimes called "blackshirts," local members of Mussolini's militia who were armed, who were usually paid and provided guidance and assistance to the Germans. They threatened the farmer and his son in an effort to find out where the Paggi family was hiding. The father pleaded ignorance, the thirteen-year-old denied with great firmness that he knew anything, the Fascists were already taking out their guns, but the German said "Niente *kaput*" (No kill), and they went on their way. This is an example of local, willing, would-be executioners and of the Nazis on whom they relied for guidance.

Thus, those farmers and their family members who were protecting Jews in various ways, either hiding them on their property, or participating in supply lines, were very well aware of the dangers they could encounter in 1943–1944. They also prepared supplementary hiding places, such as natural or manmade caves or holes in the ground, barns, and escape plans such as putting their guests in a back room from which they could easily jump out of the window. They hid Jews in the caves in the daytime and made contingency plans for how to get them to a more remote location if and when such places proved too dangerous. Elena Servi and her family of six, plus a sister's fiancé, were hidden and lived in a cave near Lake Mezzano, some way to the east of Pitigliano. When Edda Servi and her siblings visited them they seemed to be living in comfort; they had plenty of food, and the cave even had curtains![25] Angelo Biondi's parents lived on a remote farm near Sorano, between the plateau and the mountain. At the request of his uncle and aunt, they hid two elderly people, Dario and Teresita Servi, who had originated from Pitigliano but were living in Grosseto. Angelo's parents generously gave them their own bedroom at the back of the house, a room from which they could escape through the low window and hide in the bushes or a cave in the forest in case of danger. One rainy night, there was loud knocking on the door; assuming it was Fascists or Germans, the Jews slipped outside to hide, as the Biondis fearfully opened the front door. There, they found some of their relatives who had fled from a German *rastrellamento* (round up) going on near their home, in reprisal for an earlier action by partisans. The relatives were seeking refuge with Angelo's parents. Everyone breathed a sigh of relief; they called back the Jews, and lit a big fire in the hearth to warm themselves up.[26]

## FEAR

Edda Servi, however, discusses instances when refuge was refused. She mentions the frequent rejections of the four young people who, having exhausted their previous hiding places, wandered aimlessly from one farm to the next in an area where the farm people did not know them. Even those who did know them often would not let them in out of fear of reprisal.[27] In 1943 and 1944, as mentioned, many others besides Jews were in hiding in central and northern Italy, and depended on local farming families, but numerous studies show that, despite their fear, ordinary rural people would come through with support. A study of the experience of Allied soldiers in hiding attests to this. One young woman who was helping to host and feed these soldiers was crying with fear as she served them a meal, but she did it nonetheless.[28] Farms would be burned down, women raped, and their menfolk would be executed, in reprisal for hiding enemy soldiers or Jews. The Nazis were notorious for responding to attacks from the Resistance by executing many probably innocent people, in a proportion of ten for one.

Recognizing the righteous who saved Jewish lives, protected downed allied airmen, fed the partisans, and hid Italian deserters should not obscure the complexity of those terrible times when fear of hunger and of the Fascists and Nazis was also accompanied by fear of the admittedly far smaller threat of the partisans because of reprisals. Thus, those who sometimes turned Jews away are also completely understandable, though less laudable, under such extreme circumstances of testing.

## PARTISANS

There were also those heroic local *pitiglianesi* who joined the partisans to fight Fascism and Nazism either in the forests and hills or in the cities. Edda Servi mentions a former schoolmate, Sesto, a bookish type turned Resistance fighter, who welcomed her and her siblings with touching joy by turning somersaults when they first approached the partisans (*Child,* pp. 202–204).

Another admirable though tragic case, a different type of partisan, is that of a markedly older non-Jewish man, Ostilio Brozzini. He was a typographer from Pitigliano who joined the Resistance in Rome. Rather than fighting in the forests and woods, he was probably a most valuable forger of identity papers on behalf of the Resistance. Born in 1879, he was of an age where he might have acquired his professional skills and independence of thought around the turn of the century at La Lente, the printing house run by the radically minded Osvaldo Paggi in Pitigliano. Arrested by Fascists in Rome in December 1943 as an "undesirable element," he was deported at the age of sixty-five on a transport to Mauthausen and shot to death at a sub-camp, the castle of Hartheim, in July 1944.[29]

## COUNTRY DEFIANCE VERSUS URBAN CONFORMITY

It is important to view what was going on in the province of Grosseto in the 1940s in the context of agrarian upheaval in Italy. The peasants' achievement of a more equitable relationship with their landlords had been violently crushed by the incipient Fascist movement in the early 1920s, as we have already noted; the Fascist squads succeeded in provoking resentment as well as fear. There is no doubt that this feeling, as well as dislike of the Germans after the many Italian casualties of World War I, persisted into the 1930s and 1940s. Whether it was resentment, a hypothetical native Tuscan obstinacy, the canniness of peasants who realized that the Fascist madness could not last forever, their basic human decency and courage, or a combination of all of these, the small farmers in the countryside were often willing to defy both Fascists and Nazis, and protect Jews as well as other groups. In the towns, though, Fascist orthodoxy reigned more nearly supreme. In Grosseto, which had witnessed the massive Fascist violent demonstration in 1921, the provincial prefect and his secretary were arch-Fascists, and even the bishop of Grosseto, whose actions will be examined later, may have been a fellow traveler. The few Jewish families in Grosseto, who were mainly from Pitigliano in the first place, except the Nunes family and a few others who went into the camp, sought refuge elsewhere: some near Pitigliano, along with at least one Polish family who also went into hiding.

## PITIGLIANO'S FASCISM

Pitigliano itself, however, with a Fascist mayor and a population that felt insecure in the new environment, became more frigid toward its Jews. The town's good reputation of friendship toward Jews apparently wore thin at this time. Local Jews felt themselves erased. Though partially reassured by a few local Fascist party members, they understood haltingly that they could not be spared the roundups and deportations. In the town, like the Christians themselves, they knew they were vulnerable and exposed. Perhaps the increasing centralization, regimentation, and homogenization of the Fascist state, which must have been overwhelmingly impressive in this small provincial town, led some townspeople to put aside their hereditary support of their own Jews out of fear. All the more credit goes to the independence of those who secretly defied the state. Thanks to tip-offs provide by some friendly *pitiglianesi*, and some practical help, many Jews were able to take refuge in the countryside with the farmers. All those who fled the town survived, but the imprisonments and deportations did ensnare especially Jews without close connections in the area. Some local Jews also gave themselves up and were imprisoned. There are stories of local townspeople who were Fascists but did not denounce local Jews they came upon in the countryside (see above); however, particularly from Grosseto, anonymous letter writers denounced the presence of Jews. The carabiniere who was doing his job by arresting Azeglio Servi and his wife, after they had voluntarily returned from three days in the countryside, said to them, "Why on earth did you come back to be arrested?"

As Alessandro Portelli writes,

> What is the relation, within the same person, between the neighbor who saves individual Jews and the Fascist activist who supports the government that is trying to kill them all? Between this private virtue and public complicity or indifference . . . lies the impervious region that separates and connects the concrete and this abstract, the personal and the ideological, private life and history. . . . Some do see the neighbor, at least: many who did not oppose either Fascism or the war took risks and paid prices to help runaways, draft dodgers, persecuted people.[30]

The carabinieri of Pitigliano were not willing to take such risks, at least not at that time, in late 1943. As Ariel Paggi says, they were not even pro-Fascist, but nevertheless did their "duty" (or made sure they would keep their jobs) by arresting Jews.

Postwar developments, such as the townspeoples' generous reconstruction of the synagogue and the Jewish *locali* (school, library, matza oven, mikva) and the founding of a Jewish museum in Pitigliano, in the 1990s and early 2000s, as well as the setting up of an exhibit in the Grosseto area in 2002 about the Holocaust period and Italian complicity, have been attempts to acknowledge the bad times of persecution, fear, and shame. All these issues, though, will be examined further in subsequent chapters.

## NOTES

1. The description of Fascist attitudes in Pitigliano may be compared with the detailed descriptions of Ferrara and Torino and how national directives impacted on a local level in Livingston, *Fascists and the Jews of Italy*, esp. ch. 5, pp. 160–196. Our oral source is the interview with Edda Servi by Vivienne Roumani-Denn and Judith Roumani in September 2011, transcribed by Elisa Septimus.

2. For more on this topic, see chapter 1.

3. No doubt many peasants or *mezzadri* (sharecroppers), temporarily beaten into submission, were skeptical as to whether the Fascist unions represented their true interests. It could be viewed as a transformation of the classic class struggle, in which socialist forces were beaten underground, until under war conditions the Resistance to Fascism and Nazism took shape and began a new active phase, often under the aegis of socialist or Communist leaders, from about 1943. See Bosworth, *Mussolini's Italy*, esp. ch. 6.

4. Galimi, *Fascismo a Grosseto*, p. 208.

5. Enzo Collotti, ed., *Ebrei in Toscana e tra occupazione tedesca RSI: Persecuzione, depredazione, deportazione (1943–1945)* vol. 1, *Saggi*, vol. 2, *Documenti* (Rome: Carocce editore, and Regione Toscana, 2007). See vol. 2, p. 255.

6. Ibid.

7. See Luciana Rocchi, "Ebrei nella Toscana meridionale: la persecuzione a Siena e Grosseto," in Collotti, ed., *Ebrei in Toscana* vol. 1, p. 286. Also Luciana Rocchi, "La persecuzione degli ebrei nella provincia di Grosseto nel 1943–44," pp. 8–14 in *La Persecuzione degli ebrei nella Provincia di Grosseto nel 1943–44* (Grosseto: Istituto Storico Grossetano della Resistenza e dell'età contemporanea (ISGREC), 1996, 2002). The slim book or brochure accompanied an exhibit with the same title, shown in Grosseto in January–February 2002 and now installed in the museum of the town of Ribolla as a permanent exhibit, which I viewed in June 2018). With thanks to Luciana Rocchi, to Adolfo Turbanti who facilitated my visit, and Gabriella Pizzetti, the curator. This site was chosen to house the exhibit perhaps because of the area's anti-Fascist, pro-Socialist, and pro-Communist traditions, and the local mines, which sheltered the Resistance and possibly some Jews.

8. Interview with Marco Servi, recorded for the USC Shoah Foundation in Southern California, Code 45587, accessed via USHMM.

9. ASG, Regia Prefettura, Lettere 1943–1944.

10. Rocchi, *Persecuzione* pp. 8–9.

11. A slap in the face was an effective part of the "ordinary violence" that was tolerated and encouraged during the entire period of Fascism. Michael R. Ebner documents the process of low-level terror in *Ordinary Violence in Mussolini's Italy* (Cambridge: Cambridge University Press, 2011). See esp. p. 243.

12. In an interview quoted by Luciana Rocchi in Collotti, *Ebrei in Toscana* vol. 1, p. 258. "In questo senso, particolare significato assumono le descrizioni di Eugenia ed Elena Servi, adolescenti nel 1938, di condivisione a Pitigliano di tutti i momenti di vita sociale e anche religiosa della città per ebrei e cristiani, e di contro, sopratutto per Eugenia, il 'male oscuro,' che la rinchiuse in un silenzioso e passivo isolamento, dopo." (In this sense, the descriptions by Eugenia and Elena Servi, who were teenagers in 1938, of Jews and Christians sharing in all the moments of social and religious life in Pitigliano, and, in contrast, the "obscure evil, obscure pain," indicates a deeply felt sense of rejection, isolation and depression that closed off especially Eugenia in silent and passive isolation later on.)

13. Interview with Gino Servi, recorded for the USC Shoah Foundation in Southern California, accessed via USHMM.

14. "Una delle prime conseguenze delle leggi razziali fu che la mia mamma perse le cosidette amicizie, cioè le relazioni tra signore dello stesso ceto: le famiglie altolocate, si fa per dire, con cui era abituata a fare le passeggiate o scambiare visita l'allontanarono" (*Bambino*, p. 19).

15. "Ebrei arrestati in provincia di Grosseto e deportati," list provided by Luciana Rocchi, Collotti, *Ebrei in Toscana* vol. 1, pp. 319–323.

16. In Rome, Florence, and other large cities the Germans themselves carried out independent *razzie* (raids) to arrest large numbers of Jews without initially informing the Italian authorities (such as the infamous one in Rome on October 16, 1943). See for example, Robert Katz, *Black Sabbath: A Journey through a Crime against Humanity* (Toronto: Macmillan, 1969). However, in order to find the Jews, they often needed the help of Italian Fascists. Shira Klein give a short list of instances in which the Germans made arrests and then discusses the overwhelming number of examples of arrests by Italian Fascists, very often on the basis of tip-offs from Italian civilians. Klein, *Italy's Jews*, pp. 115–120.

17. Interview by Judith Roumani and Jacques Roumani with Elena Servi, founder and president of La Piccola Gerusalemme organization, November 2011. In the extended, filmed interview, *Il Pane della memoria,* directed by Luigi Faccini, Elena said that the person sending the message was the leader of the Fascist Party in Pitigliano.

18. Interview with Marcella Servi by Judith Roumani and Jacques Roumani, www.covenant.idc.ac.il, *Covenant Global Jewish Magazine* 2.3 (Aug. 2009); reproduced by permission of Judith Kolp Rubin, for the Rubin Center, IDC.

19. Interview with Marcella Servi by Judith Roumani and Jacques Roumani, www.covenant.idc.ac.il, *Covenant Global Jewish Magazine* 2.3 (Aug. 2009); reproduced by permission of Judith Kolp Rubin, for the Rubin Center, IDC.

20. Interview cited above.

21. See Paggi, *Bambino*, p. 50.

22. See the extensive discussion of the evolution of the situation in Snowdon, *The Fascist Revolution in Tuscany 1919–1922* (Cambridge: Cambridge University Press, 1989), esp. pp. 80–93.

23. Interview with Gino Servi, recorded for the USC Shoah Foundation in Southern California, accessed via USHMM.

24. See a discussion of different types of Fascists in Martin Clark, *Modern Italy: 1871 to the Present* 3rd ed. (Harlow, London, New York: Pearson, 2006), p. 262. They could be officials holding specific positions in the hierarchy, or members of the militia, or more lowly squadristi, often called thugs.

25. *Child*, p. 230.

26. Interview with Angelo Biondi, by Judith Roumani and Jacques Roumani, October 25, 2011.

27. *Child*, pp. 227–232.

28. Roger Absalom, *A Strange Alliance: Aspects of Escape and Survival in Italy* (Florence: Olschki, 1991).

29. See Eugenio Iafrate, *Elementi indesiderabili* (Rome: Chillemi, 2015), p. 89.

30. Alessandro Portelli, *The Order has been Carried Out* (New York: Palgrave, 2003), p. 88.

*Chapter 4*

# Hiding like Animals, in Caves, Barns, and Farms; and the Righteous Gentiles of Southern Tuscany Who Risked Their Lives Protecting Jews

### THE PAGGIS GO INTO HIDING

The first Jewish family of Pitigliano to go into hiding in 1943 was the Paggi family. Ariel's mother made a point of being well-informed despite, or rather because of, no longer being allowed their Telefunken radio. Soldiers returning from the front told of atrocities[1] and defeats while the government was still touting victory. "After the Armistice the family started getting worried especially Dina who was actively getting information about what was happening to Jews where the Nazis were in control; since we did not have a radio the only pieces of information came from those who could listen to Radio London and from the returnees from Russia, Germany and surrounding countries" (see note below). A loudspeaker was attached to the Albergo Guastini in town; for important occasions everyone, including Jews, gathered on the street outside to listen to broadcasts: for example, on July 25, 1943, the announcement that Mussolini's government had fallen, but the war was continuing. Ariel Paggi remembers standing on the drawbridge opposite the hotel, listening. His mother's friendship with the Polish governess of a highly ranked Fascist official in the town, as well as a naturally skeptical turn of mind, led her to insist that her family leave Pitigliano[2] and take refuge with a farmer whose family had often had dealings with them and whom they could trust. A list was in the hands of the carabinieri of all the Jewish families in Pitigliano; the family had already experienced her husband Manlio's arrest and forced internal exile in the south three years previously. They had been friendly with Rabbi Abramo Disegni, who had briefly lived in Pitigliano with his family, and had recently left for Palestine. The Paggis had discussed moving either to Palestine or America, but left the decision until it was too late to make travel arrangements. In September, the Germans had entered town and set up regional headquarters in the old castle in the main square.

The Paggis initially consulted with the Pellegrini family even though Ariel Paggi's aunt owned a farm, and they could count on the loyalty of their tenant farmers. Ernesto Pellegrini was the *mezzadro* (tenant farmer) of their cousin, Dario Servi. Pellegrini brought in Vincenzo Dainelli, whose son was receiving math tutoring from Manlio. Another account tells that Manlio made a direct appeal for help, via the son. Since the Dainellis responded positively, six members of the Paggi family immediately walked the three kilometers to the Dainelli farm, where they were installed in the stable that the son cleaned out for them. Only two people in town knew where they had gone; others were given to understand that the family had left the area.

As we have seen, Manlio always tried to provide some service, such as tutoring, in return for the hospitality of their hosts. Even little Ariel, who was seven years old, would pick up fallen wild pears, put them in his smock, and bring them to the mistress of the house, declaring that they were for feeding the pigs. Thus, all the members of the family tried to make themselves useful, but the problem with this refuge was that it was too close to the highway, where German traffic passed constantly. In addition, the visits of other farmers to the farm meant that the Jews had to run out to the barn or into the forest to hide. Even the barn was not safe, as visitors might have some reason to come and look at the livestock. The Paggis soon realized this and Manlio, "*il babbo*," began looking for a safer refuge with the help of his student, Luciano Dainelli.[3] At the same time, Aunt Wera, Aunt Efsiba, and the grandmother were still in town, winding up their affairs. Wera entrusted their valuables partly to the lawyer Focacci and partly to the sisters of the local convent, as well as to Marina Felici's family. The Felici family came through again, contacting the family of Stefano Perugini, who had purchased a small farm from them; The Peruginis agreed to shelter the Paggis and became the second of five farming families who sheltered them over the next ten months. Zia Wera had reached an agreement with a grocery shop in town that would accept their ration coupons, even though they were no longer valid. Zia Adele's *mezzadro* tenant, Agostino Guazzerotti, agreed to continue providing them with farm produce. From January 1944, onwards, Adele's farm would be confiscated along with other Jewish property, but it seems that Guazzerotti was not bothered by the new administrator and continued to provide the family with food.

Suddenly, the remaining family members in town received notice that they had to report to the police station in a couple of days. The round-ups were beginning. The grandmother and aunts rather rashly set out in a cart in broad daylight to join the family in hiding. This presented a problem for those sheltering the Paggis, both because of their numbers—they were now nine—and because it was likely that the latest arrivals would have been spotted. The farmers began scattering the extended family in different refuges (figure 4.1). The carabinieri of Pitigliano, a few days later, started searching for the three women who had not turned themselves in, but the search was perfunctory. They searched only the roads and not the farmhouses.[4] Where do we place these carabinieri along the spectrum of active resistance, passive resistance, bystanding, and collaboration? As discussed previously in relation to the writings of Alessandro Portelli,[5] some individuals varied in their behavior, a concern for their "duty" (i.e., preserving their jobs and good relations with the regime in power) vying with intermittent (perhaps unreliable) voluntary humanitarianism.

To sum up the experience of the Paggi family, and passing over their next three refuges, it seems that there must have been a fairly large number of rural farmers and their families and a few town dwellers, too, who supplied them, gave them advice or activated contacts, held their valuables, and more, and may have had some idea of where the family might be, or at least that they had not left the area. This informal network of numerous protectors, helpers, and confidants earned and deserved the family's trust and did not betray them

It is hard for us today perhaps, in our atomized, self-interest-driven society, to imagine a long-standing network of relationships between Jews and Christians, going back many generations, whereby a Jewish family could ask local families, who are not well off, not related and not of the same race and

**Figure 4.1  Cave Dug Out by the Perugini and Bisogni Families for the Paggi Family.**
*Source*: Courtesy of Ariel Paggi, 2009.

religion, to host and hide them indefinitely, undergoing considerable inconvenience, stretching scarce resources of space and food, and facing real danger from the occupying Germans and the local Fascists.

## LIVIO SERVI'S FAMILY GOES INTO HIDING

Livio Servi's family also decided to entrust themselves to farmers. His daughter Elena has discussed her experiences in an interview with Ariel Paggi, a film, and our interview, among others.[6] Her family, like that of Ariel, had close relations with non-Jews in Pitigliano, but while the perhaps outspoken mathematics teacher Manlio Paggi had been exiled as a subversive, Elena's family seems to have preserved good relations with some of those who had become Fascist officials in Pitigliano. These interfamily relations predated Fascism, perhaps by many decades, and between the families, perhaps, the new ideologies of Fascism and antisemitism may have seemed like mere irrelevant details. As a child, Elena played with the neighbor's daughter. The father, though he was a Fascist official, in reaction to the new ostracism, swore that he would never prevent his daughter from playing with Elena. Nevertheless, this Servi family was warned that they should go into hiding and that their lives were in danger. Elena's father, Livio Servi, who earned a medal of honor in the First World War, according to Ariel Paggi's notes, had not looked upon the arrival of Fascism with disfavor, although he was never an active member.[7] Rumors had seeped through of the fate of the Jews of Rome after October 16, 1943, as well as knowledge of the notes that had been thrown by Roman Jewish deportees as they passed through the nearby town of Orvieto from the cattle cars beginning the long journey to the death camps. Elena's family had received warnings to go into hiding not only by friends but also by the sister of a guard who worked for the leader of the Fascist Party in Pitigliano, the implication being that it could have been the boss himself who wanted to get the message through to them. Livio, his wife Olga Bemporad, and their daughters decided to hide in the countryside before they could be arrested, and they left on November 11, 1943. They had informed a few trusted non-Jewish families, including the Carrei and Ragnini families, who seem to be townspeople who were their friends.

The first hiding place of Elena Servi's family was the farm of Ernesto Pellegrini, who was the *mezzadro* of their Servi cousins in Grosseto and with whom the Paggis had also stayed. Elena's father Livio, who like his relatives sold fabrics, occasionally had business dealings with the tenant farmers (*Il Pane della memoria*). Elena emphasizes, though, that they were sometimes sheltered by farmers who did not know them, such as when they were far away, in the next county.[8] Like the Paggis, the Servis remained on the Pellegrini farm for only a short time, and moved on to two other places in December and January. It is probable that they had heard that the Pellegrinis had hosted the Paggis, and that is why they had turned to them first. The third refuge was the farm of Eliseo and Angelo Conti, where an informer who was a neighbor on bad terms with the Contis denounced their presence (termed "una spiata"), so they had to leave quickly.[9] Umberto Calò, the fiancé of one of the Servi daughters, joined them here for a while until he joined the partisans.

The Contis found another refuge for the Servi family, this time to the south in the neighboring county of Farnese, a place called Dogana. Umberto, in poor emotional condition because his father had been arrested by the Nazis, joined them again, but the new hosts had to ask them to leave as they were too many to shelter. They took shelter in various farms, including one that belonged to the Fascist leader of Pitigliano, Cavallari, obviously without his knowledge, but with the protection of his tenant farmer. Eventually they stayed in a well-concealed cave near Lake Mezzano. Various families provided them with food and fresh sheep's milk and furnishings for the cave. Most of these supplies were gifts, but the Servis did occasionally pay small sums or render services such as repairing clothes for the farmers. The Sonno family would send someone riding by each morning, on either a black horse, meaning danger, or a white horse, meaning safety, as frequent Nazi and Fascist searches were happening in the area. The Servis stayed in the cave for three months where they often received visits from non-Jewish and occasionally Jewish friends.

Their host Francesco Sonno was a close friend of Maresciallo Troisi, a member of the nearby village of Valentano's carabinieri. They met often, Sonno surreptitiously picking up information that would help the Jews he was protecting.

Meanwhile bombardments and battles were going on in the area. Elena relates that the family would bath in a waterfall near the cave. In early June of 1944 they were surprised by French soldiers who were looking for the waterfall, and thus they realized that the Allies had arrived in their region, and they were now free. There was little rejoicing, because the Allies continued to engage in battles with the Germans, and had just bombed Pitigliano's bridge and the town itself, mistakenly killing many civilians.

Elena tells us (figure 4.2) that the conditions over the winter of 1943–1944 had been extremely harsh, as the family had trekked on foot over and over again from one hideout to another. She describes what to her were the most dramatic incidents:

> I remember walking at night in the snow, another time when we had been at Mezzano and we had to flee at night, and then the time in the cave, after seven

**Figure 4.2   Interviewing Elena Servi.** *Source*: Photo by Jacques Roumani, 2011.

months away from home, in a cave . . . . And returning to Mezzano, in the snow, in single file, we didn't have proper shoes, we were lacking everything. It's a long story. . . . Returning from Manciano, we had to cross the river, the bridge was gone . . . we had very light shoes, only Babbo had a pair of strong shoes, and, while we walked, my mother, my sisters and I, my older sister had light shoes, I saw a vein on her leg that was turning green, from the cold, and at that moment I was seized with a feeling of hatred for Mussolini, that he was doing this to my sister. . . . I felt so bad inside, even though I was a young girl, with my two hands I would have killed Mussolini! My Babbo, who had been such a strong and optimistic man, never recovered from these hardships. He died in 1950.

## THE CHILDREN OF AZEGLIO SERVI AND SARA DI CAPUA GO INTO HIDING

The story told by Edda, Gino and Marcella Servi, our third family and distant relatives of Elena, is if anything even more dramatic. They received a warning months before, in mid-1943 from a German soldier—a very unlikely quarter. Specifically, as Edda tells it, he was an Italo-Austrian interpreter from Alto Adige near the Austrian border who was stationed in the area, and who had fallen in love with Edda when he saw her in Porto Santo Stefano. He later traveled to Pitigliano from Sardinia, obviously absent without leave, to warn the family about unspecified atrocities that the Germans were committing against Jews, and to urge them to flee. Edda's father calmly rejected the idea, saying that he had no money, nowhere to go, had committed no crime and that therefore they had nothing to fear. The soldier even suggested that the family take refuge with his mother in Alto Adige. This must have been shortly before the Allied bombing of Rome in June 1943, long before the deportation of the Roman Jews in October. Edda at the time was engaged to her first cousin, who lived on the coast; she wrote to tell him about the incident. Her cousin immediately broke off the engagement. Upset by the broken engagement, Edda went to discuss her feelings with her local priest (see previously on p. 19). Both she and her father discounted a very serious warning.

In November 1943, the four older siblings, two brothers and two sisters, between twenty-one and thirteen, took to the countryside, on their father's request, surviving there for almost a year. They were constantly on the move, their lives at risk, while their parents and the youngest sibling turned themselves in and were interned in the local internment camp where they barely escaped deportation.[10] As with the other Jewish families, the parents, and primarily their father, took the initial decisions and charted the family's survival strategy. In the Paggi case, however, the mother played a very important decision-making role. Ariel Paggi has characterized Edda's story as somewhat melodramatic, but the basic events that befell them have been corroborated by her siblings and others. Her memoirs are pithy and unsparing, marked by a certain justified resentment concerning that period of her life and the family's sufferings, even if her vivid imagination has added somewhat to these.

Azeglio Servi, who was born in Pitigliano, married a girl from Rome who never felt she quite belonged in this provincial place. She would describe Pitigliano as the village of donkeys and flies.[11] Though Azeglio was the assistant rabbi, he was even suspected of having married a woman who was not Jewish, because she was considered so elegant. She was, in fact, from an old Roman Jewish family, and Azeglio Servi and Sara Di Capua named their daughter Edda after Mussolini's daughter, to mask somewhat Azeglio's anti-Fascism.[12] The family's, or rather Azeglio's, decision to go into hiding was taken hastily and late, on November 27, 1943, when they received another urgent warning from an army officer's wife, Signora Maddalena, their upstairs neighbor.[13] Because he was the person responsible for the Jewish community he felt it best to remain in town with his wife, who in any case would not be able to stand the rigors of life in the countryside, and with Mario, their youngest child. They did try the countryside for three days and returned to town. The four older children left immediately without finishing supper, grabbing only a few things, such as the father's boots, their kitten, and the ricotta dessert their mother had been about to serve. They went initially to the home of their former wetnurse, where they deposited the family jewelry (finding in the morning that the kitten had eaten all of the ricotta dessert and then disappeared) and moved on early the next morning to the countryside. One of their underpaid father's sidelines was helping the *mezzadri* to do their accounts and representing them vis-à-vis their landlords when it came time to make their annual payments in kind or in cash. The impoverished tenant farmers were most appreciative of his support. This network of loyal clients served his children well when they would knock on doors with letters from their father. Not everyone would accept them, especially people who did not know them, and the four young people seem to have trekked back and forth across the region even more than other Jewish refugees. Often they would split up into groups of two, to make it more likely that they would be given shelter, but sometimes they slept outside. As mentioned before, Jews were not the only people asking the country folk for refuge. Several types of fugitives were competing for scarce food and the ability and willingness of the rural farmers to conceal them, while Fascist militia and Nazis were out hunting for them.

## JEWISH RESISTERS

Eventually the four Servi siblings, especially the boys, became active with the Resistance. About a thousand Jews across Italy actually joined the Resistance. Some even returned from safe havens such as Switzerland or Palestine to fight. Jews, Michele Sarfatti writes, had a special commitment, and even those who concentrated on their own survival and that of their families actually were resisting extermination policies too and thus could be classed as resisters.[14] Claudio Paggi, a descendant of Osvaldo Paggi originally from Pitigliano, and the son of Bruno Paggi, is an example of a Jew who had found safety but returned to perish in battle. Bruno had taken refuge in Venezuela and Claudio with his mother, Milena, and younger siblings escaped to Switzerland. Claudio returned, eventually managed to cross the lines and joined the Allies in Bari, in southern Italy. He then enrolled in a special Jewish platoon with Tito's resistance forces, in Yugoslavia. He died in a field hospital in Bosnia in February 1944, and was buried in a mass grave.[15]

## COUNTRY PEOPLE

The Jews of southern Tuscany definitely would not have survived had it not been for the brave individuals who secretly defied the local Fascist and Nazi authorities to protect them. Among the townspeople, help given the Jews was secretive and timid, but among the exposed country people, it was wholehearted and generous to the point of risk for themselves.

A number of rescuers passed Yad Vashem's rigorous requirements of documentation by witnesses and were honored in person or through their descendants in 2003 and 2007 as Righteous Gentiles in ceremonies held in Pitigliano and in Livorno.[16] Ariel Paggi and Elena Servi have made the lists of rescuers, Paggi's being followed by a detailed account of the families' actions and how they saved the Paggi family and their relatives, the Saduns, culminating in recognition by Yad Vashem on March 18, 2002. The list of persons who helped save the lives of Elena Servi and her family is even longer.[17]

Other rescuers and helpers have been acknowledged less formally, for example in Ariel Paggi's autobiography, *Un Bambino nella tempestà*, where he mentions some who helped his family, such as townspeople Marina Felici, Mr. Focacci the attorney, and farmers such as Gilberto Palombi and Agostino and Piero Guazzerotti. When he does not remember or never knew the name of someone who helped the family, one can sense bitter regret at not being able to give an appropriate acknowledgement. Edda Servi also mentions in her book those who aided her family, most notably the German/Austrian/Italian soldier, Nino Bernabe, the lady from upstairs, Signora Maddalena, who pretended to be a loyal Fascist but urged them to leave when arrest was imminent; and Sesto the welcoming student partisan from Pitigliano, all described with gratitude. She mentions without naming those farmers who would give the Jews food but not shelter, out of fear that they would be caught, and others in whom compassion would prevail over fear, allowing the young Jews to stay. After almost a year of wandering, wearing the same summer dress she had left home in, Marcella felt that she had become a "wild child," always hungry, and so poorly dressed that the nuns who eventually provided a celebratory meal to the victorious partisans would not let her in, until she put on a child-sized Fascist youth group uniform they found abandoned in their closet. She wore this together with her communist red beret.

It seems that the younger the child, the greater would be the trauma of separation from parents and home, and of having to adopt a life of hiding, begging, and wandering. In general, country women came through for the children, as other evidence from the Holocaust years in many other places in Italy and elsewhere testifies. It is significant that the Servi teenagers stopped at the home of the family's wet nurse first, even though it was only to entrust her with their jewelry. Other sources, such as the evidence of Roberto Bassi, who was hidden in an orphanage in Rome, or the film *Besa: The Promise*, which chronicles the concealing of Jewish refugees in Nazi-occupied Albania, attest to the importance of non-Jewish women in protecting Jewish children.[18] Ariel Paggi, a seven-year-old separated from his parents, was housed on a nearby farm and blended in with the farmers' children, missing his family terribly *(Bambino*, p. 64) but being far safer and learning how to shepherd their sheep.

Others who protected Jews in the Pitigliano area were the doctors at the hospital who sheltered several elderly Jews and declared them unable to be moved (figure 4.3). In addition, a few socially marginal, poor Jews were left alone and were not expected to report to the internment camp.[19] Jews who had converted or inter-married were also not permanently detained, although some converted Jews were arrested and then released, such as Jolanda Paggi from the nearby village of Petricci. They stayed free, mostly unmolested, for the duration of the war.

**Figure 4.3  The Hospital in Pitigliano, in which a Few Elderly Jews Were Hidden.**
*Source*: Photo by Judith Roumani, 2018.

There are apparently only a few instances of church officials in the province protecting Jews, unlike in other parts of Italy. Perhaps it is because Jewish rescue organizations, such as Delegation for the Assistance of Jewish Emigrants (DELASEM), never reached here. This may seem surprising to those who know that DELASEM was particularly active elsewhere in Tuscany. Among the various instances of assistance to Jews, I have found no evidence of DELASEM help in the province after a thorough search of the archives of DELASEM's funder, the American Jewish Joint Distribution Committee (as well as published sources about the organization). This fact only underlines the isolation of the Jews of the province of Grosseto from national or international networks and their need to rely on their own contacts. No direct group appeals for help were ever made to the local clergy. The Paggi family trusted the local nuns enough to leave some family valuables with them. Edda Servi recognized two local priests, a Don Giovanni, and Don Omero Martino. Little is known about the rescue of Jews by the bishop of Pitigliano, Stanislao Battistelli, but he does seem to have made efforts to help individual Jews.

What were the motivations of the saviors of Jews? Since there were so many, especially among the country people, was their sense of responsibility a vestige of the age-old harmonious relations between Christians and Jews in the area, or simple human solidarity? Interviews with the descendants of the Righteous Gentiles shed some light on this. Angelo Biondi in our interview describes the situation thus: "The Jews who did not go to Roccatederighi, those who took refuge in the countryside around Pitigliano, Manciano, and Sorano, were all saved. I have also talked with Gino Servi . . . who told me, 'I have never found a door that was not opened.'" Biondi adds:

> There used to be, in our area, unfortunately now less so, a very strong culture of solidarity, both in the towns and in the countryside. Now it is less so, because modern society does not encourage these moral and ethical aspects. So people made themselves available to help those who were in need, not only Jews, but others.[20]

Biondi continues:

> After the war, there was a silence about these things. The local people simply did not look for medals or recognition. When they were questioned many years later, they responded "We did what we did because we thought it was the right thing to do." But it was normal to help those who were in need, even incurring risk to do so. For example, the episode I told you about, they were perfectly aware of what might happen, but they helped anyway.

Though Angelo Biondi's parents together with their siblings, Angelo's uncles and aunts, protected Jews in their homes before he was born, they have not been honored by Yad Vashem, because the parents, and even their older son who was a witness, have either passed on or in his case was not able to testify for health reasons. Thus an informal certificate system has been set up locally, whereby those who are not officially recognized by Yad Vashem but nevertheless did shelter Jews are awarded certificates by the rescued Jews in a local ceremony. Biondi's parents sheltered Dario and Teresita Servi of Grosseto and their son, a family who first took refuge in Pitigliano itself and later in this more remote area of the countryside. Angelo Biondi and Ariel Paggi have been working together, Angelo told us in 2011, still conducting interviews, in a race against time while a few of the rescuers were still with them: "So we have been trying to collect them (testimonies), trying to fill the gaps with a substantial part of what has been missing from this important story, important in terms of morality, civilization, ethics, and solidarity" he said.

Another view was provided by Giovanna Dainelli Mazzoli, who together with her husband runs the Albergo Orientina next to the Jewish Baths, Bagnetti degli Ebrei. The *albergo* and *bagni*, hidden in the Valle Orientina, down a sharply winding narrow lane and invisible from the main road, might have made a hiding place had they not already been associated with Jews. Giovanna's grandparents, Adele and Vincenzo Dainelli, were the first to accept extended families of Jews, starting with the Paggi family, at their farm very close to the *albergo* but also close to the highway. Thus it was particularly risky for them, though they wished to protect Jews. Vincenzo owned another farm, in the area of Pantano to the south, to which he would transfer his charges, still taking total responsibility for hiding and feeding them, until they would find some other, safer arrangement.[21] Luciano, the Dainelli's son and Giovanna's uncle, was particularly helpful and responsible toward the Paggi family. Giovanna, who is acquainted with the broad outlines of her family's heroic actions, says:

> I was born after the war, but I always heard in the family about the Jews who were saved and hidden during the war. Adele and Vincenzo hid them in valleys and caves. It wasn't safe to keep them on the farm, because it was located only a few kilometers from Pitigliano, it was too close to the conflict . . . too close to the road. So they had to hide them for a while in the caves, after they had cleaned them up and put them in order. They were not there for very long, perhaps a month or something like that. Then they moved them somewhere else. . . . They had arranged that if there were a *spiata* [denunciation] or raid they would say that they were from the north [Giovanna probably means the south of Italy] so that they had already been liberated, and that was it.[22]

She described relations between Christians and Jews in the early part of the twentieth century in response to my question about whether her parents were friends of the Paggis and the Servis, the Jews they protected:

> During those years, everyone knew everyone and they were all fond of each other; even if some were Jews and some were Christians, they loved and respected each other normally.

To sum up, it is never easy to understand why some people would risk their lives for others. So many reasons and excuses could be given for not acting altruistically, for not becoming a hero. Pitigliano's Jews could not avail themselves of the organized escape routes and were helped by priests and nuns to a far lesser extent than in other parts of Italy.[23] Thus they had to turn to the ordinary, country people.

It is worth pointing out for comparison what were the options for Jews in other parts of Italy. The DELASEM network was founded to aid foreign Jews. From 1943 as the danger intensified it was engaged in hiding both foreign and Italian Jews. When it was too dangerous and the organizers themselves had to go into hiding, they entrusted their mission and funds to local priests and bishops.[24] DELASEM, the church, or the Resistance were, at varying times and inconsistently, able to aid Jews, temporarily, or even save their lives. Organized rescue activities did not exist in Pitigliano, where the Jews had to rely on their own devices and personal networks. It was more a case of "Si salvi chi puo!" (Every man for himself!) as Azeglio Servi said to his children, with the aim of encouraging them as he sent them off into hiding, though he himself was the most responsible and self-sacrificing among the Jews of Pitigliano, behaving like the proverbial captain of the sinking ship.

Pitigliano's Jews appealed to the local farmers with whom their families had had relationships for centuries; most of the farmers did not fail them. Activating these relationships for survival was almost their only choice, and it turned out to be successful. Of the local Jews who went into hiding, none lost their lives. We have to take into account that the many small occasions when professed Fascists or sympathizers would turn a blind eye, such as the clerk omitting the stamp that said "Jewish Race" on Edda Servi's identity card, the grocer who accepted the Paggis' ration cards when they were no longer valid, or the several occasions when Jews of Pitigliano such as the seven- or eight-year-old Ariel Paggi knew that Fascists recognized them but there were no consequences, also contributed to saving their lives. The local Jews who turned themselves in, and the foreign Jews who did not have the network of long-standing relationships, ran much higher risks, even though their lives in captivity initially seemed much more comfortable, even attractive to those in hiding. The next chapter will discuss life in the local internment camp, where conditions were quite unique, but in the opposite way.

## NOTES

1. One article tells how some Italian soldiers outside Italy, under orders from the Nazis, behaved. James Vitarello, "In World War II, Italian Army Refused to Persecute Jews," *Washington Jewish Week*, May 27, 1999, p. 17. In this case, ordered to bury alive 400 Jews of a Russian village, in order to save bullets, they refused, and were punished with two weeks of starvation during which several Italian soldiers died. Naturally, one cannot generalize from just one case, but a few other instances of similar behavior have come to light. On the other hand, numerous accounts of atrocities that Italians, both soldiers and civilians committed during Italy's wars, have emerged. See, for example, Angelo Del Boca, *Italiani, brava gente?* 2005 (Vicenza: BEAT, 2014).

2. "Dopo l'armistizio la famiglia si cominciò a preoccupare soprattutto per iniziative di Dina che si attivava nel'informarsi che cosa accedeva agli Ebrei dove comandavano i nazisti; essendo privi di radio le uniche informazioni venivano da chi poteva ascoltare Radio Londra e dai reduci dalla Russia, dalla Germania e dai paesi circonvicini." *Bambino*, p. 45. Interviews by Ariel Paggi, "Famiglie coinvolte nelle vicende del period," Also Paggi's book *Il Muro degli ebrei* (Livorno: Belforte, 2018), pp. 130–132. Apparently the Paggis went into hiding a month and a half after that, requesting help from the Dainellis on September 15, 1943. See also www.db.yadvashem.org/righteous/family.html.Item ID=8875347.

3. See Paggi, *Bambino*, pp. 45–49.

4. Paggi writes, "I militi, e di questo va reso onore al Maggiore Lucetti, agirono, ma senza troppo zelo" *Bambino,* p. 54. (The militia was active, but without too much zeal, and for this Major Lucetti should be honored.)

5. See the last footnote of chapter 3.

6. *Il Pane della memoria*, directed by Luigi Faccini. Elena Servi has frequently been interviewed, especially by travel magazines, as the founder and president of La Piccola Gerusalemme Jewish-Christian organization which manages the synagogue, Jewish museum and other Jewish sites in Pitigliano. Our interview on October 24, 2011, Ariel Paggi's interview with her (n.d.), and the documentary, enable her to describe her experiences in considerable detail.

7. "Livio had been a courageous fighter in the First World War and won the cross for fighting in the field of battle. Over the years he had been one of the Jews of nationalist and patriotic sentiment and had not viewed with disfavor the arrival of Fascism while not taking part in political activism, even though he had been induced to take out party membership in 1933 when it became you could say compulsory." (Livio era stato un valoroso combattente nella prima Guerra mondiale avendo ottenuto anche la croce al merito di guerra sul campo. Nel corso degli anni era stato tra quelli ebrei di sentimenti nazionalisti e patriottici che non aveva però guardato con sfavore all'arrivo del Fascism pur senza svolgere alcuna attività politica, anche se era stato indotto a prendere la tessera durante gli anni trentatré quando divenne per così

dire obbligatoria.) Paggi, "Famiglie coinvolte nelle vicende del periodo." Of course, for a Jew membership would have ended in 1938 with the racial laws.

8. My interview with Elena Servi, October 24, 2011. Also *Il pane della memoria*, dir. Luigi Faccini. With thanks to Natalia Indrimi, director of the Centro Primo Levi, New York, for access to the video.

9. Here we have an insight into the thinking of informers of the time. Though the reward for turning in a Jew was a kilo of salt, a valuable commodity in an age before refrigeration, this neighbor was motivated by his rivalry with the Contis, whom he wished to see punished.

10. Edda Servi Machlin, *Child*, and in interview by Vivienne Roumani-Denn and Judith Roumani, September 2011. Edda also has a videotaped interview in the archives of the United States Holocaust Memorial Museum, as does her brother, Gino Servi. (Edda also published several cookery books, based on the Jewish cuisine of Pitigliano, and including descriptions of her childhood, such as baking matza for Passover.)

11. Marcella Servi Siegel, interview by Jacques Roumani and Judith Roumani, December 2007, published in *Covenant Global Jewish Magazine*, 3.1 (August 2009) www.covenant.idc.ac.il; and with Judith Roumani and Vivienne Roumani-Denn, filmed interview in 2009, unpub., transcribed by Elisa Septimus. Also Edda Servi, *Child*, for example, p. 30. Marcella told us in her interview that her mother had an even worse name for Pitigliano, *il caccatoio* (shithouse), related to the lack of indoor plumbing in her day (theirs was the first family in Pitigliano to install an indoor bathroom in their home).

12. Edda says that to her knowledge he was the only Jew in Pitigliano not to have taken out membership in the Fascist party, as such membership was a passport to a job. *Child*, p. 32. See also above, note 7 on Livio Servi. See chapter 2 on Azeglio's anti-Fascism and on his cousin, the Zionist leader Dante Lattes.

13. The Jews found it necessary to leave the town just as refugees from the big cities were fleeing to places like Pitigliano. In January 1944 their properties were officially confiscated. Most of Pitigliano's Jews who returned needed to evict squatters from their homes at the end of the war.

14. Michele Sarfatti, *Jews in Mussolini's Italy* (Madison: Univ. of Wisconsin Press, 2006), esp. pp. 202–211. Naturally, Jewish resisters were among the most committed and courageous. Two Jews he mentions who returned to fight the Nazis are Gianfranco Sarfatti, who returned from Switzerland, and the famous Enzo Sereni, who came from Palestine. Both were killed in their efforts.

15. Vera Paggi, intrigued by the total silence in the family concerning her uncle's fate, only in 2003 discovered his diaries and Claudio's father's 1946 correspondence, to understand the facts of his death. In the reticent early postwar years, it was considered appropriate to hide such tragic news. Claudio's mother, though she may have suspected something, apparently never gave up the illusion that her son might return one day. His father was actually in correspondence with the doctor who treated Claudio and who witnessed his death. Vera Paggi, *Vicolo degli azzimi*, pp. 199–204.

16. Here are the rescuers, at least those known at present: Martino Bisogni, and Maria Mazzieri-Bisogni, his wife; Vincenzo Dainelli, Adele Pacchiarotti-Dainelli, his wife; Luciano Dainelli, their son; Agostino Nucciarelli, Annunziata

Simonelli-Nucciarelli (his wife); Stefano Perugini; Adele Mozzetti-Perugini; Sam Perugini, their son; Domenico Simonelli; Letizia Serri-Simonelli.

The list is from Yad Vashem archives, "The Righteous among the Nations." Db.yadvashem.org/righteous/family.html Item ID=8875347.

17. Francesco Sonno, Fortunato and Maria Sonno; Ernesto and Francesca Pellegrini; Eliseo and Leonida Conti; Angelo and Rosa Conti; Quinto and Aveneria Sarti; Piero and Lucia Vagnoli; Cica family; Settimo and Gismonda Maccari; Adriano and Clorina Manetti; Emilio and Pasquina Torrini; Guido and Pia Nicolucci; Ferdinando and Ines Cini; Arnaldo and Lea Vetrulli (brother and sister).

18. See Michael Shapiro, "Women and Hidden Jews under Fascist Rule: Roberto Bassi's Evidence," *Shofar* 31.3 (2013), 103–114; *Besa, The Promise,* a documentary film, directed by Rachel Ghoslins, JWM Productions, 2012; see also Judith Roumani, "Film Review: *Besa, The Promise,*" *Sephardic Horizons* 3.3 (Fall 2013), www.sephardichorizons.org/Volume2/Issue3/roumani.html.

19. My interview with Ariel Paggi, unpub.

20. Angelo Biondi, interviewed by Judith and Jacques Roumani, October 27, 2011 (this quote and the following one).

21. Interview conducted on October 26, 2011, with Giovanna Dainelli Mazzoli, by Judith Roumani.

22. In other words, they should pretend to be ordinary Italians from the south, perhaps Rome, who had fled to avoid the Allied bombings. The fact is that if they were discovered by local Fascists, or Fascists with Germans, this story would not have been believed and they would probably have been recognized as Jews, potentially endangering not only the Jews but also the Christians who were hiding them.

23. See, for example, Susan Zuccotti, chapter 10, "Survival in Italy" pp. 201–228 in Zuccotti, *The Italians and the Holocaust: Persecution, Rescue, Survival* (New York: Basic Books, 1987), esp. p. 213, where she writes with regard to help from priests and nuns: "In all probability, then, the word 'network' should be used with caution, and the word 'organization' is not applicable"; see also Alexander Stille, *Benevolence and Betrayal,* pp. 230–233; Ivo Herzer, Klaus Voigt and James Burgwyn, eds., *The Italian Refuge: Rescue of Jews during the Holocaust* (Washington DC: Catholic University of America Press, 1989) (e.g., pp. 178–204, on the rescue of the children of Villa Emma).

24. Alessandro Cassin, "DELASEM: The Unhailed Organization that Assisted Thousands of Jewish Refugees" (interview with Donato Grosser). March 26, 2014, www.primolevicenter.org/printed-matter/delasem.

*Chapter 5*

# At the Mercy of the Church and the Fascists

*The Obligingly Hospitable Bishop Galeazzi of Grosseto and the Experience of Jews Who Turned Themselves In*

## RESCUE BY THE CHURCH

Pope Pius XI had tried to oppose the worst of antisemitism in Germany and Italy, but his voice had been effectively stifled in the late 1930s until and especially after his death in 1939. His successor, Pope Pius XII, seems to have avoided any mention of Jews and their suffering, as research has attested, even when knowledge of the Holocaust had indubitably reached him.[1] Susan Zuccotti examines assertions that the pope gave explicit instructions to save Jews, that Jewish expressions of gratitude, such as that of Golda Meir, to the pope after the war were proof that he had exerted himself to save Jews, and that he had personally saved hundreds of thousands of Jews. The controversy continues, with the claim that documents newly found in the Vatican Secret Archives prove the latter.[2] Many scholars are likely to remain skeptical, though, until the further opening of March 2020, and the processing of the newly available material, render decisive information. Shira Klein in *Italy's Jews* (2018) has written: "Currently available documents suggest that the Vatican never issued an order to help Jews, and that priests and nuns acted of their own accord" (p. 122).

Some Italian bishops took their cue from Pius XII and remained passive, but others, especially individual priests and nuns lower down in the hierarchy who interpreted signs of silent compassion on the part of their own bishops as a green light, worked energetically to save Jewish lives at much risk. Perhaps they did not know that the pope, whatever his motives, was largely passing over the plight of Jews and imagined that they were expressing his implicit wishes in helping them. Or perhaps it was their own indignation and compassion that compelled them. When the Jewish rescue organizers in the DELASEM organization had themselves to go underground in such cities as Genoa, Milan, and Florence, they entrusted their funds and their mission to sympathetic clerics.[3] The priests and other church people, from bishops to nuns, who rose to the task and helped rescue Jews knew that their status would not spare them from danger if arrested. On the contrary, some priests received harsher treatment than did laymen. Some who stand out are Father Maria Benedetto (Père Marie-Benoit) in Rome, Cardinal Pietro Boetto of Genoa, and his secretary, Don Francesco Repetto, as well as many more humble clerics, such as the young priest who was summarily executed below the city walls of Lucca, in northern Tuscany, for sheltering Resistance members and Jews.[4] The network of priests and nuns who protected Jews in the convents and monasteries of Florence from the Fascists and Nazis is truly admirable.

## THE CHURCH IN THE PROVINCE OF GROSSETO

None of the general studies (except Simon Levis Sullam briefly, in *The Italian Executioners*) seem to mention the peculiar case of the province of Grosseto and Bishop Paolo Galeazzi of Grosseto. The Italian scholar, Luciana Rocchi, of the research center in Grosseto (ISGREC), and author of several works on the subject, expresses the clear opinion, based on Bishop Galeazzi's actions, that he was probably a Fascist, despite the fact that clerics were not supposed to hold political allegiance.[5]

How do the church's actions in southern Tuscany, in particular the province of Grosseto, compare with its members' heroic record in other parts of central and northern Italy? Unfortunately, the best word one can use is "ambiguous." A study of the church's own documents issued in central Italy during the war years refers to pastoral letters issued by the bishops of the area. Church officials were officially limited to neutrality in their dealings with all of the following: the Fascist militia and police, the two post-September 1943 governments of Italy (north and south), the Allied forces, the Nazi forces, and the bands and committees of the Resistance. This was no easy task. Achille Mirizio's summary of the subjects of these pastoral letters, steering between Scylla and Charybdis, among such general theological discussions as the advent of suffering through the sin of man, includes "Biasimo ai pochissimi sacerdoti coinvolti in fazioni politiche" ("Censure of the few priests involved in political factions"), reminders that Christians should observe the fifth commandment against murder, and "Il cordoglio dei vescovi per le deportazioni" ("The compassion of the bishops over the deportations"). This last sentiment, despite what springs to our minds now, is not likely to have implied deportations of Jews to death camps. Both during and after the war for many years the fate of Jews was fused in Italian minds with deportations of political prisoners, some of whom were tragically killed by the Nazis but not in the proportions by which Jews were murdered. Elsewhere, we find bishops urging comfort for suffering family members who were ignorant of the fates and destinations of their (Christian) loved ones, which leads us to think that deportation by the Nazis was put on a level with internal exile of political dissidents to southern Italy prevalent in earlier years. Thus the bishops in their pastoral letters tended to stay on the level of theological abstraction, of Christian virtues, and of generalized compassion for the sufferings of political dissidents, rather than calling in any way for compassion for the concrete and much greater suffering of Jews.[6]

We first examine the record of Pitigliano, which had the largest Jewish community, where Bishop Stanislao Battistelli's behavior seems to have been positive, although he once publicly (perhaps to conform to Fascist expectations) urged the social boycott of Jews, and then the record of Grosseto and Bishop Paolo Galeazzi. Finally, we will describe life for imprisoned Jews at the camp of Roccatederighi. This camp, under the aegis of Bishop Galeazzi, was one of the few internment or concentration camps in Italy set up on church property and the only one with the active collaboration of the local church.

## THE CHURCH IN PITIGLIANO

In Pitigliano, the church and the Jewish community, particularly the rabbi, had a centuries-long tradition of cooperation. Angelo Biondi tells us that according to local tradition, the bishop was responsible for visiting the synagogue occasionally to inspect the holy books, the Torah scrolls, and make sure that as books holy also to Christians they were being well taken care of. Obviously this was a mere formality, but it did bring the religious leaders into contact. Presumably, by the early 1940s, in the absence of a rabbi in Pitigliano, Bishop Battistelli would have had this same commitment to the assistant rabbi, Azeglio Servi. Thus, according to Biondi there was a certain trust between the leadership of the two communities. The family of Azeglio Servi maintained friendships with two priests, as recounted by his daughter, Edda (e.g., *Child,* p. 130).[7] Ariel Paggi (2009) mentions certain possible actions by the local bishop to help Jews: Don Stanislao Battistelli, he suggests, may have obtained the release of one or two Jews from the internment camp by forging baptismal certificates (*Bambino,* p. 59).

Francesca Cavarocchi, basing herself on Luciana Rocchi, with regard to Pitigliano mentions:

> a certain solicitude shown by Bishop Stanislao Battistelli, who took upon himself to warn local Jewish families of the danger, suggesting though that they enter the camp of Roccatederighi as a concrete way of saving themselves.
>
> (una certa sollecitudine dimostrata del vescovo Stanislao Battistelli, che si incaricò di avvertire del pericolo le famiglie ebraiche locali, prospettando tuttavia l'ingresso nel campo di Roccatederighi come una concreta possibilità di salvezza).[8]

There is a contradiction here, as the danger that faced the Jews was of being arrested and sent to Roccatederighi, exposing themselves to possible deportation, whereas Bishop Battistelli is portrayed as advising the Jews to go there to avoid danger. None of the Jewish interviewees from Pitigliano have suggested that they did receive any warning or advice from the bishop or the church. There is another contradiction that emerges relating to a later stage: one wonders why the bishop would have initially suggested to some Jews that they enter the camp, but then possibly obtain the release of two by forging baptismal certificates. It is possible, of course, that he changed his mind about the camp over the course of its existence, becoming more aware of the fate of the Jews in Europe and realizing belatedly that this camp was part of the machinery set up for their destruction. We do know that various Jewish families entrusted their valuables to the local nuns, meaning that the nuns in the convent and probably the bishop as well were aware that the Jews were leaving to hide in the countryside.

Bishop Battistelli may actually have assisted in the hiding of four Jews in Pitigliano's hospital over about eight months, by interceding with the doctors to shelter them. This is undocumented, but highly possible (again, Ariel Paggi is the source for this). Ariel elaborates on this bishop's possible help in providing false conversion certificates:

> In the archive of Roccalbegna there is a letter from the Fascist Federale and the local mayor addressed to the prefect of Grosseto in favor of Jolanda Paggi [a converted Jew] who had brought up her children in the Catholic faith. Possibly it was actually the bishop of Pitigliano, Stanislao Battistelli, within whose diocese the village of Petricci fell, who actually helped her, as he also tried to save Clara Piperna, a Jew [from Rome] who had taken refuge in Selvena and who was arrested after being informed on; the bishop produced a false baptismal certificate.
>
> (Nel archivio di Roccalbegna esiste una lettera del federale e del Podestà locali indirizzata al Prefetto di Grosseto a favore di Jolanda Paggi che aveva

educato i figlioli alla religione cattolica. Forse in realtà in soccorso di lei venne il vescovo di Pitigliano Stanislao Battistelli, nella cui diocese era Petricci, il quale si adoperò anche per salvare Clara Piperna, un'ebrea rifugiata a Selvena che fu arrestata a seguito di spiata; il vescovo produsse un falso atto di battesimo.) (*Bambino*, p. 59, and *Muro*, pp. 244–45, 248)

Thus, to the credit of the bishop of Pitigliano there is one actual case and another presumed case (if we follow Ariel Paggi) of his forging documents to help Jews, in addition to his probable role in hiding four in the hospital. My research on Bishop Battistelli in the Archivio Storico Diocesano of Pitigliano has brought no evidence whatsoever of the forged certificates among the many documents concerning this bishop, but it is not surprising that such infraction of canonical law would not leave a paper trail. Documents pertaining to civil status signed by Bishop Battistelli that I found are very informal, more like handwritten notes with a simple rubber stamp added, such as certificates of *confermazione* (confirmation), and another of *stato libero* (unmarried status). It would not be surprising if he had written notes certifying to their conversions in order to help Jews or former Jews and then added the official stamp only to the original in the hands of the person involved, without depositing copies in the archives. Therefore, it is quite possible that Bishop Battistelli saved some Jews in this way.

Paggi implies above that Jews in the province of Grosseto did not need the help of clerics because there were no mass arrests and not a large number of "spiate," many of the Jews who were arrested having voluntarily presented themselves to the carabinieri when they were summoned. However, I cannot see why they would not have benefited from rescue by the church since after arrest they were placed in the same danger of deportation as Jews elsewhere, if not more so; everyone apparently assumed that they would be safe under the wings of Bishop Galeazzi of Grosseto. For comparison, Marcella Servi gave a sad appraisal of the fate of her Jewish relatives in Rome who converted to Christianity to be rescued by the church. Jews who had not been sent to Auschwitz had often taken refuge in convents and emerged as Christians. So, as she regretfully said, either they were dead, or they were dead to their relatives.[9]

As already noted, Grosseto Province seems to have been largely out of reach for the DELASEM network of Jews rescuing Jews, and subsequently of clerics rescuing Jews. Had there been an actual appeal for help from the local community, DELASEM no doubt would have tried to respond to the best of its limited ability. In the absence of such an appeal, however, naturally neither the rescue network nor any clergy was brought in. Some funds to help Jews were later sent from Genoa to Grosseto, and I hypothesize these might have been used to alleviate the living conditions, such as providing more food, for the internees in the camp. By this time (late 1943 and 1944) such funds were handled by the clergy, possibly by the bishop of Grosseto himself. The bishop did, in fact, occasionally hand out some small gifts, which would probably have been some kind of food. Enzo Collotti's contributor, Francesca Cavarocchi, concluded that "no episodes of help by the church in the Pitigliano area have been found."[10] Thus, perhaps the actions by the bishop of Pitigliano, Don Stanislao Battistelli, were the only exception. Bishop Battistelli seems to have been very cautious and circumspect in his actions, though they were successful as far as they went; he covered any assistance with his remonstrances against fraternizing with Jews.

## THE CHURCH IN GROSSETO AND BISHOP PAOLO GALEAZZI

To turn to Bishop Paolo Galeazzi, he had actually been a local priest in Terni just across the border in Umbria before being appointed bishop of Grosseto. During the First World War he was a military chaplain attached to the prestigious Bersaglieri regiment of riflemen (whose characteristic is that they would run rather than walk when marching). He was also apparently sympathetic to Fascism, even though clerics were not supposed to take political positions.[11] In 1943–1944, the Vatican had not recognized Mussolini's new government, the Republic of Salò, and, therefore, there was no need for the bishop to pay it the special homage ("omaggio" is his own term) which he did nevertheless (figure 5.1).

An article Bishop Galeazzi wrote deploring the actions of the Allied armies which bombed the Grosseto area actually earned him criticism from the Vatican. He contributed a chapter about the bombing of Grosseto to *Perfida Inghilterra*, a 1943 work of Fascist propaganda with about thirty contributors and an introduction by Goebbels. The outraged tone of his chapter and the context in which it was published go beyond what was considered appropriate for a neutral man of the church. He described in horrific detail the sufferings of the dying victims, and accused the Allies of deliberately targeting civilians. Bishop Galeazzi's article was termed "inopportuno, perché politico," (inappropriate, because it is political), and he may even have received "un rebuffo" (a rebuke) from the Vatican.[12]

In response to Bishop Galeazzi's allegations that American pilots were deliberately targeting civilians, American ambassador Harold Tittmann asked for proof before he would approach his government. Monsignor Tardini wrote that the Holy See could easily find the proofs and make a good case. He implied though that Bishop Galeazzi was not neutral, and it would not be enough to ask him. "The latter in a letter to the Holy Father stated that

**Figure 5.1 Bishop Galeazzi of Grosseto on the Steps of the Cathedral, Surrounded by Fascist Leaders, 1940s.** *Source*: Courtesy of Luciana Rocchi and ISGREC.

Grossetto is a city without any military targets, except for an airfield which is held by the Germans and is one of the largest in Italy (this was almost a detail of little importance)."[13] Cardinal Maglione also wrote a note suggesting that they ask Conte Galeazzo Ciano, Mussolini's foreign minister and son-in-law, and a native of the region, for details.

Bishop Galeazzi apparently had connections with Mussolini and with Mussolini's son-in-law, the young foreign minister Galeazzo Ciano. In the words of Angelo Biondi,

> It's true that he had relations with the Fascists, yes. He had relations with Mussolini himself and with Galeazzo Ciano for example. The relations, it seems, were oriented toward a series of activities he was promoting, that is the construction of churches in areas of *bonifica* (agricultural development). For example, during the Fascist period, the area of Albarese was colonized or settled by people who came from Veneto (Venice area) to Maremma, which was a special development area. Grosseto still suffered from malaria and there were a series of problems of this sort. . . . Whether or not he was a Fascist, that we cannot know.[14]

Years after the war, Bishop Galeazzi, likewise, showed what might be viewed as continuing loyalty to Fascism. Against all evidence, he defended a notorious Fascist who was accused of several mass murders. There are also indications, not proofs, it is emphasized, that Bishop Galeazzi may have helped the same person evade justice, with the possible help of the Vatican.[15]

There are multiple examples of the church's being drawn to Fascism and to the right, because of its instinctive and long-standing aversion to "godless" socialism and Communism. Research in the Archivio Storico Diocesano of Pitigliano has revealed many instances of the church's aversion to Communism and secularism in the 1940s. A civil marriage was described as "concubinage"; Communism was idolatry, and so forth. Bishop Galeazzi's own aversion to Communism and leaning toward Fascism as its main opponent were, thus, expressions of the culture of the Catholic Church in Italy at the time. The question then is how far he might have gone along the path of pro-Fascism.

It is intriguing, though not a basis for any conclusions, that there are certain similarities between Bishop Paolo Galeazzi and Count Enrico Galeazzi, known as "the Engineer." The count, together with his half brother Dr. Lisi-Galeazzi, an ophthamologist and the pope's most trusted physician, was a close confidant of Pope Pius XII. The Galeazzis were from Umbria, though I have not found evidence that the bishop and the two brothers were related. Luciana Rocchi, who has also considered this question, refers to circumstantial evidence derived from a common origin in Umbria and a confluence of interests, but emphasizes that there is as yet no hard proof of a family connection.

Count Enrico Galeazzi was the Vatican's official architect. He was interested in promoting sports among young Catholics and constructed a number of stadiums around Rome that are still used today. There is even a Galeazzi prize for sports that is still awarded every year in Italy. Besides being a builder like the bishop, like the pope the count was most troubled when the Allies briefly bombed Rome, destroying lives and properties in San Lorenzo, an area near the main railway station. In 1943, he was sent, or perhaps volunteered, as a special emissary from the pope to request Roosevelt and the Allies not to bomb the city.[16] Two documents prepared in Vatican City are of particular interest. One dated September 8, 1934, describes Enrico Galeazzi's achievements. Though a young man, the writer says that he rose in papal favor over older architects:

> One is astonished at how Galeazzi has received priority. . . . Most recently he has been called on to form part of the Pontifical Mission to Buenos Aires, and for this purpose has been appointed specifically to the Secret Order of Sword and Cape.

The writer continues to discuss this special favor, reserved usually for nobility, and predicts that Enrico Galeazzi will be nominated an official of the Azione Cattolica organization.

A later document, dated July 8, 1942, no longer expresses outrage, but shows resignation to the two brothers' influence over the pope, though there are still complaints. "At the Vatican the usual malcontents point out the influence that the Galeazzi brothers, intimate friends of the Pontiff, are gaining."[17] As already noted, one served as his cure-all doctor, though he was labeled a quack, the other continued to undertake delicate missions to the Americas on the pope's behalf. Bishop Galeazzi, like Count Enrico Galeazzi, was highly concerned about church property in his province. Thus, parallel origins, passions, and a modus operandi hypothetically link these two Galeazzis. Despite our lack of documentation, it is hard to imagine that these Galeazzis would not have aided in cementing Paolo Galeazzi's relationship with the pope and his influence at the Vatican.

The bishop of Grosseto was also, probably, on cordial terms with the recently appointed prefect of the province of Grosseto, Alceo Ercolani. The bishop's network of high-level ties both with the Vatican and with Fascists had won him special consideration in terms of extra funding for his church-building ambitions in the province, linked to the government's *bonificazione* [development] efforts. His goal was a church and a nursery school in every parish. Galeazzi succeeded in raising funds for, and eventually building, an impressive basilica in the provincial capital dedicated to the memory of those who had died in the Allied bombings (and in which he was eventually laid to rest), a number of churches, a seminary, and a nursery school in every parish. He would obviously have made an influential ally in the province.

## BISHOP GALEAZZI, PREFECT ERCOLANI, AND THE CAMP AT ROCCATEDERIGHI

When Prefect Ercolani took the initiative of approaching Bishop Paolo Galeazzi in early November 1943, to allow the Fascists to set up an internment camp—"camp di concentramento" in Italian—for Jews at his summer property in Roccatederighi (figure 5.2), Galeazzi readily agreed to rent it to him. After the war was over, Galeazzi claimed that he had done it under duress, that Ercolani told him that the decision had already been made. No evidence of such pressure exists, but if so it might have been the normal Fascist way of getting things done. The language the bishop responded with implies eagerness rather than duress. The Fascist government did not actually have the authority to requisition church property to use for its own political purposes. Rather than acquiescing, Galeazzi could have consulted with his superiors in the Vatican about what to do. Instead, he signed an informal, but full lease by which he would receive quite a large rent from the Fascist provincial government and would house and feed interned Jews.

**Figure 5.2** Bishop's Seminary Near Roccatederighi, 2018. Used as a *campo di concentramento* for Local and Foreign Jews, 1943–1944. *Source*: Photo by Judith Roumani, 2018.

The camp was supposed to charge the Jews for their meals.[18] The government would build a security fence and provide about twenty guards, fully armed with machine guns and grenades. The bishop would provide five nuns who would take care of the food and three male orderlies, all of whom would receive salaries from the provincial government. The outrage was still evident in Marcella's voice: "He rented, rented you understand, he rented [his seminary to the Fascists] to put the prisoners there and he made extra money by having . . . nuns prepare the food, and charge what was then an enormous amount of money for each prisoner. So an innocent he was not."[19] It was a potentially lucrative deal for the bishop and fulfilled the ambitions of the prefect.

The Roccatederighi camp was set up most expeditiously; it was ready to receive inmates in a few days. Prefect Ercolani, himself, was actually asked to explain why he had acted ahead of instructions from the ministry in Rome, which was indeed about to order such camps all over the parts of Italy still under Fascist-Nazi control, to impose "internment with a view to deportation."[20] A stiff letter to him from the ministry points out that this should have been a ministerial decision, which would have included the ministry's appointing a director for the camp, rather than the prefect. He, thus, joined Bishop Galeazzi in being castigated by his superiors for pro-Fascist zeal.

The lease document, together with other correspondence including a letter from the bishop, with what had he been Jewish would have been called incredible *chutzpa*, is reproduced in Collotti.[21] The letter claims payment of unpaid rent after the war from the postwar post-Fascist Italian government (pp. 89–91). In the original document, the bishop addressed the Fascist government with the phrase, "in prova di speciale omaggio verso il nuovo Governo" ("as proof of special homage to the new government"),[22] the then-new government being Mussolini's Nazi-allied government in Salò. In his copy of the lease sent to the postwar government, this phrase was obliterated. The bishop was never, to our knowledge, asked to explain, even after the war.

## FASCIST CONCENTRATION CAMPS FOR JEWS IN ITALY

What were the implications of interning Jews in camps? Mussolini's government in Salò was already subservient to German wishes. With Fascist collaboration, the Nazis had begun since October 1943 to arrest Jews in the large Italian cities, such as Rome. As of December 1, the Fascists were doing it for themselves. Jews were deported to extermination camps, mainly Auschwitz. As Alberto Giordano and Anna Holian suggest (2014), "Anyone with common sense could see that interning the Jews meant making them available for the Germans to seize them whenever they wanted and therefore exterminate them."[23] Rumors had been flying around for some time among Italian Jews, church officials, and Fascist government officials, not to mention the Allies, about the terrible fate that awaited Jews who were handed over to the Germans and deported. During the previous summer, Azeglio and Edda Servi had been made aware of the situation. One can only say that they discounted the well-founded warning they had received. Interning Jews amounted to deliberately putting them in harm's way, which is precisely why many Jewish families, even from information-starved Pitigliano, began going into hiding at this time.

Valeria Galimi discusses the degree of political knowledge among the internees within various Fascist camps. She compares two other camps in central Italy, Bagno a Ripoli and Civitella. The first camp was full of political prisoners who were well aware of the possible fate awaiting them; the second was full of families of Libyan Jews who happened to have British citizenship and included many children and elderly. When they had a chance to go free, in the confusion surrounding the Armistice in September 1943, many of the latter chose not to, as they believed they had nowhere to go and no means of support. This latter group was eventually deported to Bergen-Belsen. They obviously did not know the risks they were running by voluntarily staying in the camp.

The Jews in the Roccatederighi camp, at least the Italians, seem more like the Libyans. They were largely unaware of the terrible destiny of those who were deported, though they may have had suspicions. Azeglio Servi writes in his diary[24] in a neutral tone that those who were transferred were being taken to the "new" camp at Fossoli, the first destination after Roccatederighi. He may be implying that "new" might even mean "better." But the new camp at Fossoli which had been set up in conjunction with the Germans was designed to speed up the deportations. Despite the previous warning he had received, Azeglio could not imagine that Fossoli was the ante-chamber to Auschwitz. His daughter Edda also relates that as a good and uncomplicated man, there was nothing worse her father could imagine than people being sent to the north to work hard at jobs for which they had not been trained.

The new arrests and new camps for Jews were in stark contrast with what had happened only a short time earlier. In August 1942, a little over a year before the opening of the Roccatederighi camp, the Jews of Yugoslavia, then partially occupied by Italy, had been in grave danger. The Ustasha (Croatian Nazi allies) were massacring Jews and Serbs. Many Yugoslav Jews fled to the areas occupied or controlled by the Italian army, which set up a camp for them. The Germans requested, via Ambassador Bismarck in Rome, that they be handed over for deportation, and Mussolini signed off, "Nulla osta" (no objection) on the plan. But nothing actually happened because Italian army officers, whether out of humanitarianism or a reluctance to bow to German orders, did not act. Eventually, the Jews interned in this camp were transferred to Korčula, an island off Italy, where they were put up in hotels and *pensioni* (guest houses).[25] Galeazzo Ciano, the foreign minister, was intimately involved in the early stages of the affair,[26] and may even have relayed some of it to his provincial connections in Grosseto. In defense of Bishop Galeazzi one could speculate that he might have thought that setting up a camp for Jews in his area would somehow protect them, as some of the Jews of Yugoslavia were protected by the Italian army. He did not have the same Italian army, however, which by then had disbanded, part of it now regrouping as a close Nazi ally under the Republic of Salò. Nor did he seem to have any strategy in case of danger; so, in the end, many of the Jews under his tutelage were deported to their deaths.[27]

Returning to the bureaucratic moves that laid the groundwork for the catastrophe, the minister of the interior had reproved the over-enthusiastic Prefect Ercolani on December 7, 1943, with these words:

> Subject: Roccatederighi Concentration Camp: . . . inform you that the constitution and organization of concentration camps is the responsibility of this

Ministry. I thus request that you provide clarifications regarding the institution, providing detailed information on the [illeg.] of Rizziello.[28]

In stiff language, the minister stated clearly that Ercolani overstepped his authority in setting up the camp and, especially, in appointing its director himself. Ercolani waited until December 25 to respond, no doubt waiting for events in other parts of Italy to catch up with him. He stated that he had waited in vain for details and thought that it was urgent. His Excellency Buffarini had given the order to set up "campi per il concentramento dei cittadini di razza ebraica" (concentration camps for citizens of the Jewish race) at the meeting in Florence and Ercolani had considered the matter "urgente ed indifferibile" (urgent and not deferable).

His efficient camp director Rizziello reported in January 1944 that he had room for thirty more Jews, if beds could be provided. On February 24, Ercolani inquired with the chief of police in Rome as to where he should be sending the Jews, in view of "the approaching of the war actions" ("l'avvicinaria delle azioni di Guerra"); "Therefore kindly communicate where they should be sent" ("Prego, pertanto volere compiacersi comunicarmi ove gli stessi debbono essere tradotti"). He only had to wait until March 1, when a scrawled note from the Ministero dell'Interno informed Ercolani at his northern headquarters of Paganico that "they should be sent to the camp of Fossoli dei Bagni" ("dovrano essere trasferiti in quello di Fossoli dei Bagni").

Thus, assuming the hypothesis that Bishop Galeazzi wanted to protect the Jews, events outflanked him. If he had ever indeed intended to save Jewish lives by making himself responsible for them, he did not succeed, but rather put more lives in danger through his acquiescence and implicit approval of Ercolani's arrangements.

## ROCCATEDERIGHI CAMP

In the meantime, though, more needs to be said about how the Jews came to be caught in the dragnet of the Roccatederighi camp. On November 28, 1943, about twenty Jews were arrested by the carabinieri in Pitigliano. Most had responded to instructions to present themselves. Azeglio Servi, his wife Sara, and their nine-year-old son, Mario, had been hiding on a farm for three days. Because of his city-raised wife's infirmities and inability to adapt to the rough country living (e.g., no farmer had either indoor or outdoor plumbing), and Azeglio's sense of responsibility to the other members of the community, generally very old or very young, who had not gone into hiding, they returned home and presented themselves for arrest at the required hour in front of the café in the main square. All the Jews who presented themselves were put in a bus that began a no doubt uncomfortable journey into the hills to the north of the province. The four Servi teenagers who had gone into hiding had been told that the bus would pass by on the highway the next morning, and they rushed to a spot overlooking the road. There was nothing they could do to stop the bus, and they watched in anguish as it passed bearing the other members of their family. The internees eventually arrived at a large villa, the bishop's summer palace/seminary, surrounded by greenery and of course the new barbed wire fence and heavily armed guards.[29]

Luciana Rocchi describes the guards and their equipment: "Twenty militia, armed with automatic guns, machine guns, an appropriate number of hand grenades for each armed guard, and a barbed wire fence, patrolled night and day to prevent escapes and passing of messages. All this was to guard eighty prisoners, including elderly people, women and children, giving an external appearance that reminds us of the concentration camps of the Reich."[30] Along with the militia, there were also the camp commander or director, a commander of the militia, and, ominously, three agents of Public Security (Pubblica Sicurezza, PS). The bishop was also in residence with some of his seminarians, his sister, three male orderlies, and a kitchen staff of five nuns.

Vera Paggi's documentary film about life in the camp provides the sense of a rather Spartan and unadorned villa, isolated in the mountains.[31] In December 1943, when the Jews from Pitigliano arrived, there were already three Jewish families from Grosseto in residence. Everything had been set up with surprising speed and efficiency. The Jews had to keep their own rooms tidy but otherwise had nothing to do. Soon other inmates, mainly foreign Jews, joined them for a total of about eighty Jews. The various accounts differ as to exact numbers.

Different prisoners have relayed totally different impressions of this camp. Eugenia Servi, born in 1928, maintained that this was the happiest year of her life. She was about fifteen years old while at Roccatederighi. After experiencing five years of racial laws, and what must have been a stifling atmosphere for a Jewish teenager in Pitigliano, she was happy to be out of the town. "For me it was like a vacation in the country" ("Per me e stata una villeggiatura").[32] She enjoyed the park surrounding the villa, the mountain air, the friendliness of the guards, and her family's supervised shopping trips to the nearby village. They were even allowed to visit the dentist. A dozen or so foreign Jewish families were brought there and Eugenia appreciated their company. She admired their culture and the fact that all of them spoke three or four languages. She became particularly friendly with a younger girl, Edith Singer, who was later deported in the direction of Fossoli. No one close to Eugenia talked about the risk of deportation, and the pleasant and undemanding life continued until the following April for most of the inmates.

They could not celebrate the Jewish holidays but, on the other hand, they had not asked to, Eugenia tells us. The bishop sometimes distributed some extra food or treats. Eugenia's impression of Bishop Galeazzi was that he was "a lovely person [una persona deliziosa]." Until quite recently, perhaps on the basis of Eugenia's testimony, the bishop of Grosseto was still being praised in his province for having heroically saved Jews.[33]

Perhaps her view of internment was colored by her family's specific situation. Eugenia's father Tranquillo Servi and his brother were liberated after one month at Roccatederighi on condition that they regularly drive a truck to Volterra, a medieval town on a mountaintop in central Tuscany, to collect a load of salt, a most valued commodity, for the camp and probably for Grosseto and Pitigliano. They also picked up tobacco from Florence. This was very dangerous work as Allied planes were constantly strafing and bombing vehicles on the roads and partisans were on the watch for those collaborating with the Fascists. On one trip Tranquillo's brother Adelmo was badly beaten up by partisans.

Eugenia and the rest of her family stayed a little longer in the camp but were soon set free at their father's insistence. Rather than return to Pitigliano they stayed on a farm. Initially, they were under surveillance but later went into hiding like other Jews of Pitigliano. Eugenia's father early on had convened a meeting to persuade the Jews of Pitigliano already in hiding to hand themselves over for internment. He told them that there was no danger and pointed out the comforts and food at the bishop's villa.

Ariel Paggi's family and Tranquillo Servi's own relatives, Azeglio Servi and family, consider that Eugenia's father played a negative role, saving his own immediate family but putting other Jews in harm's way. Perhaps he and his family self-defensively never changed their minds about the situation, as many years later Eugenia still presented the internment camp in positive terms. When Eugenia's father tried to persuade other Jews to go into the camp by saying that the camp needed Jews to function, Ariel Paggi's sharp-witted mother Dina Sadun understood immediately what was going on, as Ariel writes. She set the example for the others present by refusing his offer, as all those who went into hiding did. Their belief was that Tranquillo had struck a deal to promote entry into the camp for other Jews while arranging for his family's and his own early release, which events confirmed. Edda and Marcella Servi, his nieces, also relate this incident but give credit to their brother Gino for seeing through Tranquillo's arguments. Eugenia's younger sister Carla has written a memoir defending her father.[34]

A far different view from Eugenia's emerges from the memories of Tranquillo's brother Azeglio's family. His two sons, Lello and Gino, had taken to the forest. Running considerable risk of arrest because all the interned Jews of Pitigliano knew them, they actually managed once, by posing as delivery men, to visit their parents and younger brother at the camp, according to their sister. Sara, their mother, suffered intensely during their visit as she could not embrace them and express her love and concern.

The food was meager in the camp and the inmates lost weight during their stay, except for those such as Tranquillo's family who were allowed to bring their own money and go out to buy extra food. When their imprisonment was over, Marcella Servi tells us, her parents and little brother Mario were like skeletons. Women lived in one dormitory and men in another, so families were separated. Mario stayed with his mother until his tenth birthday; then had to move to the men's dormitory. We hear stories of Azeglio dressing up in his wife's clothes and singing arias as part of the camp's home-made entertainment, but this was early on in their imprisonment.

Then the mood became somber. Marcella tells that Azeglio had entered a light-hearted and joking man, but came out psychologically broken and prematurely aged. He had been a somewhat naïve idealist, according to his children, someone who when warned to go into hiding had responded with naïve pride in his record as a loyal and law-abiding Italian that he had nothing to fear. Even in 1943, some Italian Jews still apparently trusted the Fascist system. Thus, their disillusionment must have been all the more intense and painful, especially for a sensitive person like the assistant rabbi, when they could no longer deny its evil intentions toward Jews.

The only written account by an inmate is the short diary, just four pages long, that Azeglio Servi kept in the inside covers of his prayer book. Listed are the names of Jews who were deported in two transports from Roccatederighi in April and June 1944. Less than a handful survived. The Servi family was overlooked for deportation by a miracle, according to the children. Though the families were supposed to be taken in alphabetical order, by some sleight of hand the list began at the beginning of the alphabet, then skipped to the end of the alphabet, and for the second transport it progressed backwards, thereby earmarking the foreign Jews but sparing the local Jews. On further examination, this turns out to be less of a miracle than a deliberate strategy. One can imagine how the carefree mood darkened once the transports began. Through it all the bishop was said to be giving undefined "moral support," whatever that was.

At least one and probably another of the Jews converted to Christianity and was saved. Another young Jewish woman fell in love with one of the guards and also seems to have been freed, because they later got married. Probably the bishop was hoping that by his apparent calmness and supposed "moral support" he would inspire more conversions. It is hard to imagine what he could have been saying to comfort the Jews whom he himself was co-responsible for putting in danger. As Luciana Rocchi and Paolo Pezzino both point out, and as Primo Levi has also written, survivors are likely to have some sort of gratitude to anyone who saved them or, as in the case of the bishop perhaps, who managed to prevent their selection. The actual selections, and strange manipulations of the alphabet, were officially made by the "militi," the Fascist guards and the camp commander, Rizziello. They very likely did these in consultation with the bishop. All the Jews of the town of Grosseto and most Jews of Pitigliano were passed over in the selections for the transports. The second transport (like the first) consisted entirely of foreign Jews, Jews from Livorno, those only indirectly connected with Pitigliano, or otherwise "out-of-towners." A group of foreigners escaped shortly before the camp was liberated. Whoever deserves praise for not selecting the thirty-four Jews who escaped deportation, also deserves blame for the forty-six who were, of whom thirty-three at least[35] ended their lives in Auschwitz. The whole unpleasant charade and tragic deceit of the Roccatederighi camp ended two days after the last transport on June 7, 1944.

In those days, and especially under the Fascist state, ordinary people, even Jews, seem to have been what we would consider today unduly impressed with uniformed authority, especially spiritual authority and its trappings. It must have provided them with a sense of comfort and the feeling that they were in good hands. Perhaps that is why some of the Jews who were interned clung to the illusion that the bishop was somehow protecting them, when in fact he did less than nothing to prevent, and actually allowed, the deportations. Their voices dominated the discourse on Roccatederighi for many years.

Bishop Galeazzi did not receive any reproof for his collaboration with Fascist and Nazi designs, but went on to serve as bishop of Grosseto until his death in 1971, for a total of thirty-nine years. He even served briefly on the Second Vatican Council, which dealt with the church's relations with the modern world and with other religions. He was one of the church fathers who served in the first session, but not in later sessions. There were four sessions; thus it is not possible that he would have been able to vote on the document involving Jews, *Nostra Aetate*. As a conservative type of bishop, probably such deliberations were not to his taste, and he withdrew voluntarily.

## ASSISTANT RABBI SERVI BETWEEN TWO BISHOPS

In his brief diary, the assistant rabbi Azeglio Servi does not mention any particular relationship he might have had with Bishop Galeazzi. Servi mentions that his *siddur* (prayerbook) was his chief companion and solace during those months. Considering that Azeglio decided to go to the camp because of his sense of responsibility toward the Jews of Pitigliano, one would think that he might have been more proactive, might have tried to establish a special relationship with the bishop in order to improve the Jews' conditions in some way, or might have engineered their escape. Apparently Jewish prayer services except perhaps a seder on Passover were not held, even though we read elsewhere of regular Jewish religious services being held in internment camps. For example, they were held in the much larger southern camp of Ferramonti, which had three synagogues. After all, Servi was an assistant rabbi who by that time was probably used to not having a *minyan* (quorum) of ten Jewish men for synagogue services in normal times. Here, he was in the presence of dozens of Jews with plenty of free time. Whether Azeglio asked and was refused by the Jews themselves (likely of secular culture) or by the camp administration, or whether, as the then fifteen-year-old Eugenia Servi confidently asserts, the Jews never asked, we do not know.

Azeglio had been much closer to the bishop of Pitigliano, Stanislao Battistelli, whose bishop's palace was the hulking former Orsini castle, the most impressive building in the town, requisitioned by the Nazis. There probably had been some smoldering issues between the two bishops, since Pitigliano had been demoted from the status of diocese or bishopric in 1924 over vehement protests from local Catholics and made subject to Grosseto until it was promoted again from 1932 on, with the appointment of Monsignor Battistelli. However, this lasted only until 1952. From 1952 to his death in 1981 Bishop Battistelli went on to serve first as bishop, and then as bishop emeritus of Teramo and Atri, near the Adriatic. He was a church father who participated in four sessions of the Second Vatican Council. After his departure in 1952, Pitigliano was demoted again to form part of the bishopric of Grosseto for a few years.[36] It is likely, in my view, that Azeglio Servi, having lived all his life in Pitigliano, and having had more to do with the rival bishop, may not have felt comfortable with approaching Galeazzi. Or he may have done so but been decidedly rebuffed. In any case the actual running of the camp was done by its director, Gaetano Rizzielli, appointed by Prefect Ercolani rather than the bishop. One can also imagine that Azeglio's state of mind was one of frustration and perhaps a sense of paralysis and pessimism over those seven months of imprisonment, leading to depression and despair as he saw the deportations begin.

## VIEWS ON BISHOP GALEAZZI

To this day, researchers are baffled by the behavior of Bishop Galeazzi. Angelo Biondi expresses it thus:

> It was a concentration camp, so it would have been better to have it requisitioned than to rent it out for the purpose, so the bishop does have a certain co-responsibility. It is not easy to make a judgment today, with the criteria of today. The

bishop was the friend of some local Jews and it is possible that he thought he might be able to protect them in some way. He himself had moved to that same building after the bombardment and so, being present, and there are testimonies by some Jews, including some from Pitigliano, who speak well of the bishop, and see his attitude, his moral help, as a form of protection. So it is hard to judge this situation. We would have to go into it in great depth, in a balanced way, to really understand the situation. But certainly it is most perplexing.

It may have been those whom Galeazzi favored and made sure to save, or whom the director saved with the bishop's tacit approval, who spoke well of the bishop. Galeazzi may very well have implicitly established a hierarchy of Jewish lives worth saving: first, those who converted to Christianity or in some other way rendered services he appreciated; second, the few Jews of Grosseto; third, Jews from Pitigliano, temporarily not within his purlieu; lastly, Italian Jews from elsewhere, and foreign Jews. His successor bishop, Monsignor Primo Gasbarri, in 1975, felt impelled to justify Galeazzi's actions and credit him with saving the local Jews. The explanation, however, merely confuses even more by claiming that some Jews preferred to be deported:

> As the front drew closer, the Germans decided to transfer all Jews to the extermination camps in Germany [in fact, as we have seen above, the decision to move them had come from the Italian Fascist government, communicated to the Italian governor of the province—J.R.]. Just before the transfer, Monsignor Galeazzi succeeded in persuading the prison camp director to let all 20 Jews of the province flee into the surrounding woods, thereby saving them from certain death, while the Jews of other nationalities preferred to follow the fortunes of transfer.

There seem to be several inaccuracies here. This account is in contrast to Paolo Pezzino, and most sources, who state that it was some of the foreign prisoners who managed to escape. Also, by the time of the suggested escape of local Jews (see chapter 7 for an attempt at reconstructing the sequence of events and which contradicts this), the others, mainly foreign Jews, had already been deported. Galeazzi's defender continues, "The Jews of the Province of Grosseto [perhaps actually the lone voices of Eugenia Servi, her father, and the Nunes family of Grosseto, as Azeglio never registered a public opinion, though his children have, and it was not positive] have always expressed their gratitude to the Bishop who, in full and sincere respect of their religious beliefs, treated them as his children, sharing with them the sadness of an unjust imprisonment and personally confronting danger for the sake of their liberation."[37]

Ariel Paggi notes in his discussion of Bishop Galeazzi that soon after the war his own family lived in Grosseto for a few years, where Ariel attended middle and high school. In Grosseto, in contrast with Pitigliano, there were still antisemitic pronouncements whenever the subject of religion came up in school. He considers that Bishop Galeazzi set this antisemitic tone. He describes:

> What in my opinion was stubborn hostility on the part of Bishop Galeazzi toward Judaism. I can cite my personal experience. There was a substantial difference between the priests of Grosseto and those of Pitigliano in how they dealt during the religion class with the subject of Jews. In Pitigliano they glossed over it, while in Grosseto, among all the religious teachers with whom I came in contact in the various schools, only one, Don Gaggioli in the middle school, did not accuse the Jews of deicide in order to portray the Holocaust as a just punishment."[38]

Paolo Pezzino in "Ebrei in seminario" is of the same opinion as Paggi and believes that Bishop Galeazzi embodied a form of "razzismo inconsapevole" (unconscious racism).[39]

It should be remembered, too, that Grosseto had received bombardments that caused serious casualties, as apparently there was a large German airbase nearby. Thus, the bishop's move to a separate wing of his summer palace in the hills together with his seminarians, his sister, a team of nuns to cook for them, and orderlies to clean, would appear to be more a matter of self-preservation than sacrifice.

Given Bishop Galeazzi's apparent sympathy for Fascism, his collaboration with the ruthless head of the province in putting Jews in danger in an internment camp, and his acquiescence in sending the Jews to deportation, it seems that the defenses of his reputation are largely whitewashing by those who could not bear to consider a bishop a collaborator due to his untouchable position.

## ALCEO ERCOLANI, PREFECT OF THE PROVINCE

Prefect Ercolani's motivations are not hard to determine.[40] It seems to have been a mixture of a desire to enrich himself, antisemitism, and zeal to show he was ultra-Fascist, all combined. In earlier years, he and his family seem to have had financial problems (his wife's family's business had a bankruptcy), which may have partly impelled his career ambitions. He attempted to have his membership as a *squadrista* (Fascist squad member) backdated, to increase his salary. He did achieve the well-paid position of governor, prefect or "capo di provincia." At the same time as arresting Jews and moving them to the internment camp, he instituted measures to expropriate their businesses, farms, apartments, and personal property, indicating perhaps a financial motive. The first expropriations, which took place even in cases where businesses had only one Jewish co-owner, took people by surprise and provoked appeals for clemency, which were rejected. Proceeds from the auctioning of Jewish property were supposed to be given to the local Fascist Association, which was in deficit. There are claims, however, that some amounts disappeared along the way, even went straight into the prefect's pocket. Ercolani's own words are that he planned to cover the initial outlay for the camp from the income derived from selling Jewish possessions: "In order to cover initial expenses, I have taken a hundred thousand liras from the general funds of this Prefecture, that will then be replenished from the proceeds of the possessions and real estate belonging to said Jews."[41]

Ercolani seemed inclined to adopt a harsher attitude toward Jews than even the Mussolini government. He inquired at one point whether the German Nuremberg Laws were to be applied. This shows a propensity to adopt the Nazi attitude toward Jews rather than the slightly more flexible Italian one, according to Luciana Rocchi.

Ercolani had served in East Africa, Spain, and Russia. He was decorated with seven medals for bravery in war; he tended toward the extreme type of the ambitious, cold-blooded, ruthless Fascist who surrounded himself with persons like himself. In March 1944 he ordered twelve young men from the village of Istia to be executed after a summary trial. Afterwards, Ercolani sent a letter of commendation to the executioners. The victims were not members of the Resistance but rather unarmed draft evaders.[42]

The German administration for Tuscany, based in Livorno, praised Ercolani for the Istia incident and indicated him as a model: "[The deeds of] the prefect of Grosseto, who had already distinguished himself on the Eastern Front, where he gave excellent proofs as a battalion commander and was decorated with the German military cross, and who now is the head of the province of Grosseto, these measures are indicated to the prefects and heads of provinces as worthy of imitation." Valeria Galimi holds that in Ercolani's case "we are confronted with a lively desire for loyal collaboration."[43]

Alceo Ercolani's personality emerges clearly also from other initiatives and actions of his. Following the meeting in Florence called by the Ministry of the Interior in November 1943 to brief the prefects on future plans, Ercolani had anticipated his instructions.[44] The concern behind this urgency, from his point of view, was that Jews who were under house arrest, or still free in their own homes, could flee at any time.

By February 1944, as the battleground was approaching and there would be renewed risks of the Jews' escaping from the camp, Ercolani wrote to the head of police of Mussolini's republic to request instructions as to where the prisoners should be transferred, receiving instructions to send them to the new camp at Fossoli. On April 18, 1944, the first transport of Jews from Roccatederighi was made on his orders, and on June 7 a second one, two days before the camp was dissolved. Ercolani was obviously one of those fanatical and cruel types who tend to rise to the top and take the reins in war, showing his true mettle in the March and April incidents.[45]

During his tenure, Ercolani received many anonymous tip-offs and what he called anonymous complaints from citizens of the province. Many must have concerned hidden Jews or the Resistance. Fulfilling ancient resentments between neighbors, they also involved other citizens not conforming to Fascist expectations. By April 6, 1944, the Fascists ruled only half of Italy, and the Allies were slowly advancing northwards and about to take Rome; thus, the wish for anonymity while settling old scores was understandable. There was a very active police surveillance of anyone suspected of marginal or "undesirable" behavior. In a public proclamation Ercolani described how he would deal with the unwillingness of anonymous letter writers to reveal their identities. The public announcement from Ercolani entitled "Anonimi" stated: "First I throw anonymous letters in the waste basket and then I disinfect my hands." ("Gli anonimi prima li cestino e poi mi disinfetto le mani.")[46] This sort of swaggering, together with their much harsher and crueler actions, was typical of die-hard Fascist leaders in the last phase of the regime.

Thus, in the heat of the war, this over-zealous and ideological prefect exhibited cruelty in his treatment of draft evaders and cupidity and active collaboration in the Holocaust in his handling of Jews. If his zeal for Fascism and the Axis cause can be comprehended on an ideological, factual level, his cruelty to draft evaders and treatment of Jews are still horrific.

## THE BISHOP AND THE PREFECT

Bishop Galeazzi, single-minded but with different priorities, a successful politician who achieved his ambitions for his province by allying himself with the Fascist government over the years, was probably nonplussed by the zealous prefect. If the bishop had ever hoped to save "his" (local) Jews, he realized that the staff of the seminary, the director, and the armed militia patrolling day and night, were all in the pay of Prefect Ercolani, and would carry out the latter's orders. Galeazzi was no doubt shocked by the March incident, the mass execution at Istia, and perhaps feared that the same could happen at Roccatederighi. His stipulations in the rental contract with the prefect[47] may have hinted at some sort of idea to save Jews, but he organized nothing of the sort.

Today, the compound has two potential entrances or exits; the one used now is from an upper road. There is a gate that leads to what may have been a short driveway for trucks and buses arriving on the same level as the building. The other approach today is totally blocked by overgrowth, to the point of being invisible. Far below, there is an iron gate and two stone gateposts marking the dramatic flight of steps leading up from a lower road. The steps and gate are now hidden under the creeping vines and bushes. In 1943, this approach was open and accessible. One might assume that even then the buses that brought Jews in and out of the premises and trucks that made deliveries may have entered from the more practical upper gate, while only pedestrians were able to enter and exit from the lower gate. It was more of a striking architectural feature than a practical entrance, giving importance to the villa from the bottom, and from the top commanding magnificent views. Another escape route usable in 1943–1944 might have been from the chapel at the rear of the building, which also had a few steps leading to the outside that were used by local villagers attending Mass. In any case, no escapes took place at the bishop's initiative. Bishop Galeazzi in the end merely managed perhaps to influence the selection of which Jews would be deported in the first and second transports, postponing for later the probable deportation of local Jews from his own province.

If one assumes that the bishop's intentions might have been pro-Jewish, then he greatly underestimated his own prestige as the bishop of Grosseto, whose moral authority even over Fascists could probably, in those waning days of the Fascist cause, have prevented the deportations, if only he had taken a stand.

## NEGATIVE VIEWS OF ROCCATEDERIGHI CAMP

Azeglio Servi apparently spoke to his daughter, who was not in the camp, of daily interrogations at Roccatederighi. Edda writes in *Child of the Ghetto* of frequent beatings, though she does not say that her father was affected. Her statements are at odds with the more positive picture presented by Eugenia Servi and by other local Jews. "Their parents, Azeglio and Sara di Capua, interned in the Roccatederighi concentration camp, were interrogated daily, because Ercolani wanted to capture the four children. The interrogators, though, did not succeed in their attempt."[48] It is possible that local Jews still in the area of Tuscany, such as Eugenia, felt constrained voicing any criticism, whereas Edda, living in New York and writing a memoir in English, did not have such inhibitions regarding the camp. There is also a chance that because she lived for many years in the United States, and read and heard about the Holocaust, she might have projected the accounts of other, harsher internment/concentration camps onto Tuscany. But, according to the documents, there were three security personnel assigned to the camp; perhaps their task was to interrogate. Conflicting, selective, and revised memories obscure our perception of what really went on at Roccatederighi, just as the invading vines and forest obscure our view of the bishop's seminary itself.

## NOTES

1. See Giovanni Miccoli, *I Dilemmi e i silenzi di Pio XII*, 2000; BUR Storia, 2007, esp. p. 437. Miccoli maintains that the pope may have been trying to protect his neutrality in the hope of eventually having some influence over the Nazis, but let any opportunity pass until it was too late. Rather than having a strategy, he and his hierarchy did not seem to have any real idea of how to act when faced with the unheard of barbarism of the Nazis.

2. See for example, Susan Zuccotti, "Pope Pius XII and the Rescue of Jews during the Holocaust: Examining Commonly Accepted Assertions," in *Pope Pius XII and the Holocaust,* ed. Carol Rittner and John K. Roth (London and New York: Continuum, 2002, 2004), pp. 205–220. In September 2014, the Vatican organized a lecture by Andrea Riccardi upon opening a new phase of its Holocaust-era archives. See Daniele Piccini, "Demolita la leggenda nera su Pio XII," (The Black Legend about Pius XII has been demolished) *Avvenire Roma Sette* Oct. 5, 2014, p. 4.

3. Liliana Picciotto has skillfully documented cases of rescue by clerics in *Salvarsi: Gli Ebrei d'Italia sfuggitti alla Shoah, 1943–1944* (Milan: Einaudi, 2017) as has Shira Klein, *Italy's Jews* (2018). An older source also has excellent descriptions of how some Italian clerics rose to the challenge of saving Jews, converted or unconverted, Italian or foreign: Susan Zuccotti's *Under his Very Windows: The Vatican and the Holocaust in Italy* (New Haven: Yale University Press, 2000). Zuccotti also mentions bishops who were pro-Fascist and not willing to help Jewish refugees: the bishops of Perugia, Modena, Mantua (pp. 258–259), and the cardinal patriarch (archbishop) and church hierarchy of Venice (p. 266). An even older source is Ivo Herzer et al., *The Italian Refuge*.

4. See Susan Zuccotti, *The Italians and the Holocaust: Persecution, Rescue, Survival* (New York: Basic Books, 1987), pp. 207–217 on priests who rescued Jews, as well as the note above.

5. According to John Cornwell, such a sentiment would not have been unusual, even under Pius XI. See *Hitler's Pope: The Secret History of Pius XII* (London and New York: Penguin, 1999, 2008), which quotes the bishop of Terracina's extravagant blessing on the duce in 1935, and states that "such sentiments appeared to welcome an alliance between the Holy See's vision of the Church as a universal 'sovereign society' and Mussolini's fantasy of a temporal empire in the making" (p. 175).

6. Achille Mirizio, "Repertorio di Fonti Archivistiche per la Storia della Chiesa in Toscana (1938–1948)" in Bruna Bocchini Camaiani and Maria Cristina Giuntella, eds., *Cattolici, Chiesa, Resistenza nell'Italia centrale* (Bologna: Il Mulino, 1997). See especially pp. 506–507, for 1944, "Beati coloro che piangono" and "Lettere sugli attuali momenti," as well as another chapter in the same volume by Achille Mirizio, "Fede, autorità e buon senso: Chiesa, vescovi e clero in Toscana negli anni quaranta," pp. 321–360.

7. One was Omero Martini, discussed previously. In 1970, Edda took her children to visit Pitigliano. "On our way back toward our hotel, we stopped in front of a courtyard where an old priest was sitting alone. He looked at us for a moment, then got up and, leaning heavily on his cane, he tottered to embrace me. "La figlia di Azeglio!" (Azeglio's daughter!) murmured Don Giovanni, his eyes brimming with tears." *Child*, p. 21. She does not say why the priest had such affection for her father. Since there do not seem to be any other references to a Don Giovanni, I would like to suggest that "Don Giovanni" might actually be Don Gennaro Fortunati, a vicar of the cathedral of Pitigliano who advised the Resistance and assisted in the Battle of Pitigliano in early June 1944. At that time he was a member of a Resistance committee and cautioned the partisans to be measured in their treatment of imprisoned Fascists and Germans. There is no proof as yet that he saved any Jews, but his moral support (if he was indeed one and the same as "Don Giovanni") could have meant a lot to Edda and her family. See *Banda Armata Maremmana*, pp. 173, 178.

8. Francesca Cavarocchi, "L'Organizzazione degli aiuti," in *Ebrei in Toscana*, vol. 1, pp. 388–389.

9. Interview with Judith Roumani and Vivienne Roumani-Denn, Jerusalem, 2009.

10. Francesca Cavarocchi, "Non sono stati rinvenuti episodi di soccorso ecclesiastico nel Pitiglianese." Ibid.

11. There was also, of course, the basic underlying fact of "Enemies in Common" that made bedfellows of the church and Fascism, in the face of socialism and Communism. See Kertzer, *Pope and Mussolini*. esp. pp. 227–240.

12. Bishop Galeazzi's article is in Sindacato Interprovinciale dei Giornalisti Lombardi ed., intro. Joseph Goebbels, *Perfida Inghilterra* (Lombardy: Sindacato Interprovinciale dei Giornalisti Lombardi, 1943). The Vatican's reaction is in *Le Saint Siège/Holy See* vol. 9, pp. 280–281, and Luciana Rocchi, *La Persecuzione*, p. 11.

13. "Questo in una lettera al S. Padre dichiarava che Grosseto è una città senza obbiettivi militari, ad eccezione di un campo di aviazione che è in mano ai tedeschi e che è tra i più grandi d'Italia (quasi fosse questo un particolare . . . di poco interesse)" (Tardini, quoted in *Le Saint Siège* vol. 9, pp. 280–281).

14. Interview with Angelo Biondi. Similar information is in Ariel Paggi, *Bambino*, p. 58.

15. Email communication from Luciana Rocchi.

16. Though his mission was somewhat changed during his journey in Sept. 1943. See http://paulonpius.blogspot.com/2010/10/story-of-enrico-galeazzi-1943.html. Cornwell, *Hitler's Pope*, provides more details regarding the pope and Count Enrico Galeazzi and Dr. Lisi-Galeazzi, his half-brother and the pope's physician, who treated (or according to many sources, medically mistreated) the pope until the end. These

two Galeazzis were certainly extremely close to the pope and his sister and official housekeeper, Pasqualina. Cornwell, pp. 176, 200–201, 351, 354–356. For numerous further insights on the obviously talented Count Enrico Galeazzi, and on his less than talented stepbrother, and their close relationship to the pope, see Robert Ventresca, *Soldier of Christ: The Life of Pope Pius XII* (Cambridge, MA: Belknap Press, 2013), pp. 110–112, 137, 141, 237, 291, 295, 301.

17. In 1934: "Si stupirà come proprio al Galeazzi sia stata data la priorità . . . . Il Galeazzi ultimamente è stato chiamato a far parte della Missione Pontificia a Buenos Aires, e per questo è stato nominato appositamente Cameriere segreto di Spada e Capa."

In 1942: "In Vaticano, dai soliti malcontenti, viene rilevato il predominio che stanno prendendo i fratelli Galeazzi, intimi amici del Pontefice."

Both documents are in the file Archivio Centrale dello Stato (ACS), files on prominent personalities, "Enrico Galeazzi," Pacco 546, Fasc. 70, No. 60.

18. Marcella Servi, interview with Judith Roumani and Vivienne Roumani-Denn, 2009.

19. Interview with Marcella Servi, ibid.

20. See Liliana Picciotto, *L'Alba ci colsi come un tradimento: Gli ebrei nel campo di Fossoli, 1943–44* (Milan: Mondadori, 2010), chapter 2, "30 novembre 1943: 'Tutti gli ebrei nei campi di concentramento'" pp. 28–33. All the eventual camps are listed, and the author states that in the provinces where no camp was set up, local prisons were used for the Jews. The book's title is a quote from Primo Levi. The quote in our text is from Robert Gordon's preface to Carlo Spartaco Capogreco, *Mussolini's Camps Civilian Internment in Fascist Italy* (London and New York: Routledge, 2019), p. xiv: "'Police order no. 5' of November 30, 1943, issued by the newly established northern fascist Republic of Salò, which stripped all Italian Jews of citizenship and decreed their internment with a view to deportation." The actual order may be viewed at campifascisti.it/scheda_provvedimento_full.php?id_provv=3. It was in fulfillment of the declaration of the Congress of Verona which that month declared "That those belonging to the Jewish race be considered foreigners. During this war they belong to an enemy nation"—a belated extension of the 1938 racial laws.

21. Collotti, *Ebrei in Toscana* vol. 2, pp. 86–87.

22. Op.cit. pp. 89–91.

23. Anne Knowles, Tim Cole, and Alberto Giordano, *Geographies of the Holocaust* (Bloomington: Indiana Univ. Press, 2014), chapter 3, "Retracing the 'Hunt for Jews': A Spatial-Temporal Analysis of Arrests during the Holocaust in Italy," by Alberto Giordano and Anna Holian, p. 100.

24. A laconic, four-page account written inside the covers of Azeglio's prayerbook, and apparently conserved by his eldest son Gino Servi, until its publication. With many thanks to Luciana Rocchi for permission to reproduce it.

25. This is how the Ladino singer from Bosnia, Flory Jagoda, and some of her family, were saved. See "Interview with Flory Jagoda," Rosine Nussenblatt, *Sephardic Horizons* 1: 3 (2011) https://www.sephardichorizons.org/Volume1/Issue2/Articles_V1I2/Flory_Jagoda.html and https://www.sephardichorizons.org/Volume1/Issue4/jagoda.html. They lived for two years on the island, before escaping to Bari in southern Italy.

26. For an account, see Susan Zuccotti, *Under His Very Windows*, pp. 117 and 125.

27. ACS, file "Roccatederighi," Busta No. 142, Fasc. 18, Inscr. 2 'Mobilitazione Civile' Inscr. 33, Grosseto 1940–1944."

28. "Oggetto Campo di Concentramento di Roccatederighi: . . . far presente che la costituzione e l'organizzazione dei campi di concentramento, come è noto, sono di compito di questo Ministero. Li prego per tanto di fornire chiarimenti cerca l'istituzione favorendo dettagliati notizie sul [illeg.] di Rizziello." Ibid. This scrawled messsage was also typed into a note from the minister, dated December 7, 1943, addressed to Ercolani, the "capo della provincia."

29. *La Persecuzione degli Ebrei nella Provincia di Grosseto nel 1943–44* (Grosseto: Istituto Storico Grossetano della Resistenza e dell'età contemporanea, 1996, 2002), p. 10.

30. "20 militi, armati di mitragliatrici, fucili mitragliatori, un congruo numero di bombe a mano per ogni milite, ed un reticolato di protezione, sorvegliato notte e giorno per impedire fughe e comunicazioni. Il tutto per sorvegliare 80 detenuti, tra cui vecchi, donne, bambini, offrendo un imagine esterna che ricorda i campi di concentramento del Reich." Ibid.

31. *Roccatederighi: Campo di Concentramento,* DVD directed by Vera Paggi, 2007. With thanks to Ariel Paggi. When she filmed the villa a few years ago it was totally neglected and unsurprisingly looked forlorn and depressing. My own visit in June 2018, confirmed this. In 2008, a plaque had been set up (ten years later stained with lichen and barely legible) to commemorate the deportation of the Jews. It does not list their names. A novel for young people also exists on the topic: Laura Paggini, *Pesante come una piuma* (Lecce/Livorno: Edizioniyoucanprint, 2014).

32. Interviewed in Vera Paggi's documentary. There is also an interview of Eugenia in the Visual History Archive of the University of Southern California Shoah Foundation.

33. "Ancora oggi sulla stampa locale il vescovo sia ricordato come 'amico premuroso e anche salvatore di alcuni ebrei'" (the bishop is still remembered today in the local press as "a caring friend and even a savior of some Jews") *La Nazione,* February 13, 2002, as Paolo Pezzino writes in "Ebrei in Seminario," *La Rivista dei libri* www.larivistadeilibri.it/2002/05/pezzino.html.

34. Carla Servi. *Una Infanzia perduta: Fra storia e memoria (Grosseto, 1943–1944)* (Empoli: Ibiskos Ulivieri, 2012).

35. For discussions of the numbers in different accounts and detailed tables listing names and fates, see Ariel Paggi's book, *Il Muro degli ebrei: Roccatederighi e la Provincia di Grosseto (1943–1945)* (Livorno: Belforte, 2018). Paggi in his book concludes that it is not possible to pin down the numbers precisely.

36. See www.catholic-hierarchy.org/bishop/bbatti.html.

37. "Con l'avvicinarsi del fronte, i tedeschi avevano deciso di trasferire tutti gli ebrei nei campi di sterminio di Germania. Alla vigilia del trasferimento, Mons. Galeazzi riuscì a persuadere il direttore del campo di prigionia a far fuggire nei boschi circonstanti tutti i 20 ebrei della provincia, salvandoli così da sicura morte, mentre gli ebrei di altra nazionalità preferirono seguire la sorte del trasferimento." "Gli ebrei

della provincia di Grosseto si sono sempre dimostrati riconoscenti al Vescovo che, nel pieno e sincere rispetto della loro credenza religiosa, li aveva trattati come figli condividendo con loro le tristezze di una iniqua prigionia e sfidando personalmente il pericolo per la loro liberazione." The words of Bishop Primo Gasbarri, quoted by Francesca Cavarocchi, in Enzo Collotti, ed., *Ebrei in Toscana tra occupazione tedesca e RSI*, p. 388.

38. "Quella che secondo me era un'ostilità pervicace del Vescovo Galeazzi verso l'ebraismo. Posso citare questo fatto personale. C'era una differenza sostanziale tra i preti di Grosseto e quelli di Pitigliano nell'affrontare durante l'ora di religione il tema degli ebrei. A Pitigliano si sorvolava, mentre a Grosseto, tra tutti gli insegnanti di religione con cui sono venuto a contatto nelle varie scuole, solo Don Gaggioli alle Scuole Medie non accusava gli ebrei di essere il popolo deicida per giustificare l'olocausto come giusta punizione" (*Bambino*, p. 58).

39. Pezzino, Paolo. "Ebrei in Seminario." *La Rivista Dei Libri/The New York Review of Books* (2002). www.larivistadeilibri.it/2002/05/pezzino.html.

40. Alceo Ercolani is well represented in the files of the Central State Archives (ACS) in Rome. See Min. dell'Int. 1814–1956. Direzione Generale Pubblica Sicurezza 1861–1981. Divisione polizia politica 1926–1945. Fascicoli personale 1926–1944. Busta 464. In a letter he sent to the duce on February 15, 1944, Ercolani declared himself dedicated to the duce heart and soul, and ready to die for him. This might just be the rhetoric of the day, but Ercolani was indeed ultra-zealous.

41. "Per fare fronte alle prime spese, ho rilevato lire centomila dai fondi in genere di questa Prefettura, che saranno dipoi reintegrate dal ricavato dei beni mobile ed immobili, di perteneza di detti ebrei." ACS, "Roccatederighi." Letter from Prefettura di Grosseto to Ministero del Interno, November 25, 1943, signed Alceo Ercolani.

42. A folded copy of a large poster, dating from March 1944, in the Archivio di Stato of Grosseto stated that any "renitenti alla leva" (draft evaders) would be subject "alla pena di fucillazione," (to be shot); as we see the prefect did actually enforce this.

43. "Il prefetto di Grosseto, già segnalatosi sul fronte orientale—dove ha fornito ottime prove come comandante di battaglione ed e stato decorato della croce militare germanica—e che oggi è anche capo della provincia di Grosseto . . . queste misure sono state segnalate ai prefetti e ai capi di provincia come degne di imitazione" Galimi's translation to Italian from the German. She adds "Ci troviamo di fronte ad un vivo desiderio di leale collaborazione." Valeria Galimi, "L'Internamento in Toscana," in Collotti, ed., *Razza e fascismo, La persecuzione contra gli ebrei in Toscana* (1938–1943) *Saggi* (Rome: Carocci, 1999), p. 557, note 218.

44. The meeting in Florence was in fulfillment of the Verona Assembly of November 14, 1943, at which it was decided that all Jews in Italy without distinction were to be arrested.

45. Many examples of such Fascist behaviors are provided in Angelo Del Boca, *Italiani, brava gente?* and in Michael Ebner, *Ordinary Violence*.

46. A poster reproduced in Giulietto Betti and Franco Dominici, *Banda armata maremmana* (Arcidosso: Effigi. 2014), p. 39.

47. Letter from Bishop Galeazzi summarizing the contract: "Without creating any obligation for any entrance that would be left free, during the stay of the Jews, at the

director's discretion and with the explicit understanding that when the camp ended the entrance would remain open or closed at the sole wish of His Excellency the Bishop." "Senza creare alcuna servitù per qualsiasi accesso che sarà lasciato libero, durante la permanenza degli ebrei, a discrezione del Direttore e con intesa esplicita che a termine del campo gli accessi stessi rimarranno aperti o chiusi a solo beneplacito dell'Eccellenza il Vescovo." One wonders what the bishop had in mind when creating this clause. Did he envisage himself perhaps leading the Jews to freedom and rescue, or was he making sure he would have an escape route for himself? Letter, Grosseto, Sept. 19, 1944, to Ministro dell'Interno, Roma. Reproduced in Luciana Rocchi, *La Persecuzione*, p. 53.

48. "I loro genitori, Azeglio e Sara di Capua, internati nel campo di concentramento di Roccatederighi, furono interrogati quotidianamente, perché l'Ercolani voleva mettere le mani sui 4 ragazzi. Gli aguzzini, peró, non riuscirono nel loro intento." *Banda armata maremanna*, p. 239. Also *Child*, for example, p. 193.

*Chapter 6*

# Foreign Jewish Refugees Who Fled to Tuscany

*Early Experiences*

### FOREIGN JEWS IN ITALY

Large numbers of Jews in central and northern Europe turned to Italy as a haven or as an escape route, especially after Kristallnacht (November 1938). Each family or individual had their own hopes and plans, often frustrated by Italian bureaucracy and official antisemitism, though such people frequently found kind individual Italians whose small actions helped them along their way. Anna Pizzuti has compiled statistics which report that 8,810 Jewish refugees became "internati" or "confinati" (both mean internees, to different degrees) in Italy during the Fascist period. If they were not in internment camps, they were usually billeted with Italian families, received a very small, intermittent stipend, and reported to the local police station at frequent intervals to ensure that they would not flee. Pizzuti's statistics also include the following information for many: the date or year of birth (7,582), their place of origin (3,548), whether they belonged to a family unit (5,128), and who were their fathers (8,191) much more often than who their mothers were (1,551). We also learn to which camps they were eventually sent (in 7,640 cases) and the progress and outcome of their internment in 6,829 cases.[1]

Statistics, though, tell neither about the persecutions and anguish these foreigners experienced before they took the decision to uproot themselves and flee to Italy and beyond, nor about their hopes and plans, and very little about the very different outcomes they encountered on Italian soil as they were faced with making ever more excruciating decisions with life or death consequences. Many had tickets or hoped to buy tickets to sail to the Americas from such ports as Genoa or to embark for Palestine from Trieste. When war broke out in September 1939, and trans-Mediterranean crossings were halted, many foreign Jews found themselves marooned in Italy. Their temporary visas allowing them to stay in Italy were not extended, and they searched in vain for other destinations, while the Italian government was requiring all foreign Jews to leave.

## INTERNMENTS IN SOUTHERN TUSCANY

The "Saga of a Child"[2] is the story of Walter Mundstein, who was born in Vienna. His family tried to reach Palestine via Italy, but got stuck in Benghazi, Libya, and in 1941 returned to Italy to a camp in Cosenza (perhaps Ferramonti). Later they became "free internees" at Civitella Marittima in the north of the province of Grosseto. The fourteen-year-old boy escaped to the woods and joined the partisans for nine months. He was caught in June 1944 and sent to Germany to an unnamed concentration camp; he then managed to escape and waited near Verona for the Americans. He eventually refound his family, which had apparently avoided arrest, in Rome. This is the story of just one family of foreign Jews who were marooned in the province of Grosseto, one of the luckier families.

The pattern of internments in southern Tuscany may not have been unique to the region. Many people, Italians and foreigners, were displaced in Italy during the war. As time went on, especially by late 1943 after the Armistice with the declaration of the Republic of Salò, the Nazi invasion, and the Allied offensive, ordinary Italians perceived safety in the countryside, where there was less danger from bombing. A number of foreign Jews were interned by Mussolini's government in and around the small town of Arcidosso in southern Tuscany, high up in the hills in the north near Monte Amiata. This is not exactly a ski resort, but a simple town catering to vacationers and hikers escaping the summer heat. Others were interned in Civitella Paganico, where Ercolani established his northern headquarters, and in nearby Roccalbegna.[3]

Around 1940, some of the male refugees among the foreign Jews had been sent south to the large internment camp of Ferramonti, near Cosenza, an inhospitable and unhealthy malarial zone. Some of their families later joined them. Manlio Paggi of Pitigliano had been sent south to another camp closer to Naples, Tricarico. Very different views of all the southern camps are expressed. Vatican representatives who visited reported satisfaction, although they offered substandard housing, poor drainage, the risk of malaria, and little food. There was little medical care except that provided by prisoners who themselves happened to be doctors and nurses and could manage to organize their own clinics. There was also no new clothing, even for those who had been there for several years and were practically in rags.[4] As Carlo Levi writes, "Christ stopped at Eboli." Prisoners must have been very anxious to leave these camps, even after the Allies had arrived.

Ferramonti and other internment camps in the south were liberated by the Allies in August and September 1943, and the inmates scattered. Some prisoners were taken northwards as the Fascists withdrew. Some heads of families who had been separated from their families who had remained in the north sought to rejoin them in Fascist territory, which they could have seen as the more "civilized" part of Italy. Also, perhaps, they may not yet have had faith that the Allies were going to hold on to southern Italy, as they had seen how battles in North Africa had waged back and forth; cities such as Benghazi had changed hands several times. Returning northward, foreign Jews found that what they had once perhaps considered a more comfortable place of refuge was no longer such, and those in central and northern Italy were almost all arrested by the end of 1943.

Imprisonment in the gulag of Italian camps had been for several years a most common fate for political opponents, subversives of all types, and even people who were socially marginal, "indesiderabili." A sentence of assignment to one of the camps followed arrest for the most trivial of offenses. Banishment and imprisonment in various forms came with different names but amounted more or less to the same thing.[5]

The small town of Arcidosso to the north of Grosseto had by far the largest number of foreign Jews in so-called free internment in 1943 (twenty-three in one source, twenty-eight in another).[6] Free internment meant that they were apparently free to come and go, billeted on Italian families, but obliged to report to the police at a fixed time every day. Foreign Jews did whatever they could to earn a living beyond the meager government allowance, improve their diet, and recompense their generally kindly hosts for small favors. In Roccalbegna, one foreign Jew was a furrier and raised rabbits. Another foreign family raised geese and had promised to invite local Italians to a feast when they had fattened them up (Ariel Paggi, interview with unnamed elderly residents of Roccalbegna). Unfortunately, the family was arrested before this could happen.

We shall follow the destinies of five families, one couple, and one individual who found themselves trapped in southern Tuscany, in the province of Grosseto—just a few among the many foreign or non-local Jews there. The foreigners were intelligent, principled, well-educated, and resourceful. They were also more acutely aware of the threats facing Jews than Italian Jews were. These qualities were not enough to save them, as their choices and options narrowed. All these stories reveal the contradictory behaviors of Italians toward these foreign Jews, after the Italians had been subject to five years worth of the Fascist regime's antisemitic propaganda. Most of the stories have to be pieced together as "paper lives," the lives of individuals traceable only through documents after their total disappearance, a term originated in Italian by Ana Pizzuti.[7]

Figure 6.1  Painting by Egon Mosbach, Internee at Arcidosso, Prisoner in Camp of Roccatederighi, Died in Subcamp of Auschwitz Untitled, 1943. *Source*: Courtesy of Adriana Bargagli.

## EGON MOSBACH

Egon Sigmund Mosbach (born March 1892) was the son of Albert Mosbach from Iserlohn, Germany. He was a single man, but perhaps was once married, and possibly had a daughter somewhere. He had no relatives with him in Italy. By 1943, he would have been fifty-one years old. The Mosbach family had moved to Iserlohn from Bruchsal. Johanna Helene Mosbach, Egon's sister, married Ludwig Strauss in Iserlohn. One of her sons, Siegbert Strauss, moved to New York in 1939 and was followed by the rest of the family in 1940. Their uncle, Egon, though, had fled to Italy, where he first lived in Urbisaglia, in the Marche, and later in Arcidosso. It is not known whether he intended to join his relatives in America or was trying to reach Palestine. He is said to have been a traveling salesman by profession. In Arcidosso he painted watercolor landscapes and gave one or more to a local shopkeeper in gratitude for providing him with some extra foodstuffs above the meager rations (figure 6.1). Adriana Bargagli, the shopkeeper's daughter, wrote to me:

> Your letter, completely unexpected, has greatly moved me and touched me, and has taken me back to distant but unforgettable times. At the time, in 1943, I was 11. I remember those young people, interned, because they were Jews, in

the small village of San Lorenzo, not far from Arcidosso. They came to shop in the grocery shop that my father Vezio Bargagli ran. Because of the war, food was rationed, so my father generously gave them extra bread and other foods . . . just basic necessities. Even though he was loyal to the regime then in power in Italy, my father had not forgotten how to be a man and a Christian, and did not approve of certain inhumane decisions, such as racial and religious persecution. One of these young people, to thank him for his benevolence, made him a gift of some small watercolors that he had painted during those sad months of imprisonment and I send you a photo of one that still remains.[8]

Other paintings were given as gifts to Egon's hosts, the Bigi family, before the carabinieri came to arrest him in November or December 1943 on the orders of Ercolani. Painting, a hobby he must have practiced before his exile to this area of beautiful Tuscan landscapes, could have been of great comfort to this refugee. Together with about thirty others, Mosbach was transferred to Roccatederighi camp, where he was imprisoned until April 1944. A young adult novel about Roccatederighi by Laura Paggini[9] portrays a painter, obviously Mosbach. In one scene, when a child who is observing him comes closer, he sees that the painter is not reproducing the magnificent landscape in front of him; he is painting a flat landscape, a scene from the town of his childhood. There is little conversation between the painter and the boy, probably because the historical sources regarding Mosbach are so meager.[10] The real Egon Mosbach was sent in the first transport in April from Roccatederighi camp, in one of the old buses, to Fossoli di Carpi, the large transit camp near Parma, and thence by train to Auschwitz.[11]

The only trace of his existence and his passing through Italy consists of the few paintings he left there and the tales attached to them.

## TURTELTAUB FAMILY: EDMUND, GERTRUDE, HANS, AND WALTER

The family of Wolf Meier Turteltaub and his wife, Amalia, was originally from Galicia; they emigrated at the end of the nineteenth century due to the severe economic situation, as well as pogroms. By the turn of the century they were living in Vienna where their two children, Edmund and Eva, were born. In 1903 twins were born, and after two more moves, the family was living in Innsbruck, where they founded a textile company in 1911.

Their son Edmund graduated from technical high school in 1917 and began studying chemical engineering in Vienna and Munich. He later worked for a few years in Innsbruck as a transportation engineer. He married Gertrude Popper, a Czech Jew, and they occupied a rented room until the birth of their son, Hans, when they moved to a room over the new family store in Dornbirn. Soon another son, Walter, was born. The storeroom, family quarters, and salesroom all shared the same premises. Profits were probably extremely low, due to the antisemitic boycott. Although Dornbirn was known as a nest of Nazis ("un nido bruno") and several letter bomb incidents are recorded, the few local Jews were not seriously bothered until 1933. With the Anschluss in 1938, life changed irrevocably for the Turteltaubs, as it did for all Austrian Jews. Nazis surrounded their house at night and shouted antisemitic chants, according to their landlord's son. The Turteltaubs stayed on, though, while others fled; Edmund had been appointed a member of the local synagogue's executive board, while the synagogue itself had been reduced to twenty-seven souls. The six-year-old Hans began primary school in September 1938, while the family at the same time had applied for and received passports, meaning that they did not see a future for themselves in Austria. On Kristallnacht in November, the seventy-year-old father was roughed up and put into so-called "preventive detention," together with two other family members. The landlady received threats for renting to Jews and felt obliged to ask them to leave. Little Hans was thrown out of school. In January 1939, the whole family received Jewish identity cards. Their fingerprints were taken, and like all Jews they were given the names "Israel" or "Sara."

After the cancellation of their lease, the Turteltaubs went to join the extended family in Vienna. Sympathetic friends from Dornbirn later visited in June 1939, and Edmund, the father, in a letter to their former landlady Rosa Walter reported that he had found work in Uruguay. They had a reservation and tickets to sail from Genoa on September 2. In July, they left for Milan, where many foreign Jewish refugees were living. The last known photograph of the family, taken in August 1939, shows them in Milan looking confident and optimistic. However, the outbreak of war, on September 1, erased all chance for their departure the next day. They seem to have returned to Milan, and Edmund sent a telegram to Rome requesting exit visas for Bolivia, which were denied, but from June 1940 on, all foreign Jews were subject to "internamento libero." Other members of the Turteltaub family, Edmund's sister and her son along with other nephews, had fled illegally to Trieste in early 1939, whence they reached Palestine on a clandestine ship. Edmund's brother, Fritz, managed to reach Britain. Other family members were eventually deported to Riga, Terezin, and Lublin, or Auschwitz, where they were murdered.

Edmund's request to extend their stay in Italy was also rejected: desperate to leave, these foreign Jews had no way of doing so. Edmund was put in an internment camp in central Italy, Isola Gran Sasso. The rest of the family seems to have stayed in Milan, until they were all put under arrest and sent to the large southern camp of Ferramonti, in Calabria, where the family reunited in February

1941. Though the physical conditions were very basic, and there was always the risk of malaria, the internees had a school, synagogues, and the help of sympathetic local clerics and neighbors. The Turteltaubs were no longer there when the camp was liberated by the Allies. Gertrude had fallen ill with Hodgkin's disease and received radiation treatment in a hospital in Rome in October 1941. After her treatment, they somehow ended up in internment in Arcidosso.

We do not know why they were in Arcidosso; perhaps they had sought to be there because they had a preference for northern or central Italy as being more salubrious than the south, or perhaps they were sent there since Arcidosso had a large number of empty rooms and small hotels for tourists. There was also a deliberate Fascist policy to send Jews to such remote villages because it would be harder for them to leave. Though one might have thought of such villages as potential places of refuge, foreign Jews stood out, and their obligation to report to the police station at a fixed hour every day made any mobility very difficult. Cooperative villagers helped find housing in some cases. For example a Signora Pierini enabled one of three Jewish families to lodge in an empty house in Roccalbegna, according to Ariel Paggi. Here, a crucial confusion shows up. Did the cooperative Italians think they were helping the foreigners or the Fascist government that was interning them there when all they wanted was to leave Italy? If the Turteltaubs had sought to go north to Tuscany on their own initiative, it turned out with the benefit of hindsight to have been a terrible mistake.

Life in Arcidosso was pleasant; over twenty German-speaking foreign Jews from Austria or Germany were there. There was beautiful scenery and a small Italian government allowance for each internee. In addition, local people tried to ease their lives in small ways. Anna Periccioli, a villager from Arcidosso, wrote a moving account of her memories of the Turteltaub family over their roughly two years in the town when she was a child.[12]

Edmund Turteltaub was tall and dressed elegantly in Austrian style; he was a consummate chess player, as was his son, Hans. He was also a skilled raconteur, presumably by now in Italian, telling stories of his life and travels; his wife spoke less Italian. They were often invited to Anna Periccioli's home in Arcidosso. Her father was the local postmaster. The foreign Jews who came to the post office were ushered into a back room, to wait until everyone else had been served, upon which the postmaster himself would serve them. Anna remembers Hans being sent to buy milk, and sometimes being pushed out of the line because people did not want to wait behind a Jewish boy. Anna, herself, would buy the milk for him, while he waited outside with her grandmother. In summer, the Periccioli and Turteltaub children would wander the fields and lanes, picking wild cherries together. The Pericciolis would invite the Turteltaubs to the cinema when the occasional film was being shown. Three Italian friends of the Jewish family (Ferruccio Innocenti

Periccioli, Carlo Rossi—an elderly socialist woodworker—and their friend Signor Ambrogi, according to Clara Ambrogi, interviewed in Arcidosso by Ariel Paggi) offered to hide the Turteltaubs when the danger of imprisonment became clear in early December 1943, but Edmund refused, saying that he did not wish to endanger his friends.

Finally, on December 12, 1943, Prefect Ercolani's plan went into effect and the Turteltaubs were arrested by the local carabinieri and taken to Roccatederighi camp as part of the group of foreign Jews living in Arcidosso. Before the trip, the whole family was imprisoned overnight in the local police station, where Anna and her sister went to see them. They were all huddled together in a corner. Anna's sister threw them a beret, while another, unnamed woman who had black market money obliged Edmund to take it. "It could be useful," she told him.[13] Thus, though one might have expected some hostility to Jews in the town of the province where the highest number and the highest percentage of arrests, or 100 percent of foreign Jews took place,[14] there were several who helped and would have done more if the Jews themselves had not perhaps underestimated the danger. Even though by December 1943, much was known, who among these isolated ordinary people knew for certain what awaited the Jews in Roccatederighi and after?

## WALDMAN FAMILY

The Waldman family was of Polish origin, although two members were actually born in Paris. Franciska, born in 1893, and Alberto, born in 1909, as well as Srul Beer, born in 1890, were stateless persons of Polish origin who reached Milan from Paris. Henrietta Zundler, born in 1891, also stateless and of Polish origin, was married to a Waldman. They followed a path similar to that of the Turteltaubs. They spent some time in the Ferramonti camp but later were interned in Roccalbegna, another small hill town near to Arcidosso and Roccatederighi. They were arrested by the carabinieri on December 7, 1943, and sent to Roccatederighi.

## DAVID AND OLGA POLLAK

David Pollak, son of Samuele, and his wife, Olga Gottlieb Pollak, were a childless couple. He was born in Vienna in 1886, said to be of German citizenship. He had also been in Ferramonti, and they were later interned in Civitella Paganico, a local town in the north of the province, which became the northern headquarters of the provincial government. They were arrested on December 12, 1943, and taken to Roccatederighi. David Pollak was thus fifty-seven years old at the time.

## THE ROSENFELD/SINGER FAMILY

We have much more information and a special insight into the story of the Rosenfeld/Singers. The family, including the young Edith Singer, were Jews of Hungarian origin from Yugoslavia: Ernst, Ernest, or Ernesto Rosenfeld was born in 1907 in Szanta Bakaka, Hungary; Szerena or Serena Rosenfeld Singer, his sister, was born in Szabadadka, Hungary, and was married to a Singer who was not present; and Edith Singer (Szerena's daughter) was born in 1932 in Vukova. They were accompanied by Edita, or Edith, Hafner Rosenfeld, Ernesto's wife. It is possible that the women had been protected by Italian troops from the Ustashas and brought to Italy for their protection. Ernesto had been a partisan in Yugoslavia. All of them were arrested as a result of a "spiata" (being informed on) while they were living in Castel del Piano. They had probably left their official residence and were in hiding. The reward for denouncing a Jew was tempting: a kilo of salt, a precious commodity in those days. The arrests took place on December 7, 1943, at Cinigiano, and the prisoners were transferred to Roccatederighi on December 29.

Although Azeglio Servi attempted to list all the inmates and their destinations in his short diary, he did not know the names of some of the Yugoslavians, listing them as "signora Jugoslava," for example. There was obviously a language barrier among the older generation in the camp. The eleven-year-old Edith, though, must have spoken adequate Italian, as she became fast friends with the fifteen-year-old Jewish girl from Pitigliano, Eugenia Servi. Eugenia expresses her admiration for the foreign Jews who joined them in captivity because of their sophistication and education, especially their skills in foreign languages. She talks of positive memories of socializing and playing cards in the camp.

Though Tranquillo Servi obviously knew what was good for his family, obtaining an early release for them, his young daughter, Eugenia, was devastated. She hated the idea of returning from the camp to Pitigliano, which she saw as swarming with hostile Fascists; she did not want to leave her new, cosmopolitan, multilingual friend, Edith Singer. The Jews of Pitigliano mostly spoke only Italian, and knew some Hebrew. The night before she was to leave, Eugenia sat outside on the steps of the seminary, crying profusely, "come una fontana" (like a fountain) as she said in her interview for the documentary film, and her friend, Edith, tried to comfort her. They never saw each other again. Eugenia believed that Edith and her family were deported from Fossoli and died in Auschwitz.

Edith Singer is portrayed as a major character in *Pesante come una piuma*, the young adult novel about Roccatederighi. Her premonitions of death contrast with the superficial optimism of the Italian Jewish children. Edith is transformed into the owl that haunts the place decades later. Though much is imaginary in the novel, the author of this novel has done her history homework, and thanks the researcher Carlo Groppi of the ISGREC institute for providing her with much information.

## ELDA MOSCATI CAVA, ALDO CAVA, FRANCA, AND ENZO

Other "out-of-towners" in Roccatederighi were Italian Jews. The fate of two families from Livorno is tragic, exceptions among the Italian Jews who were interned in this camp. Elda Moscati Cava, born in 1909, was the daughter of the respected Abramo Moscati and Gismonda Sadun of Pitigliano; she had grown up in Pitigliano, in fact. She married Aldo Cava of Livorno, born in 1899, the son of Adolfo Cava and Adele Giolli. The young couple established their home in Livorno. They came to Pitigliano from Livorno to seek temporary refuge. There in Pitigliano, a place where the Livornese husband had no contacts and no livelihood, they had trouble finding food, especially as Jews' ration cards had been canceled. Thus, they spontaneously presented themselves for arrest and transportation to Roccatederighi, where they arrived on December 2, 1943. Their two children, Franca, born in 1931, and Enzo, born in 1936, were with them. A week later, another Moscati family member, Elodia Colombo, joined them after voluntarily handing herself over. The option of going into a rough hiding place and being maintained by a secret network of farmers either did not appeal to them as city folk or was not offered to them as they were out-of-towners without the long-standing financial and professional relationships maintained by Pitiglianese Jews. They also may have heard the good reports of the camp being spread by Tranquillo Servi. Only those local Jews who were by nature extremely skeptical (a quality that Ariel Paggi mentions in reference to his mother), and in addition had good contacts, were capable of resisting the call. They perceived that although Roccatederighi would be a safe refuge from bombings and there would be food, it would be at best a precarious refuge from Nazi-Fascist anti-semitic designs. Thus, the Cava family, more trusting than others, made the fateful decision to enter the camp.

## PASERMAN FAMILY: MOSZEK, ANNA, DAVIDE, AND LEONE

The Paserman family was a family of foreign Jews who were particularly fortunate. Moszek (Maurizio) and Anna Paserman had arrived in Genoa from their native Poland in January 1934, where their sons Davide and Leone were born in 1935 and 1939, respectively. Their father had been employed with a private company in Genoa. Anna's teenage sister, Bruna Cukier, came for Leone's birth and could not go back to Poland because of the Nazi invasion in September 1939. The Pasermans' Polish citizenship was revoked because they had been away from the country for more than five years; under Fascist racial laws they did not qualify for Italian citizenship. Thus, they were sent to Montefiascone, near Viterbo, just north of Rome, for "confino" (house arrest).[15] The father was initially sent south to Ferramonti, but after nine months was allowed to rejoin his family in Montefiascone. In August 1942, the entire family managed to be sent to Pitigliano, following the parents' application for their children to attend the Jewish school in Pitigliano. Leone Paserman and Ariel Paggi have fond memories of being classmates, the youngest in the school. The family had good relations with the local Jews; they lived in the same building as Ariel's family. The Pasermans were as alarmed as the local Jews were when news filtered through via the grapevine of the deportation of the Jews of Rome in October 1943.

In November, Pietro Felici, a local, non-Jewish farmer, overheard a conversation among some Fascists at the "osteria" (public house), saying that the carabinieri had received orders to arrest the Pasermans and send them to the police in Florence the next morning. Felici knew the Pasermans slightly. That very night, he warned them of their imminent arrest and offered them a hiding place on a farm owned by his family and the Paoli-Bizzarris in the area of Pantano, south of Pitigliano. The desperate Pasermans followed him on foot in the middle of the night for several kilometers. There were tufa caves on the property, as in many places in the area, and they gratefully lived in one for several months. The adults never went out, only the children, who could be confused with local children. Such a life had to be much harder on the adults than on the children, who probably thought it was fun. Risking his life and not asking for anything in recompense, Pietro Felici brought them food during all those months. In early April 1944, an action by the partisans led the local Fascist leader to flee Pitigliano, so the Pasermans felt it was safe to return to the town, until the final liberation in June. According to Leone Paserman, it was not really safe yet, but his father was anxious to reopen the "forno degli azzimi" (Jewish community matza oven) and bake matza for Passover. In

July, he and Azeglio Servi together reopened the synagogue for services. Thus the Pasermans were a fortunate exception among foreign Jews.[16]

## FELSEN FAMILY

The stories of foreign Jews interned in the province of Grosseto may be compared with those elsewhere in Italy. Two examples, both of which reflect positively on the behavior of churchmen, a phenomenon less common than elsewhere in the Grosseto area, follow. First is the experience of Alfred Felsen, a member of a German or Austrian Jewish family, and who was interned in Latera near Viterbo in the province of Lazio. This family was very near the first location of the Pasermans. The Italian government requisitioned an apartment for the Felsen family in the home of a priest. The family received a small government allowance. They were not allowed out after dark, nor to have a radio. Moreover, they all had to sign in at the police station every day.

The kindly priest with whom they shared a dwelling lent them newspapers and even a record player. Alfred, who was fifteen or sixteen, joined the local olive pickers and was paid with olive oil. His sister taught German in the village. The local villagers brought them lots of food, too much for them to eat, in fact. Alfred socialized with the local teenagers. In 1942, the Felsens were told that they had to leave for an internment camp. They were picked up in a police car and taken on an eight-hour trip down to Ferramonti camp in Calabria, from which they were presumably liberated by the Allies in 1943.[17]

## LICHTNER FAMILY

According to the book, *Il Caso Lichtner,* the Lichtner family from Germany had hopes of travelling to America; like many others, they saw their hopes dashed. Mrs. Lichtner—Federica, or Friederike—was particularly active in writing letters to request help throughout their ordeal. She operated out of a sense of desperation and in full awareness of what might befall the family if they were trapped in central or northern Italy. Perhaps it was also a family strategy for the wife to approach the authorities as she might elicit more sympathy than the husband. Many times, they were disappointed. It is difficult to imagine the pressure on a family living in such circumstances. Without residence visas, she knew they would be interned and eventually deported.

They took refuge in Penne, near Pescara, in Abruzzo, where a sympathetic cleric, Archbishop Venturi, agreed to intercede for them as Jews who had been baptized as Christians. Federica appealed to the archbishop "as our situation is extremely difficult and stressful."[18] At the same time, she made an appeal to the Vatican which was turned down. The question of the Lichtners' continuing residence in Italy, while others were being deported or interned, illuminates differences between the foreign ministry and the interior ministry, as well as between the government and the Vatican, which should not have regarded them as Jewish once they had converted. Many appeals were being decided on an ad hoc basis. The Lichtners, an exception, luckily managed to avoid internment and deportation, thanks to Venturi, and survived the war.

## FOREIGN JEWS IN ROCCATEDERIGHI CAMP AND BISHOP GALEAZZI

Those two families who encountered sympathetic clerics were fortunate. In the meantime, many Jews in the province of Grosseto had Bishop Galeazzi and Prefect Ercolani to deal with.

In Roccatederighi, though Bishop Galeazzi was a remote and authoritarian figure, he does seem to have made some gestures toward the inmates. There is an account of his inviting them to attend his private chapel on Christmas Eve, and of an inmate called Maria, who must be Maria or Mary Wodak, singing for the bishop. He invited them to a Christmas dinner and another for the Epiphany. He also gave them small gifts, since the food in the camp was generally in scant supply and very basic. Perhaps the bishop had some covert design to convert these Jews, and indeed one was released on this basis, and another on the basis of having a Christian spouse and children. Apparently Bishop Galeazzi espoused the same view as Pope Pius XI, that a converted Jew was no longer a Jew, rather than the biologically based view of Mussolini. In other respects, the bishop seems to have adhered to the positions of Pope Pius XII with regard to the Jews, but even more so to those of the Fascist head of the province of Grosseto, and those of the Fascist government (by this time in northern Salò).

A rare short English article about Bishop Galeazzi in a Catholic publication begins:

> An Italian bishop rented out a wing of his diocesan seminary to house a concentration camp for Jews during World War II, according to documents recently placed on exhibit in Italy. Camp survivors recounted that conditions were not harsh and the bishop used to visit camp inmates, handing out gifts and playing with the children. But 46 of the prisoners eventually were deported to the Nazi death camp at Auschwitz. The story was reported by the Italian newspaper *Corriere della Sera* in mid-February (2002).[19]

This article did not generate any further attention in the English-speaking world. One must now add the book by Simon Levis Sullam (three pages) published in English in 2018, and the English-language article "Roccatederighi" in the *Encyclopedia of Camps and Ghettos* of the United States Holocaust Memorial Museum (2018).[20]

Bishop Galeazzi traced his episcopal or spiritual lineage back to Pope Pius IX, a mid-nineteenth century, ultra-conservative pope known for his anti-Jewish positions, such as the kidnapping of Edgardo Mortara and refusing to discredit the notorious blood libel. He also forced the Jews of Rome back into the ghetto after they had previously been freed. He was the last pope to rule the extensive temporal papal states.[21] The bishop obviously admired Pius IX, and may have aspired to belong to the "black nobility" of loyal papal supporters in Rome. A new evaluation of Bishop Galeazzi[22] emphasizes that, though he was not an actual Fascist Party member (after all, Vatican rules would not allow this), his militant personality, and perhaps earlier wartime experience as a military chaplain, accorded well with Fascism, and allowed him, in collaboration with the head of the province, Alceo Ercolani, to anticipate the wishes of the Fascists. Even his episcopal coat of arms had a militant motif, an elm tree, a hard wood used for weapons. It is seen today on many churches he was responsible for building, often helped by government funds.

Interestingly, in the biographical files of prominent Italians held in the Central State Archives in Rome, while other files contain many documents, under Paolo Galeazzi's name we find a slim file with but one document. It dates from the very early years of Bishop Galeazzi's career, and does not reflect his later achievements. It is a report dated May 1940 on his personality and achievements and his fitness for the position that he occupied for the rest of his life. He is described as "energic" but "malleable,"[23] the very qualities that later led him to fall in with the aims of the fanatical Fascist prefect. Later documents might have been removed, for one early document could not make a person prominent enough to merit such a place in the national archives.

The bishop both demanded respect for his authority and paid respect to those more powerful than himself. He had even had a major confrontation with the previous Fascist prefect. Committed to building a bishop's seminary in the center of Grosseto, though the economic situation was very bad, he claimed that the government should cede to the church a prime piece of real estate in the center of Grosseto. When he was denied, he wrote successfully to Mussolini to grant him the land.[24]

It does not seem, though, that all local Jews were mistreated at Roccatederighi.[25] The bishop's brooding, authoritarian presence would have inspired awe and fear rather than love. He, indeed, took upon himself an awesome responsibility over the lives and deaths of these local and foreign Jews, as we shall see in the next chapter.

This non-scientific sampling of the stories of foreign Jews and local impressions of those in authority gives rise to the suspicion that, to put it mildly, the clergy, with some exceptions such Bishop Battistelli and associates in Pitigliano, were less sympathetic or forthcoming in providing assistance to Jews in the province of Grosseto than in some other provinces of Italy.[26]

The diocese of Grosseto did not exactly correspond to the state's province of Grosseto. Bishop Battistelli's territory of Pitigliano was carved out from it, and part of the northern portion of the province belonged to the diocese of Massa Marittima. The superior of these bishops was Cardinal Costa in Florence. He himself set up a number of refugees in monasteries and convents as well as lay people's homes in Florence, in which Jews were often successfully hidden. However, bishops did not have to obey instructions or heed examples from cardinals who were their superiors. There is no evidence that Cardinal Costa approached Bishop Battistelli, who did save Jews, or Bishop Galeazzi, who in our analysis did not, though the full story has not yet come out. The fact that by early 1944 all the Jews of the province, both native and foreign, were either in hiding, mostly around Pitigliano, or interned in the Roccatederighi camp, under the supervision of Bishop Galeazzi and Gaetano Rizziello, the Fascist camp commander, may allow us to have a clearer picture of motivations and responsibilities, insofar as the confusion and murkiness of incomplete records, abetted by selective and unreliable memories, may allow us.

Foreign Jews found themselves interned in Roccatederighi through a series of earlier unfortunate decisions, in addition of course to the will of the Fascists. Some had delayed decisions to flee Europe. Others chose or were required to remain in, or return to, northern Italy under the Fascist thumb. They had the inevitable misfortune of falling foul of Mussolini's new 1943 policies, which were in line with Hitler's. By contrast, Italian Jews, apart from the idealistic Azeglio Servi who refused to abandon his flock, were there largely because they had been duped into thinking that the camp was for their protection. The promise of adequate food and the protective presence of the bishop led them to be unaware that they were walking into a trap by voluntarily presenting themselves for internment in the camp.

## NOTES

1. The Centro di Documentazione Ebraica Contemporanea in Milan has the most comprehensive resources on foreign Jews in Italy, in its General Index of Foreign Jews Interned in Italy 1940–1943. Francesca Cappella (5,829 entries) and Anna Pizzuti (9,337 entries) have complied two databases, both based on Italian State Central Archives, and accessible via http://www.cdec.it/ebrei_stranieri/. Only the

second one is being updated, as Cappella has unfortunately passed away. The research draws on other archives too, such as the International Tracing Service Collections in Bad Arolsen, Germany.

2. *JDC Digest*, 4:3 (July 1945), NY_AR3344_00033_00139.pdf.

3. Source is Ariel Paggi's table "Elenco degli Ebrei presenti al campo di concentramento di Roccatederighi." The tables that I consulted have subsequently been published: see Ariel Paggi, *Il Muro degli ebrei: Roccatederighi e la Provincia di Grosseto (1943–1945)* (Livorno: Belforte, 2018), pp. 279–346.

4. For details and an evaluation of the Vatican's contribution compared with that of individual priests who actually lived in the southern camps, see Susan Zuccotti, "Foreign Jews in Italian Internment Camps, 1940–1943," chapter 6 in *Under His Very Windows* (New Haven: Yale Univ. Press, 2000), pp. 82–92. See also the chapter by Carlo Spartaco Capogreco, trans. Ruth Feldman, "The Internment Camp of Ferramonti-Tarsia, pp. 159–177, in Ivo Herzer, et al., eds., *The Italian Refuge*. Also Carlo Spartaco Capogreco, trans. Norma Bouchard and Valerio Ferme, *Mussolini's Camps*. For a discussion of those who were never liberated but died at Ferramonti of various causes, see E. Tromba, A Sorrenti, and S. N. Sinicropi, *Il Kaddish a Ferramonti: Le Anime ritrovate* (Castrovillan: Edizioni Prometeo, n.d.) (for directing me to the last book I thank Rabbi Riccardo Di Segni).

5. See Carlo Spartaco Capogreco, *I campi del duce* (Turin: Einaudi, 2004), trans. Norma Bouchard and Valerio Ferme, *Mussolini's Camps*, and two articles in *Printed Matter*. "Mussolini's Camps: Civilian Internment in 1940–43," Jan. 5, 2020, n.p. (with a particularly good bibliography in its copious notes), http://primolevicenter.org/printed-matter/mussolinis-camps-civilian-internment-in-fascist-italy-1940-1943/ and Carlo Spartaco Capogreco's introductory essay to Maria Eisenstein, *L'internata numero 6*, Editori Mimesis, Milano-Udine 2014. http://primolevicenter.org/printed-matter/what-was-precisely-a-concentration-camp/

6. See the map attached to Luciana Rocchi's list of deportees, "Luoghi di arresto dei deportati dalla Toscana centro-meridionale," *Ebrei in Toscana tra occupazione tedesca e RSI: Persecuzione, depredazione, deportazione (1943–1945)* Vol. 1, *Saggi*, p. 325. Ariel Paggi assembled a list of twenty-three names of foreign Jews (either German or Polish) interned and then arrested in Arcidosso. See his table, "La ripartizione degli internati nei vari comuni della Provincia." In his "Elenco degli Ebrei presenti al campo di concentramento di Roccatederighi," he has twenty-eight names of persons arrested in Arcidosso, although the last four were Italian Jews from Grosseto and turned themselves in. On Roccalbegna and Arcidosso, see *Il Muro degli ebrei*, p. 208. See also Anna Pizzuti with twenty-seven names, www.annapizzuti.it/pdf/elenco.php.Ebrei stranieri internati in Italia durante il periodo bellico, ultima località: Arcidosso.

7. Anna Pizzuti, *Vite di carta: Storie di ebrei internati dal fascismo* (Rome: Donzelli, 2010). An older example of this technique, this one from France is Patrick Modiano's 1997 novel, *Dora Bruder*, the meticulously traced story of one young Jewish woman who disappeared into the Nazi death camps, and whose whole existence is known today only through the meager documents Modiano unearthed. As with Anna Pizzuti's book, readers are touched even through these

few pieces of paper. See Patrick Modiano *Romans* (Paris: Quarto Gallimard, 2013), pp. 643–736.

8. Signora Adriana Bargagli has kindly sent us the photo of a painting of a very simple flat green landscape with a German-looking church spire. Obviously the German Jew was homesick, drawing on his memories of home rather than the undulating Tuscan landscapes surrounding him. "La sua lettera, del tutto inaspettata, mi ha molto colpita ed emozionata e ha spostato la mia memoria a tempi lontani, ma indimenticabili. All'epoca, 1943, io avevo 11 anni. Ricordo quei giovani ragazzi, confinati, perché ebrei, nella piccola frazione di S. Lorenzo, poco lontana dal paese di Arcidosso. Venivano a fare spesa nel negozio di generi alimentari che mio padre, Bargagli Vezio, gestiva. Al tempo, per motivi bellici, i generi alimentari erano razionati, così, mio padre, generosamente, elargiva loro razioni più abbondanti di pane e di altri alimenti . . . solo generi di prima necessità. Mio padre, pur avendo aderito alla politica del regime allora vigente in Italia, non aveva dimenticato di essere un uomo e un Cristiano, ne' aveva approvato certe decisioni disumane, come le persecuzioni di razza e di religione. Uno di questi giovani, per ringraziarlo della sua benevolenza, gli fece dono di alcuni piccoli acquarelli da lui dipinti in quei tristi mesi di prigionia e di uno rimasto le invio la foto."

Email with attachment from Adriana Bargagli's daughter, Paola Bianciardi, November 30, 2018. With much gratitude to both Adriana and Paola. Ariel Paggi gives other information in *Muro*, p. 228.

9. Laura Paggini's *Pesante come una piuma* (Heavy as a feather) is an excellent self-published young adult novel in the genre of Holocaust educational fiction designed for today's younger generation in Italy. It is a very sensitive and well-written ghost story, involving the Italian and foreign Jews interned in the camp, and their premonition of the tragic end that awaited many of them. It is partially set in 2002, when the bishop's palace was still being used as a summer camp for children from cities such as Livorno, and the author's own son was sent there to summer camp. Paggini lectures occasionally on the topic of her book in Italian high schools.

10. Laura Paggini wrote to me that she does not know whether Mosbach managed to paint in the camp, but that her setting him, a historical figure who has migrated to fiction, in front of an easel with his brushes and paints at Roccatederighi is a fictional means of "giving him a caress," of expressing her compassion. See also note below.

11. This information is thanks to Ariel Paggi who saw the other paintings some time ago and has attempted without success to contact the American descendants of Mosbach's nephew. Most likely they did not know that he even existed, and thus did not show any interest. These relatives, named Strauss, settled in New York and Florida, beginning in 1939 and 1940. With thanks to Anna Sarah London for her assistance in trying to locate them, to the staff of the Survivors' Registry at USHHM for forwarding letters, and to Mark Lazerson for his help in trying to locate the other paintings, which may now be lost.

12. The Turteltaubs have since been the subject of an exhibition on the Holocaust in Dornbirn in 1996. The exhibit highlighted this family of definitely ordinary people who disappeared from the town of Dornbirn. The exhibition was part of an effort there to recuperate local history and Holocaust memories. See the brochure for the

exhibit held in November 1996, written by Martin Achrainer and Niko Hofinger, the Italian name of the exhibition being "La Famiglia Turteltaub, Via per Lustenau, 3."

13. The detailed information on the Turteltaub family has been collected by Ariel Paggi through his research at the Documentation Center in Milan, and interviews with local people in Arcidosso.

14. In Arcidosso, at least in 1922, the number of Fascist party members was low: a mere fifty. Perhaps by late 1943 it was much higher. See Galimi, *Fascismo a Grosseto*, p. 208.

15. The terms "confino" and "internamento" seem to be used interchangeably by the prisoners.

16. Leone Paserman, a prominent member of the Roman Jewish community today, has told his family's story several times. Sources used here are Leone Paserman's Preface to Ariel Paggi, *Bambino*, pp. 9–11; and the text of a brochure, "Pietro Felici ed il salvataggio della famiglia Paserman, Pitigliano 1943–1944," (Rome, February 19, 2008, Museo Ebraico, Lungotevere Cenci, Rome).

17. This interview, recorded in 1996, is from the USC Shoah archives, consulted at USHMM.

18. "Essendo la nostra situazione difficilissima e angustiosa." Giuseppe Perri, *Il Caso Lichtner: Gli ebrei stranieri, fascismo e la guerra* (Milan: Jaca Books, 2010), esp. pp. 124–125.

19. Gill Donovan. "Bishop rented property for concentration camp (World)." The Free Library. 2002 *National Catholic Reporter* September 10, 2015. http://www.thefreelibrary.com/Bishop+rented+property+for+concentration+camp.+(World).-a083667066.

20. Though the latter does unfortunately seem to contain an inaccuracy. It states that the bishop received the rent and later returned it. The opposite is in fact the case: he had not received the rent and he applied for it to the postwar government, as the documents reveal.

21. See Kertzer, *Popes against the Jews*, pp. 118–128, 166. Also idem, *The Pope who would be King: The Exile of Pius IX and the Emergence of Modern Europe* (New York: Random House, 2018).

22. With thanks to Adolfo Turbanti.

23. See ACS Paco 546. Fasc. 70 No. 62. A one-page report from Vatican City, May 23, 1940 (i.e., before the wartime events). Entitled "Mons. Paolo Galeazzi." Near the end of the document, he is described as "persona energica ed attiva" (an energetic and active person) and, tellingly, the report concludes with "E abbastanza malleabile per ciò che riguarda i rapporti con le autorità civili e dal Regime" (He is quite malleable as regards relations with the civil authorities and the Regime).

24. Valeria Galimi, ed., *Il Fascismo a Grosseto*, chapter by Luciana Rocchi, pp. 89–90. Rocchi also states here that Galeazzi's personal file disappeared from the local episcopal archives.

25. "Le guardie erano bonarie e lo stesso vescovo si intratteneva con i reclusi distribuendo doni e carezze ai più piccoli." "The guards were well disposed and the bishop himself would spend time with the prisoners giving out gifts and caresses for the littlest ones." "I lager italiani 1943–1945: Il campo di Grosseto," *Corriere della Sera*, February 12, 2002. This is contradicted by his defender Carla Servi's portrait

of him: "Ogni tanto assistevamo al breve tragitto del Vescovo che, uscito dale sue stanze, si recava fino alla chiesa: non rivolgeva lo sguardo, tanto meno la parola, a nessuno." "Every so often we witnessed the swift passing by of the bishop who, coming out of his quarters, was going to the church: he did not look at, and even less speak to, anyone." Carla Servi, *Una Infanzia perduta*, p. 26. This from an eyewitness who elsewhere is anxious to defend the bishop. Perhaps these two contrasting impressions hint at the fallibility of (revised) memory.

26. Many documented cases elsewhere of the saving of Jews by clergy are recounted in Liliana Picciotto, *Salvarsi*. She particularly focuses on networks to save Jews and others in Genoa and Florence.

*Chapter 7*

# Last Days at the Bishop's Palace for Foreign and Italian Jews

### LIFE IN THE CAMP

The bishop's palace was a palace in name only. It consisted of two large rather dingy buildings with little architectural charm, linked by an enclosed glassed-in corridor and in need of renovation. A long, steep flight of steps led up to them. The grounds were hardly gardens, basically a wild and uncultivated bushy area called a "park." Surrounding everything were the barbed wire and heavily armed guards. The bishop resided in one building, together with his seminary students, his sister, any visiting priests, and probably the two male orderlies and the five nuns who prepared the food. In the other more Spartan building, the Jewish prisoners were quartered. Where the twenty militia members and the three security men lived is unknown, but the carabinieri were probably local.

Though they had come from vastly different backgrounds, all the Jews interned at Roccatederighi shared the same surroundings and the same way of life. It might well have appeared that the future held the same fate in store for them; however, it turned out that very different destinies were being prepared for them.

Time passed slowly and heavily. Perhaps most laboriously for the men, for whom, whether foreigners or Italian Jews, playing cards and exchanging stories were poor substitutes for earning their living and working in their professions. The women busied themselves with taking care of their families, helping with the meals, helping with cleaning and tidying their quarters, and maintaining their families' clothing, making sure it was adequate for the extreme cold. The children, sensitively portrayed in Laura Paggini's imaginative young adult novel *Pesante come una piuma* and confirmed by Carla

Servi's memoir, kept busy with various games involving objects they found in nature and toys they made themselves.

The Jews were not allowed access to radios or newspapers, so any news they learned about the progress of the war came from some of the friendlier guards or from former inmate Tranquillo Servi's visits. After the early release of the supposedly ill members of the Nunes family of Grosseto, of Tranquillo himself, and later his close family members in late February, and of a couple of women with Christian connections in their families, little broke the tedium. One of Tranquillo's daughters, Bianca, became engaged to a Fascist guard, an occurrence that would have been newsworthy. Presumably, she would have been asked to convert at some point.

Some members of the Nunes family were released early purportedly for health reasons. Cesare Nunes, interviewed many years later by Giuseppe Celata, said that three members of his family were released on the basis of X-rays, implying tuberculosis infections, that perhaps had been exchanged for the real ones. The same account reports that the head of the militia guarding the Jews in the camp was none other than Vittorio Ciabatti, a close childhood friend of Cesare Nunes from Grosseto. Ciabatti was replaced, however, and sent to Bologna by the head of the Milizia in Grosseto; obviously he had been too amenable. One of his subordinates had alleged that it was the Jewish internees themselves who were running things at Roccatederighi. Cesare Nunes met his future wife while he was in the camp. She was a local, Christian girl who came to the chapel to attend Mass, entering via an external set of steps. He described her as modern and stylish. They married after the war. Cesare and the rest of his family did not need her help, though, to escape from the camp, as they had their own connections.[1] Since anyone with the connections to obtain release from the camp seems to have managed to do so, this belies the theory that the camp could have been a place of refuge and safety for Jews.

## THE FASCIST TYPE

Then, in March 1944, news would have filtered through about a shocking event in the area, the massacre at Istia. Michele De Anna was also responsible for other similar atrocities in the area.

News of these events must have inevitably reached the inmates and their guards high on the hill at Roccatederighi. Perhaps the bishop was as shaken by such excesses as the prisoners. As the war wound to a climax in this area, those who had tendencies to brutality such as Ercolani and De Anna revealed their true colors. Mussolini had been exhorting the nation for years about the need to create the new Fascist man; such a person was decisive, a man of action, battle-hardened[2] and not morally squeamish. On a local level, in the province of Grosseto, the type of Fascist who came into being and rose to the top in fulfillment of Mussolini's dreams is revealed in the Ercolanis and the De Annas. Ercolani also surrounded himself with brutish types ready to do his bidding. Francesco Frose, for example, was "a very violent and strongwilled person, of limited culture, even though last February, on the orders of Ercolani, he was given a high school graduation certificate from the classical high school of Grosseto."[3] Such were the brutish followers of a corrupt regime.

## BACK AT THE CAMP

The bishop spent some of his time in the Roccatederighi internment camp writing pastoral letters, to be distributed to his flock. There is a published list of their titles that does not include the actual texts. His letters covered a number of topics. In 1943, several of them addressed agriculture and religion. In 1944, some of his topics included "martyred Grosseto," "the tears of the pope," and, later in the year, "prayer for the tranquil fruit of justice." Later in life, Galeazzi wrote large numbers of circulars, especially in 1957. It is obvious that in 1943–1944 the bishop was deeply disturbed by the war situation.[4] In sixteen pastoral letters by Bishop Galeazzi held in the archives of ISGREC he makes not a single reference to the plight of Jews, local or foreign. In this group of letters, the bishop is concerned with disrespect toward the church on the part of local people. He merges and confuses respect for Fascism with respect for Catholicism. It is probably accurate that secularism went hand-in-hand with anti-Fascism and as we have seen there was endemic grassroots anti-Fascism in the province of Grosseto, due to its history of Fascist violence. In the bishop's pastoral letters, piety and patriotism are all mixed up. In a Lettera Pastorale of 1941 he had exhorted:

> Let us return, in delight, to our Church; let us return, to listen in devotion to the Holy Mass. . . . Let us renew our consecration . . . our prayers, for the prosperity of his Majesty the King, . . . for assistance to the strong and wise National Government, for the health and resistance of our Soldiers, for the triumph of justice, for the victory of Italy, for universal peace.[5]

Praise for the bishop from Jews who had been interned in Roccatederighi has continued to echo:

> Jews of Maremma who escaped the transfer from Roccatederighi to Fossoli have testified to his commitment to the internees, his efforts to influence the director of the camp for a more humane treatment of the internees, and some special situations that he encouraged, personally hiding some Jews from the Germans in their retreat.[6]

However, these instances of the bishop's favor always seem to be attributed, when there is specific attribution, either to Cesare Nunes, who belonged to a particularly assimilated Jewish family from Grosseto who had mostly been released early, or to the members of Tranquillo Servi's family, who had likewise been released and were not there in the final, dramatic days.

After the March 1944 Istia incident, while others at that point fell away from the Fascist cause in horror and disgust, and took into account the obvious fact that the Fascists were slowly losing, Bishop Galeazzi drew his personal conclusions: as a friend and colleague of the prefect, he still persisted in believing his duty lay in fulfilling Ercolani's wishes. Bishop Galeazzi's complex double game of providing supposed moral comfort for the Jews, while maintaining loyalty to the Fascist regime and allowing the Fascists to use his facilities as a means toward executing the terrible Nazi-Fascist plans against these same Jews (which he must have been aware of by then), smacks of either fear or hypocrisy.

## TRANSPORTS BEGIN: FIRST TRANSPORT

On April 18, a Pullman, rather than one of the gasogenous buses, was waiting to be loaded. The previous night, the camp director, Gaetano Rizziello, had drawn up a list, possibly after conversation with the bishop. The Jews were supposed to be taken away in alphabetical order. Azeglio Servi, in his short and laconic diary, also made a list of those who were loaded on that bus, with their countries of origin. His list included only three families of Italian Jews, all from out of the province.[7] The list shows that almost all those taken that day were foreign Jews and out-of-the-province Jews from Livorno in northern Tuscany (figure 7.1).[8]

They were all taken to the large transit camp of Fossoli dei Carpi, near Modena and Parma, and all (except one individual and two families) shortly thereafter (May 16) loaded on Convoy No. 10 of cattle cars bound for Auschwitz, where most of them died. Fossoli had been presented to the deportees in neutral fashion as a new camp, understood perhaps as a more comfortable one. The Jews on the first bus from Roccatederighi seem to have had little idea that it was a waystation to Auschwitz. Thus no one tried to escape along the way.

## CAMP AT FOSSOLI

The expectations about Fossoli can be explained by its previous reputation. In addition to the fact that, even late in the war, Jews from provincial corners

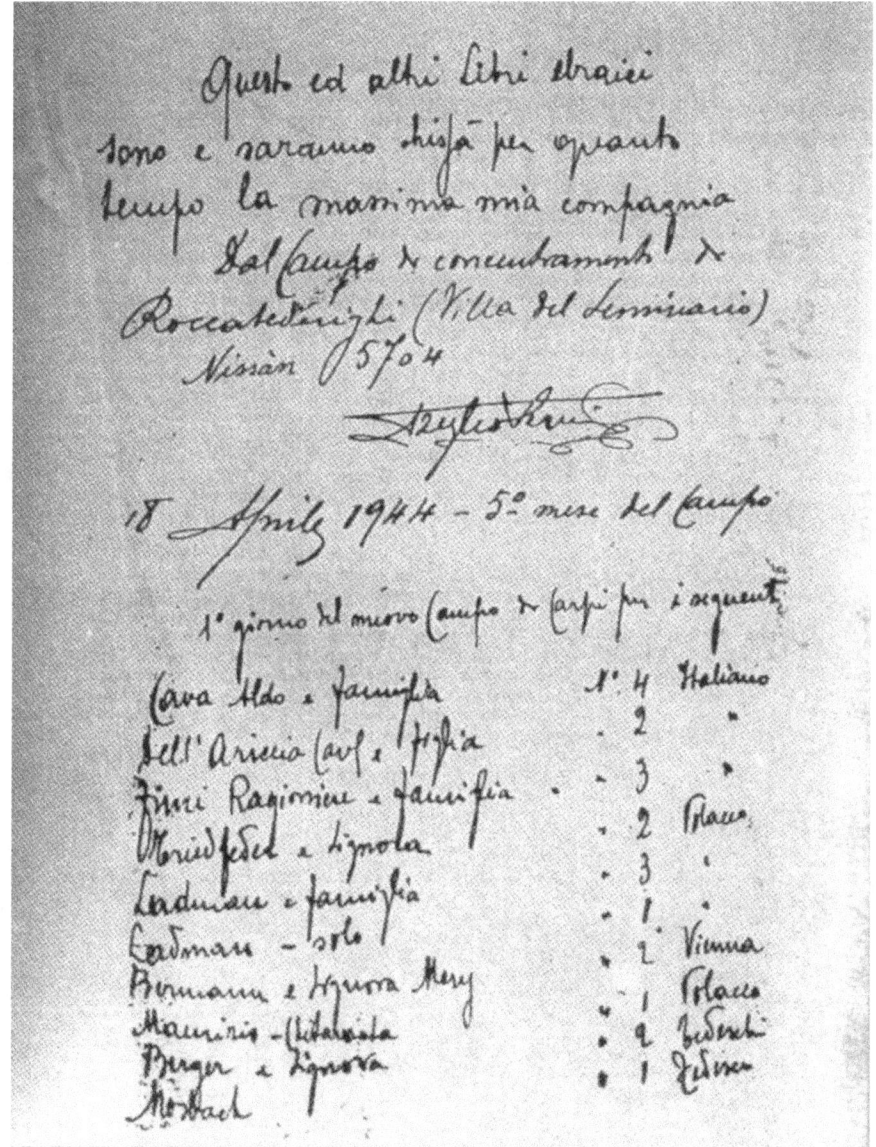

**Figure 7.1** First Page of Azeglio Servi's Diary, Included in *La Persecuzione degl ebrei nella Provincia di Grosseto nel 1943–1944*, Grosseto: ISGREC, 1996, 2002, p. 56.
*Source*: Courtesy of Luciana Rocchi.

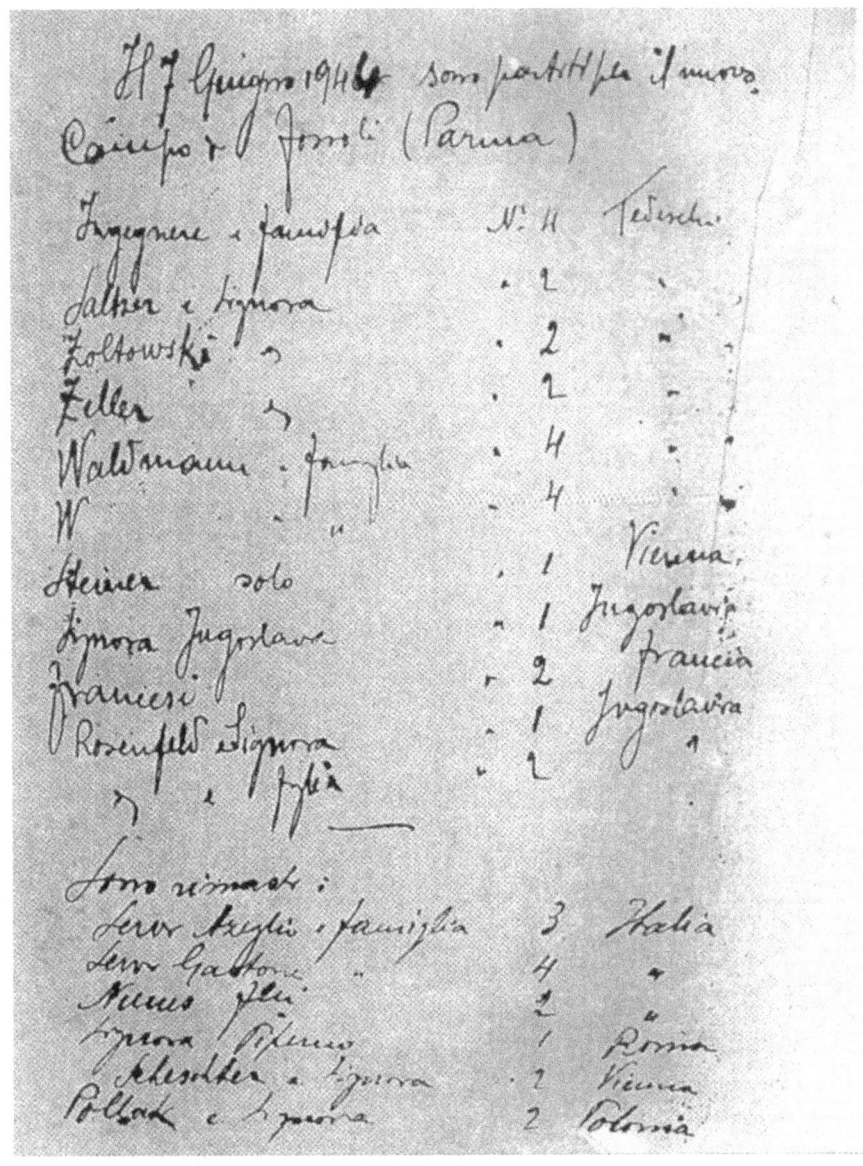

Figure 7.2  Second Page of Azeglio Servi's Diary, ibid., p. 57. *Source*: Courtesy of Luciana Rocchi.

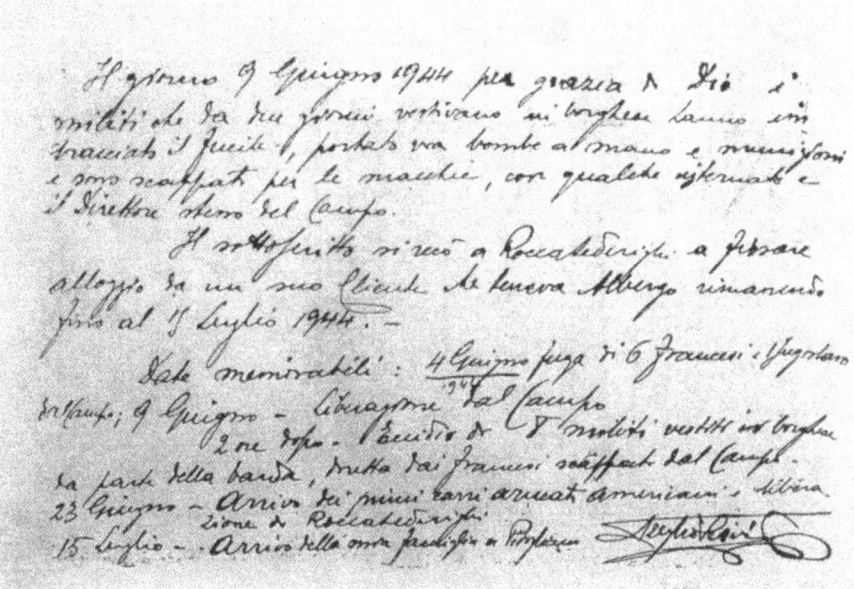

Figure 7.3  Third Page of Azeglio Servi's Diary, ibid., p. 58. *Source*: Courtesy of Luciana Rocchi.

such as Grosseto might have been prone to nurture more illusions than those who were from the cities, Fossoli had previously been viewed as a destination of privilege for those who were "misti" (of mixed blood) or "discriminati" (exempt from the most onerous antisemitic laws). Renzo De Felice related that Jews in Ferrara, with its humid climate, considered that Fossoli had better air; initially they actually hoped to be sent there. Some Ferrara Jews had presented themselves voluntarily for shipment to Fossoli:

> Mixed-race Jews, exempted from internment under the RSI laws, did everything they could to be taken to Fossoli, where the air was good and there were no risks of bombing.[9]

Primo Levi, who was initially interned in Fossoli, writes in *Survival in Auschwitz*, that those sent to Fossoli often still nurtured some hopes, until they realized, after the SS took over command on March 1, 1944, that all inmates, old and young, whether "discriminati" or not, were being deported.[10]

Fossoli was actually an old camp that had been used for British prisoners and later for Italian political prisoners. When Mussolini made the decision to intensify the anti-Jewish campaign by deporting all Jews the camp was greatly expanded and doubled in size from December 1943. The Italian RSI

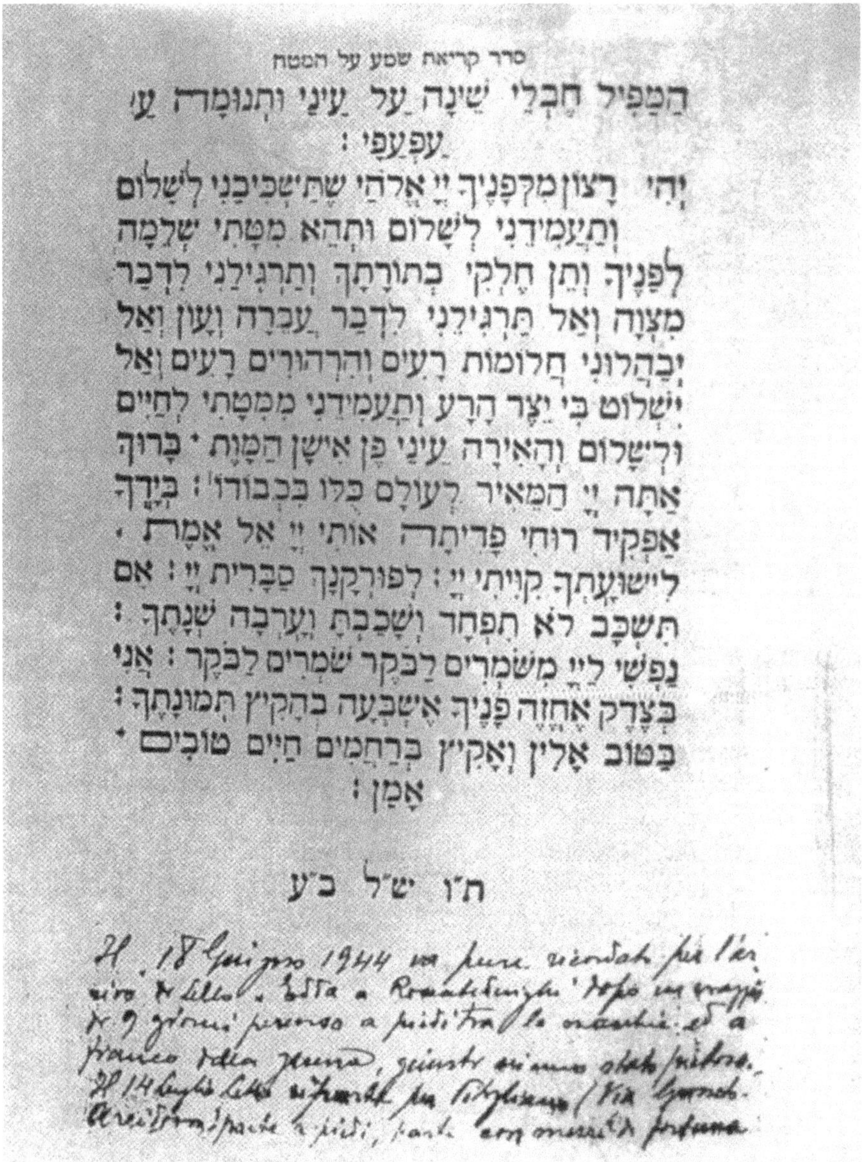

סדר קריאת שמע על המטה

הַמַּפִּיל חֶבְלֵי שֵׁנָה עַל עֵינַי וּתְנוּמָה עַל עַפְעַפָּי:

יְהִי רָצוֹן מִלְּפָנֶיךָ יְיָ אֱלֹהַי שֶׁתַּשְׁכִּיבֵנִי לְשָׁלוֹם וְתַעֲמִידֵנִי לְשָׁלוֹם וּתְהֵא מִטָּתִי שְׁלֵמָה לְפָנֶיךָ וְתֵן חֶלְקִי בְּתוֹרָתֶךָ וְתַרְגִּילֵנִי לִדְבַר מִצְוָה וְאַל תַּרְגִּילֵנִי לִדְבַר עֲבֵרָה וְעָוֹן וְאַל יְבַהֲלוּנִי חֲלוֹמוֹת רָעִים וְהִרְהוּרִים רָעִים וְאַל יִשְׁלוֹט בִּי יֵצֶר הָרָע וְתַעֲמִידֵנִי מִמִּטָּתִי לְחַיִּים וּלְשָׁלוֹם וְהָאִירָה עֵינַי פֶּן אִישַׁן הַמָּוֶת בָּרוּךְ אַתָּה יְיָ הַמֵּאִיר לָעוֹלָם כֻּלּוֹ בִּכְבוֹדוֹ: בְּיָדְךָ אַפְקִיד רוּחִי פָּדִיתָה אוֹתִי יְיָ אֵל אֱמֶת. לִישׁוּעָתְךָ קִוִּיתִי יְיָ: לְפוּרְקָנָךְ סַבְּרִית יְיָ: אִם תִּשְׁכַּב לֹא תִפְחָד וְשָׁכַבְתָּ וְעָרְבָה שְׁנָתֶךָ: נַפְשִׁי לַייָ מִשֹּׁמְרִים לַבֹּקֶר שֹׁמְרִים לַבֹּקֶר: אֲנִי בְּצֶדֶק אֶחֱזֶה פָנֶיךָ אֶשְׂבְּעָה בְהָקִיץ תְּמוּנָתֶךָ: בְּטוֹב אָלִין וְאָקִיץ בְּרַחֲמִים חַיִּים טוֹבִים אָמֵן:

ח״ו יש״ל ב״ע

*Il 18 Giugno 1944 in pure viendah più l'ar... [handwritten Italian text, largely illegible]*

**Figure 7.4** Fourth Page of Azeglio Servi's Diary, ibid., p. 59. *Source*: Courtesy of Luciana Rocchi.

government decided on its own initiative, without German pressure, to set up transit camps for Jews and begin deportations to prove that it could still make its own decisions. Three thousand Jews, including Primo Levi, were deported to Auschwitz from Fossoli. From March 1, 1944, onward, the Nazis were in charge of management of the deportations, but as Primo Levi observed there was still a great deal of willing collaboration from Italians along the way, just as we have seen at the beginning of the process at Roccatederighi.

## FOREIGNERS' ESCAPE

Sometime in May or in the first days of June 1944, a number of internees escaped from Roccatederighi Camp through the barbed wire into the woods. They were six French people and one Yugoslavian, but Azeglio does not name them, probably because he did not know them well. Cesare Nunes actually had been part of the escape plan, which involved sunbathing for several days near the fence to lull the guards into inattention. Nunes, however, did not escape at this time. Their leader, said to be Rêné Babonneau of the Foreign Legion and a close associate of De Gaulle, was wounded in the escape. He was sent to the hospital at Roccastrada. Most of the escapees joined the local partisans. These were not ordinary prisoners, it turns out, but rather a few supposedly French, probably Algerian, fighters from the Free French Foreign Legion who had been captured and somehow ended up in Roccatederighi. They felt the time had come for them to join the local Resistance, and possibly this was not their first escape attempt. They have even been hypothesized to be a "fifth column" planted inside the camp. Most likely, though, they had ended up there by pure chance. Cesare Nunes relates that he almost escaped with them, but then remembered that his brother was still inside and went back to join him; the two apparently escaped later. At the very least, this action indicates that desperation was rising. The sense that Roccatederighi was some sort of refuge must have disappeared after the April 18 transport. Most likely, after this transport, Bishop Galeazzi stopped trying to win the Jewish internees' confidence.

## SECOND TRANSPORT

On June 7, when Rome had fallen and the war front had reached the province of Grosseto, the fall of the Fascists and flight of the Nazis were obviously imminent. It was also the same day that Pitigliano received heavy bombing, which could have been audible from the camp. The camp director improvised another transport at the last minute (figure 7.2). Again, the inmates were taken in alphabetical order, but beginning from the end of the alphabet, unlike previously. Almost all the Jews taken were foreign, leaving behind the local Jews from Grosseto and Pitigliano and a few others in the camp. The last names of the inmates had been carefully analyzed, and it was determined that the local Jews of Grosseto and Pitigliano would not be on the second bus either. If the bishop and camp director believed they were saving Jewish lives, they must have known also that those Jews who were selected would stand a strong chance of losing theirs. Italians describe this approach as a "gioco delle tre carte," "playing with false cards." On the first transport, those with names from A to P were taken. On the second transport, it was those with names from Z working back to Singer. Azeglio Servi, his wife and son, another Servi family, that of Gastone Servi from Grosseto, two Nunes brothers from Grosseto, Clara Piperno from Rome, who may have had a false baptismal certificate but was still in the camp, and two foreign families, the Schusters, and the Pollaks both from Vienna, remained in the camp. It is not known why the Pollaks were not in the transport (except for the last letter of their name being "P"), though there is an explanation for the Schusters.

Two days later the camp was disbanded, and the question of whether the second transport really had to take place impresses itself. Even if Rizziello, the camp director, was still under strict orders from Prefect Ercolani, surely the bishop would have had some inkling that, with the front so close, the Fascist power was about to collapse. Bishop Galeazzi may have been satisfied with not sticking his neck out, as he had been in the past months. Some Nazis might have been present for the departure of the second bus, even though they had other very pressing issues. Nevertheless, the main actors, the camp director who was officially responsible for carrying out Prefect Ercolani's order, the Fascist militi who guarded the Jews, and the bishop, were all Italians.

Eugenio Iafrate's book *Elementi indesiderabili* raises the case of another transport, though not one from Roccatederighi. The book's introduction by Dario Venegoni is relevant to the role of Italians in the deportations from Roccatederighi:

As Dario Venegoni emphasizes in the preface to Iafrate's book, "Seen thus from close up, the case of this transport seems to be the incontrovertible proof that the RSI apparatus played an active role alongside the Nazis in the deportations. The fact is that hundreds of Italians put their experience at the service of the Nazis, pursuing, arresting, accompanying other Italians to that tragic train, and even further."[11]

Several stories are told specifically about the bus transports from Roccatederighi to Fossoli dei Carpi, and to the nearby camp of Scipione, near Parma. The long trip took the deportees near Florence. Some controversy or "divided memory" exists about the provenance of the buses used for transports. The administrators of the Pitigliano bus company maintain that they falsely claimed all their buses needed repairs and could not make the journey. Others state that the buses used were indeed theirs.[12] The claim is made that disabling of the buses was so complete it also disrupted public transportation. The conflicting narratives about how buses were found is most likely a result of not only fading memories but also memories hastily revised as the war ended, rather than long decades later.

Picciotto writes: "In Pitigliano in a single night, the drivers in the SIAT transportation system rendered all the buses unusable, for they understood that the German request for transport was intended for the transfer of Jews from the provincial concentration camp of Roccatederighi to Fossoli for deportation." The note attached to this assertion does not give any reference regarding Pitigliano, but rather to another incident near Faenza. After the war, the SIAT managers had every reason to declare that they had not been involved in deportations and had in fact saved Jews. But the other story cited by Rocchi, Paggi, and Edda Servi is more detailed, and actually names the drivers involved. Perhaps someone with access to the keys to the bus and the skill to drive it could have acted on official orders, so that a SIAT bus could have been "borrowed" without the owners' official knowledge to make the trip, though the first driver seems to have been following instructions from the company.

Paioletti also mentions that in the last days of the war, the Germans requisitioned two buses from SIAT (p. 162). He does not say, however, what they did with the buses. The SIAT facilities, he writes, included a pasta factory that was obliged to provide food for the Germans and that, when possible, the company manufactured extra pasta and send it to the partisans. Again, narratives vary, and, as in other cases, the truth may be impossible to know.

Edda Servi and Ariel Paggi write that for the first transport a partisan rescue operation was expected but never happened. Luciana Rocchi corroborates their reports.[13] The driver tipped off the Resistance and even stopped for several hours in a pre-planned location, unloading everyone from the bus while he pretended to repair it. Another twist is that the leader of one of the local Resistance groups around Roccatederighi was the son of Gaetano Rizziello, the commander of the concentration camp. Apparently, the local partisan groups were focused on fighting Nazis and Fascists, rather than on saving Jews. They would not be equipped to shelter a large group of dependent non-fighters in the forest. It could also have been that the driver tipped off the wrong group, one that did not operate in the area where he stopped the bus. No partisans appeared, and eventually the driver had to stop pretending and everyone got back on the bus again. The driver of this otherwise uneventful April transport stated that on arrival he took a look at the situation in Fossoli and did not like what he saw, so he refused to drive a second time (hinting that the company did provide a driver for a second run). We do not know exactly what bothered him, but there could have been plenty of factors. Perhaps he saw overcrowding, poor food, or lack of hygiene, or spoke with some of the Fossoli inmates. They may have told him that every prisoner who entered the camp would eventually be deported.[14] "You can fire me but I won't go there again!" he stated emphatically.

In a version of the story of the second bus, or perhaps a third bus that may have been aborted, it was asserted that Bishop Galeazzi had sugar poured into the gasoline tank to immobilize it and that the Germans could not possibly fix it in time. The bishop might have resorted to this act, in desperation, but sugar was an extremely scarce commodity. Whether there were any Germans there at the time or who they could have been is not known. Furthermore, this is not the kind of initiative the psychologically distant bishop might have undertaken, in my view. Such a deed might have been attributed to him by those who were reluctant to believe that he could have been a Fascist collaborator, or even a passive onlooker or bystander, and were looking to justify his elevated reputation. In any case, a new driver was found for the last-minute deportees from Roccatederighi and the second bus transport set off.

There is a likelihood that the second bus or truck did not go to Fossoli, but rather to Scipione, another provincial camp, in the same area, near Salsomaggiore and Parma. This other transport from Roccatederighi to Scipione has been only briefly mentioned in the literature.[15] Perhaps Fossoli could not take all of the people on the bus and some or all were redirected to Scipione. The Waisborgs, a foreign family, recounted that they were saved from deportation by the director of the Scipione camp, who was not a convinced Fascist, at least by that late date; he managed to save the lives of about twenty foreign Jews in all, though only the Waisborg family was from Roccatederighi. His children had become friends with the Waisborg children, and he maintained that the entire family was needed to work in the camp's administration. He hid them in the basement when the Nazis came to deport them, thus saving their lives. Other than this report, information on this camp is rather slim. Carlo Spartaco Capogreco refers to it as one of the previously existing camps repurposed to be a provincial camp from November/December 1943, to which prisoners from Roccatederighi were delivered (p. 294).

In the previous chapter the stories are told of how several "foreign" Jews ended up at Roccatederighi. Here they are continued, to their final destinations, as far as we know them.

## EGON MOSBACH

Our lonely painter, Egon Mosbach, never to our knowledge tried to escape. He was in the first transport that left Roccatederighi on April 18. He was not included with others in Convoy No. 10, which left Fossoli a month later. Perhaps he managed to hide within the camp or blend in with another group that had arrived more recently. He was, however, in Convoy No. 13, which departed Fossoli for Auschwitz on June 26, 1944,[16] the last date on which convoys left Fossoli directly for Auschwitz. Mosbach was probably selected for slave labor and later transferred to Birkenau. Finally, he was sent to Charlottenburg, where he perished.[17] We can state that, as far as Fossoli is concerned, the ill-starred Egon Mosbach was on the last train to Auschwitz.

## TURTELTAUB FAMILY

The Turteltaub family, Edmund, his wife Gertrude, and their sons Hans and Walter, left Roccatederighi in the June 7 transport. The entire family was included in the same convoy out of Fossoli as Egon Mosbach, on June 26. They all died at Auschwitz, the children no doubt murdered immediately.

## WALDMAN FAMILY

The Waldman family, Alberto, Franziska and Saul Behar and Henriette Cecilia, who were Polish, also left Roccatederighi on the June 7 transport. They were included in the same Convoy 13, which left Fossoli twenty days later. All died at Auschwitz.[18]

## POLLAK FAMILY

The Pollaks, David and Olga, who were from Austria, had been brought to Roccatederighi from Civitella Paganico. They were extremely lucky because they were not included in either of the bus transports from Roccatederighi to Fossoli. They escaped from the camp into the countryside together with the Nunes brothers from Grosseto. They thus benefited from local Italian knowledge of how to survive in the wooded countryside.[19]

## ROSENFELD/SINGER FAMILY

The Rosenfeld/Singer family's fate is particularly intriguing, though probably tragic. Serena and Edith Singer, mother and daughter, were on the transport on June 7 that went to Scipione. In the list of names provided by Azeglio Servi, we see "Signora Rosenfeld" and " figlia" as Azeglio may have had the impression that they were the wife and daughter of Ernesto Rosenfeld, rather than his sister and niece. Serena's brother, Ernst/Ernesto, had escaped on May 4, or on June 4 (as one finds two dates for this event in the sources) together with the non-Jewish French and Algerian former prisoners-of-war. Ernst/Ernesto had been an officer in the Yugoslavian army; after they made their break the escapees all joined up with local partisans who planned to attack the camp. He also hoped to rescue his wife, who was still inside the camp. We do not know how she escaped. Ernesto took the battle name of "Barbanera," perhaps giving us a hint as to his appearance. After the liberation Ernesto, now reunited with his wife, briefly took up residence near the Italian coast, and worked as an interpreter for the Allied forces in Piombino.[20]

A number of foreign Jews who were sent to Scipione managed to survive. There is a theory that from Scipione, Serena and Edith Singer might have been sent or escaped in the direction of Verona, perhaps in the company of three Frenchmen. Verona, however, was a major German headquarters at that time, and the trains also collected Jews for deportation from there. Thus, it is unlikely that anyone escaping would head for Verona. At this point, all traces of them are lost. They are not included among the lists of those deported and killed (*Il Libro della Memoria*[21] and the websites that continue it), but this does not mean that they survived. Rumors allege that while Ernesto may have eventually emigrated to Argentina, his niece, Edith Singer, may have reached the United States, but this is doubtful.[22]

## CAVA/MOSCATI FAMILY

The Cava/Moscati family, we know, met a tragic death. This family, as we saw, is different in that they are Italian Jews from Livorno. Elda Moscati, the wife, had grown up in Pitigliano; she and her immediate family took refuge there, most likely from the bombings. Elda's elderly father, the respected Abramo Moscati, was, in fact, one of about six Jews who were successfully concealed for several months by the doctors and nurses in the hospital in Pitigliano. They probably received support from Bishop Battistelli.[23] They were having difficulties finding food, and perhaps the younger people's connections with Pitigliano by then were rather weak, but for whatever reason they were trustful enough to hand themselves over spontaneously to the Pitigliano carabinieri when summoned in late November 1943, and thus were sent to the dubious refuge of Roccatederighi. The whole family, including the children Franca and Enzo, were taken on April 18, on the first bus transport to Fossoli. Elda boarded the bus early in order to have a front seat, as she suffered from motion sickness. From Fossoli, a month later on May 16, the family was put on Convoy 10, consisting of sealed cattle cars, to Auschwitz where they were killed immediately on arrival. One resists imagining how this trusting family, believing they had taken refuge among benevolent family friends, saw their confidence erode into doubt, then fear, then terror as the Fascist-Nazi machine swallowed them.

Livorno had a flourishing and highly educated Jewish community before the war, a prestigious *collegio rabbinico* (rabbinical college), Jewish publishers such as the Salomone Belforte Press which dated back to the beginning of the nineteenth century, and the second largest Sephardic synagogue in Europe. When the racial laws were applied in 1938, the community responded by setting up its own successful high school with highly qualified teachers and university professors. But as the situation worsened, many Jews fled the city. As a major port, it was subject to intensive bombing and, indeed, today the downtown area consists mostly of postwar construction. The roof of the magnificent synagogue was damaged in the bombings; after the war it was demolished and replaced by a much reduced concrete structure. Inside, though, one can still find some of the magnificent synagogue furnishings that had been hidden during the war. Between 1938 and 1940, the Jewish population of Livorno had already almost halved.[24] The community of Pitigliano had officially joined the Livorno community in 1931, thus theoretically reinforcing their bonds.

## NATALE, BERTA, AND GIGLIOLA FINZI

Natale and Berta Finzi, another couple from Livorno, had the special joy of welcoming a baby girl born to them while interned at Roccatederighi. Berta was allowed to go to the local hospital for the delivery. The Fascist treatment of Jews in the camp, thus, varied between humanitarianism and callous disregard for their lives. Documents reveal Natale pleading for his wife to be allowed medical care as she was expecting a difficult delivery, and this was granted. He also asked permission to return to their residence to retrieve items that she would be needing. Permission for this too was granted. Natale stayed with Berta in the local hospital after she gave birth until they received a polite note from the camp director inquiring when they would be returning to camp. A few days later they were back with a healthy new baby girl, Gigliola. Everything so far had happened in a compassionate and civilized manner. Two months later they were shipped out to Fossoli and Auschwitz. They were among the nine Italian Jews who saw themselves assigned first to the bus transport to Fossoli, and then to the convoys bound for death at Auschwitz. Baby Gigliola's new life was cut short at the age of three months, together with her parents' lives. Gigliola, upon arrival at Auschwitz, was seized, thrown up in the air, and impaled on a bayonet; her mother immediately fell down on the train tracks, dead from the shock. Her grieving husband was sent for slave labor and died soon after.[25]

## PASERMAN FAMILY

Moszek Paserman and his wife went into hiding; both survived and prospered. Though foreigners who were officially under "confino libero," free internment, they were offered a secure hiding place and a host family near Pitigliano. After hiding in a cave for several months, they emerged, in order to prepare for Passover 1944. No harm came to them in Pitigliano, and the family remained in Italy after the war. Leone went on to become the president of the Jewish community of Rome and head of the Museum of the Shoah Foundation.[26]

The Waisborg family and the Pasermans happened to be related. The Waisborgs were in Roccatederighi, though they do not appear in Azeglio Servi's lists and, as the daughter tells it, were transported in June not to Fossoli but to Scipione. She remembers the local villagers of Roccatederighi, people whose loyalties were probably more in tune with the Grosseto province's northern towns' socialist and anti-Fascist traditions, passing milk through the barbed wire for the children in the camp.

## LAST DAYS AT ROCCATEDERIGHI CAMP

The final days of the internment camp at Roccatederighi were complicated. The various accounts differ, because of "divided memory," again. Some narratives were apparently created in order to enhance the image of Bishop Galeazzi so that for many years he came off as a savior of Jews. Other narratives enhance the image of the Resistance.

My attempt to reconstruct what actually happened is dry and inadequate compared with the emotions, the terror, the relief, the confusion, that must have overwhelmed the few Jews still left in the camp. Azeglio Servi's brief account may guide us. It was perhaps written closest to the events and has an air of honesty about it, as he wrote down a sequence of events during the final days of the camp (figures 7.3 and 7.4). On June 4, he writes, the seven French and Yugoslavian prisoners escaped. Then, on June 7, the last transport took place, while the Allies approached and the partisans probably were becoming more emboldened, but not enough to stop the deportation of Jews. On June 9, the armed Fascist militi guarding the camp put down their arms and exchanged their uniforms for civilian clothing, as the Allies' arrival seemed imminent. Next, the guards, and the camp director, actually disappeared into the countryside. Since the inmates were no longer guarded, after a while, the remaining Jews escaped, also melting into the countryside. Two dramatic events occurred before they left, however. Two hours after the guards fled, while the Jews were still in the camp, Azeglio writes that the partisans executed eight of the former guards. They were identified by the French prisoners who had escaped and joined the partisans. The "Frenchmen" probably sought revenge, or justice as they saw it, because when they had tried to escape previously, several of them were caught and beaten ("almost to death") by the Fascist guards.[27] If one compares their possibly harsher treatment as Algerians with the harsh treatment of the "Africans" Jews of Libya who were interned in Civitella del Tronto, another camp in Central Italy, Fascist racism is seen in practice. African Jews, and of course Muslims, were on an even lower rung than Italian or European Jews.[28]

Azeglio and his family headed for a local hotel run by someone who had once been his client in the village of Roccatederighi, seeking shelter there. Though the owner was a Fascist and *federale* or secretary of the local branch of the Fascio, he understood at that point that it would stand him in good stead to have protected some Jews. Azeglio named June 9 as the day of the camp's liberation; he probably meant it was the day he and the remaining prisoners realized they were free since no one was guarding them.

Azeglio's diary entries do not tell when the camp director or the bishop fled. Edda Servi's account, based on what her father told her, if it can be relied on, reveals a little more. Perhaps the bishop had finally remembered that clerics were not supposed to have taken sides in the conflict, and his presence there would be compromising. By then, though, there was nothing obvious to indicate the camp's recent existence except the barbed wire fence, and the memories of the few surviving ex-prisoners.

Azeglio's list of events is thus filled in by his daughters. Edda highlights and perhaps also heightens the drama of those days in her memoir. She relies on her memory, the diary she kept, documentation supplied by her brother Gino, and corroboration by her sister Marcella and younger brother Mario, who was a ten-year-old child, for her book, published in 1995, thus many decades later. According to Edda, as the Allies approached Pitigliano, she and her brother Lello decided to travel north ahead of the front to find and rescue their parents and Mario at Roccatederighi. After a perilous trek, they arrived in the area to hear that the camp had been dismantled. They found some former inmates living in huts in the forest near Arcidosso, together with hundreds of refugees from the cities. It was no easy task to find their parents, and they feared they had been deported. Hold-out Fascists had become snipers, and fear and mistrust were in the air. Edda presents her father's detailed oral account of the end of the camp, abandoned by everyone except the last inmates. Some other dramatic events taking place prior to and during the "inter-regnum" are also recounted.

> We learned from Father that when the second bus had come . . . people were not called in alphabetical order: all the foreign Jews were taken with the exception of a couple from Vienna, the Schechters, because Mrs. Schechter had become the lover of the camp director; and the remaining Italians—after some bribing of the director and of the bus drivers—were left behind. After this, there had not been a third bus. The director of the camp and the guards had fled in fear of the Allies and of the revenge of the survivors. The bishop, his sister and his butler had also vanished, and the few Jews who had not been deported were left to their own wits. Not knowing where to go, they remained at the camp, planning to wait there for the arrival of the Allies. No sooner had they agreed on this than they saw a group of Gestapo [sic] stopping at the foot of the long flight of steps outside. The Jews immediately split into two groups, locked themselves inside two of the three bathrooms in the building, and waited for the worst. The Gestapo men looked in the dormitories, ransacked the place, and with their rifle butts sprang open the door of the one bathroom where nobody was hiding; they stole whatever food was still in the pantries and left. At this point no one wanted to remain in the camp one more minute, and they all fled in different directions in search of safer shelter.[29]

On June 18, Azeglio's two children, Lello and Edda, turned up, seeking and finding their parents in the village. It was not until June 23, though, that the first American tanks, jeeps, and armored carriers appeared to liberate the village of Roccatederighi. The eldest of the four Servi siblings, Lello, served as a sapper, disabling bombs and boobytraps left by the Germans. On July 15, Azeglio Servi and his family arrived back in Pitigliano, preceded by Lello.

Azeglio told the hotel owner in Roccatederighi that the partisans and the Allies were about to come for his head, but if he sheltered this family whom he knew to be Jews, they would intercede for him. He did so. As Edda and Lello arrived, though, the hotel was requisitioned in the meantime by the SS as a temporary headquarters. The Germans fled after five days, but not before threatening to take Edda whom they considered a great cook with them. Either they had been joking or they could not find her when they left hastily in the middle of the night. She was hiding in the attic. A battle ensued as the Allies shelled the village until the next morning, when a column of liberators finally wound its way up the hillside.

The hotel owner, in the meantime, disappeared, but was arrested and taken to the local school. Ten-year-old Mario was brought and identified him to American military police, who proceeded to beat him. The Servis later informed the partisans and others administering justice that he had given them shelter and not betrayed them to the Nazis. Edda was horrified by the violence inflicted on the former Fascists, but says she and her family were still unaware of what the Nazis had done to the Jews (*Child*, pp. 270–279, 283–285).

## WAS THERE A BATTLE AT THE CAMP?

Azeglio's account that eight Roccatederighi camp guards were executed on the indication of French escapees is contested in other publications. Luciana Rocchi states that the group of partisans who may have done this were identified as being led by a certain partisan nicknamed "Bombolo" but also that he and his men may have simply noticed the Fascists entering the woods and shot at them, and in any case six were killed.[30]

The only possible corroborating evidence of any battle, large or small, at the camp between partisans who came to liberate it and the Fascist guards is noted by Laura Paggini. She sent me a photograph of a tombstone or memorial which, when she visited in 2013, was decorated with flowers and candles.[31] When I visited in 2018, there were no flowers, but neighbors seemed inordinately upset that we were viewing the monument. The tombstone or memorial is of an eighteen-year-old Fascist killed near the perimeter of the camp, Fidelfo Falchi, whose epitaph reads "For him, who did not wish to die, dusk was fatal" ("Lui, che non voleva morire, il tramonto fu fatale"), killed by "una mano incosciente" (a cruel hand). One can surmise that this Fascist was a local boy killed by the partisans and whose family still lives nearby. Falchi was killed on the same day that the guards cast off their uniforms and ran away. The situation seems more like a case of abandonment by the Fascists and the bishop than like a battle; Falchi, himself, probably tried to escape but hesitated too long as the partisans closed in. The partisans, led by Bombolo or by Ernesto Rosenfeld, killed him as they entered the camp.

They were busy cleaning and becoming acquainted with their new arms which had been dropped from an Allied plane when the group of Nazis approached at the bottom of the long flight of steps. Here accounts are contradictory. According to Edda Servi, Ernesto Rosenfeld, who was on guard, may have started shooting and throwing grenades to delay the Nazis and give the partisans time to escape into the woods and the inmates time to hide in the bathrooms. The same incident including the attention to the new weapons and involving the same Ernesto Rosenfeld is described in *Banda Armata* (pp. 236–237). This version takes place though at Poggio Fogari. The two narratives or places seem to have become conflated. In either case, Rosenfeld seems to have behaved with courage.

Paggini emphasizes the historical basis of her novel in an author's postscript. She mentions two conflicting theories of the course of the events at that crucial time. She prefers the theory that there was an exchange of fire between the guards and attacking partisans:

> Those of the province who were liberated also related that the bishop, as the Allied army approached, had the last few who were left run away after the two transfers to Fossoli. . . . But the version according to which the camp was attacked by the partisans seems much more plausible, a proof of this being the still existing memorial stone in memory of the young militia member killed right where the barbed wire fence was in the exchange of fire on June 9, 1944.
>
> I grossetani liberati hanno anche raccontato che il vescovo, approsssimandosi l'esercito degli Alleati, fece fuggire gli ultimi rimasti dopo i due precedenti trasferimenti a Fossoli . . . . Ma sembra molto più plausibile la versione secondo cui il campo fu preso d'assalto dai partigiani; riprova ne è la lapide, ancora visibile, in memoria del giovane milite ucciso proprio adosso del filo spinato nello scontro a fuoco del 9 giugno 1944. (p. 158)

Another researcher, Heide Moldenhauer, also believes that there was a battle.[32] It is probable in my view that neither of these two theories is totally correct, but that the inmates were more or less abandoned to their own devices. The Jews remained there because they simply did not know where to go. If the Jews were liberated, why did they not leave with their liberators? Azeglio Servi did not write about either partisans or Nazis entering into the camp. In any case, they both seem to have left very quickly.

There are other limitations to Azeglio Servi's account, as he himself would no doubt acknowledge. He did not know much about another undocumented kind of life that was going on among the prisoners. Ernesto Rosenfeld had fought in Yugoslavia, and the "Frenchmen," with their leader, had fought in battles with the Free French Forces. They planned and implemented a breakout from the camp together, and eventually joined the Resistance. It is unlikely that they constituted a fifth column planted within the camp, though. The Resistance consisted of a number of small competing bands with different leaders and ideologies. They were well aware that precipitous strikes against the Nazis on their part would lead to tenfold revenge on the local population, which they needed to have on their side. Judging from the Fosse Ardeantini episode in Rome, in which Roman Jews who were already in prison were executed along with new arrests, the camp inmates would have made handy scapegoats for the Nazis, too. The fact that one of the Resistance leaders was the son of the camp commander Gaetano Rizziello may I conjecture have also held them back from entering the camp. Until the father had fled, the partisans did not enter. Apart from this, in general, they were biding their time until their actions would really help the slowly advancing Allies, rather than have a negative result. Probably most of the local Italian Jews, who did not know French, did not realize that some surreptitious planning had been going on within the camp itself, among the French speakers. An exception would have been one of the Nunes brothers from Grosseto, who was involved with the breakout. The eleven-year-old Edith Singer could have been aware of what her uncle Ernesto was planning, since she knew his past. She also knew enough not to share it with her garrulous companion Eugenia, who no doubt had told her that her own father was a friend of Bishop Galeazzi and of Commander Rizziello. It is tragic that the imprisoned fighters within the camp could not do anything to frustrate the aims of the Fascists when the deportations began. But the first busload must have convinced them that it was high time that they made their break.

## LIBERATION OF GROSSETO

Actually the camp at Roccatederighi saw its "liberation" at the same time as the liberation of Pitigliano to the south-east and some days before the liberation of Grosseto to the south. As for Grosseto, the partisans of the Vittorio Alunno band, named after a local anti-Fascist who had fallen in the Spanish Civil War, led by Ganna (Aristeo Banchi) achieved this on June 14 by occupying major buildings in the city, apparently with no Fascist resistance. On June 15, they fought a battle against retreating SS troops who came up from Rome and entered the town from the south. These must have been surprised to find the Resistance there already. Six partisans were killed and twelve Germans, as well as thirty Axis prisoners taken. The townspeople at that point proudly raised a white flag to indicate to the Allies that Grosseto was theirs.[33]

## LIBERATION OF PITIGLIANO

Rome had been liberated on June 4–5, only a few days earlier. Pitigliano was liberated on June 10–11, right after the devastating Allied bombing intended to hamper the Germans' retreat. The partisans entered the town via a little-used entrance from the west and then captured some two dozen Germans in a bicycle brigade heading north. The Germans were caught in a pincer movement between advancing Allies and from the north and west by the partisan bands. Some twenty-five Germans were killed; their bicycles were distributed among the partisans and the townspeople. The surviving Germans were locked up, some of them in a windmill.[34] The German army sent reinforcements from the north, and the ensuing twenty-six hour-long battle for Pitigliano was vicious. The province of Grosseto was the first province north of Rome to be liberated from the Fascist and Nazi yoke; therefore, Pitigliano and the concentration camp of Roccatederighi must have been two of the earliest significant locations to be liberated.

## FASCIST LEADERS OF THE PROVINCE FLEE

On June 10, all of the Fascist leaders of Grosseto, except Alceo Ercolani, who had been running his affairs already from Paganico in the north of the province, had fled north in a motorized convoy, robbing and pillaging as they went. They had extorted money, taken from an account intended for refugees, from a Grosseto bank, and opened the safe in Grosseto's Fascist headquarters and shared out the contents among themselves before fleeing. A sorry ending for high provincial officials who had given themselves such airs of superiority only a short time before. They reunited with their leader Ercolani and put themselves at the service of Mussolini's puppet republic in the north.[35]

## CLAIMS THAT BISHOP GALEAZZI WAS A HERO

After the war, it was claimed in Grosseto that Bishop Galeazzi heroically saved Jews. His successor bishop contributed to this impression (see chapter 5). It seems that a bishop, because of his prestige, may be like a pope in that virtuous actions can magically adhere to him in the minds of the faithful. The bishop who succeeded him gave an explanation that obfuscates more than it clarifies. He alleged that Bishop Galeazzi allowed the local Jews to be released, whereas all the foreign Jews actually preferred to be sent to Fossoli. This was certainly not a matter on which they were offered any choice, and it is highly unlikely that they would have chosen to be sent to there.[36] It is more likely that foreign and out-of-area Jews inside the camp simply did not have the same connections as did the Jews of Pitigliano and Grosseto[37] and thus were not able to maneuver for exemption. Luciana Rocchi writes that "neither group had available the protective networks within the camp and among the Fascist authorities that allowed the Grosseto province internees to be freed for reasons of health, or to stay in the camp until Liberation" ("ne gli uni ne gli altri disponevano di quelle rete di protezione all'interno del campo e tra le autorità fasciste che avevano consentito ai grossetani internati di essere rimessi in libertà per motivi di salute o di restare nel campo fino alla Liberazione").

One can compare Bishop Galeazzi's behavior with that of more highly placed clerics in Pisa, the archbishop, or Florence, the cardinal. There, informal networks and initiatives that helped hide local and foreign Jews went into action mobilizing priests and nuns to provide safe havens. The bishopric of Grosseto did not cover all of the province of Grosseto, however. To the east, Bishop Battistelli of Pitigliano hid Jews in the hospital and issued false baptismal certificates. To the north, the Jewish orphanage of Livorno was located in a town called Sassetta outside of Galeazzi's bishopric, in an area called Massa Marittima in the province of Grosseto. The orphans were rescued by the bishop of Livorno, Monsignor Giovanni Piccioni, and some other priests, from a train on which they were already being transported and which was halted by a bombing.[38] Such actions were not consonant with Bishop Galeazzi's personality and political sympathies. Though the tide may have been changing, Bishop Galeazzi's role is still considered "disputable" ("discutibile") and he still has his defenders. The complicated events and multiple accounts of the final days of the camp confuse more than add any clarity about the bishop's role.

## NOTES

1. Giuseppe Celata, *E poi la salvezza: Storie di ebrei strappati alla Shoah (1943-1945)* (Florence: Edizioni Medicea, 2014), p. 55.
2. Ercolani had served the Fascist government in Eastern Europe and East Africa, where the Italian army had committed atrocities in Ethiopia and Libya. I have not found details on his activities. See Angelo Del Boca, *Italiani brava gente?*
3. "E persona violentissima e decisa, di limitata cultura, pur avendo conseguito nel febbraio scorso, d'ordine del capo della provincia, la licenza di maturità classica nel liceo di Grosseto." See ACS: Copia: Min. Int. Direzione Gen. della P.S. Divisione Polizia, Frose Francesco No. 54, 28 Ottobre 1944. After the war Frose was charged for "violenza privata continuata" (continuous private violence) and sentenced to eighteen years of prison.
4. Bruna Bocchini Camaiaini and Daniele Menozzi, eds., *Lettere Pastorali dei Vescovi della Toscana* (Genoa: Marietti, 1990), pp. 111–112.
5. "Torniamo, dunque dilettissimi, alla nostra Chiesa, torniamo, per ascoltare devotamente la S. Messa . . . Rinnoviamo la nostra consacrazione . . . le nostre preghiere, per la prosperità della Maestà del Re Imperatore . . . per l'assistenza del forte e saggio Governo Nazionale, per la salute e resistenza dei nostri Soldati, per il triunfo della giustizia, per la vittoria italiana, per la pace universale." Paolo Galeazzi, Festa della Purificazione di Maria Vergine, 1941, Grosseto: Tipografia Fascista La Maremma, 1941, pp. 42–43.

6. "Ebrei maremmani scampati al trasferimento da Roccatederighi a Fossoli hanno testimoniato il suo impegno in favore degli internati, dagli interventi presso la direzione del Campo per un trattamento più umano degli "internati," ad alcune situazioni particulari che caldeggiò, al nascondere personalmente alcuni ebrei ai Tedeschi in ritirata." Giuseppe Celata, *E poi la salvezza*, p. 55.

7. Photos of the four pages of his diary, written in the inside covers of his prayer book, may be found in Luciana Rocchi, ed., *La Persecuzione degli ebrei nella provincia di Grosseto nel 1943-44* (Grosseto: ISGREC, 1996, 2002), pp. 56–59, and herein.

8. See Ariel Paggi's "Elenco degli Ebrei presenti al Campo di Concentramento di Roccatederighi e loro destino." Based on information collected from CDEC, Bad Arolsen, ISGREC, Spielberg Foundation, and USHMM. See also the discussions in *Il Muro*, passim.

9. Renzo De Felice, *Storia degli ebrei italiani sotto il fascismo* (Einaudi, 1961, 1972), p. 452: the "'misti', che esclusi dall'internamento dalle leggi della RSI, fecero di tutto per essere portati a Fossoli, dove vi era aria buona e non si correvano rischi di bombardamenti." *Jews in Fascist Italy* p. 449.

10. Primo Levi, *Survival in Auschwitz* 1958, 1959 (New York: Collier, 1961), pp. 10–12. See also the new edition of the *Complete Works of Primo Levi*, consisting of new and revised translations, ed. Ann Goldstein, Liveright, 2016.

11. "Come sottolinea Dario Venegoni . . . nella prefazione all'opera di Iafrate: 'Visto così da vicino, il caso di questo trasporto suona come la prova inconfutabile della parte attiva dell'apparato della RSI al fianco dei nazisti nelle deportazioni. La verità è che centinaia di italiani misero allora la propria esperienza al servizio dei nazisti, inseguendo, arrestando, accompagnando altri italiani fino a quell tragico treno, e poi ancora' . . ." For this assessment of the role of Italians in the deportazioni, see A. Smulevich, www.moked.it/blog/2015/06/10libristorie-di-indesiderabili. The point is made at book length in *The Italian Executioners*.

12. This story is in Paoletti, pp. 162–163, and is also told by Liliana Picciotto, "Jews during the German Occupation," in Herzer, *The Italian Refuge*, p. 132. See also *Il Muro*, p. 144.

13. Rocchi, "Ebrei nella Toscana meridionale," in Collotti, *Ebrei in Toscana*, Vol. 1, p. 298. See Paggi, *Il Muro*, p. 103 on the sugar hypothesis. Celata (*E poi la salvezza*, 2014), gives the positive report on the bishop's behavior, p. 55. Edda Servi, *Child of the Ghetto*, p. 271 writes "there had not been a third bus."

14. "Potete licenziarmi ma io non ci torno più!" Paggi, *Il Muro*, p. 144, he maintained that he said to his bosses. Luciana Rocchi writes that the first transport was indeed in a Pullman owned by the SIAT Company of Pitigliano. See also Paggi, *Bambino*, p. 67. The driver's name was Bocini. The vehicle used for the second transport is not clear, perhaps a German truck, or another Pullman, but the driver was different: a certain Nizzi. Rocchi also writes that the driver who informed the partisans of his itinerary was the first one, Bocini. Luciana Rocchi, "Ebrei nella Toscana Meridionale," in Collotti, *Ebrei in Toscana* vol 1, p. 298.

15. Ariel Paggi, *Il Muro*, p. 111.

16. A train from Fossoli would take four days to reach Bergen-Belsen, in Germany, or eight days to reach Auschwitz, in Poland. Giuliana Donati lists the convoys, numbers of prisoners, departure and arrival dates and also reproduces lists

of victims' names. Giuliana Donati, *Ebrei in Italia: Deportazione, resistenza* (Milan: Centro di Documentazione Ebraica Contemporanea, 1980).

Primo Levi had survived the trip to Auschwitz in February, noticing the close cooperation between Germans and Italians as he boarded. See Centro Primo Levi, "Primo Levi at Fossoli," http://www.primolevi.it/Web/English/Contents/Auschwitz/110_Primo_Levi_at_Fossoli.

The last convoy out of Fossoli took place on June 26, but a later one from Verona to Auschwitz on August 2 included prisoners from Fossoli, as the bridges had been bombed. Giuliana Donati, *Ebrei in Italia: Deportazione, Resistenza* (Milan: Centro di Documentazione Ebraica Contemporanea, 1980), pp. 20–25. For conditions inside the trains, see Yossi Sucary, describing the plight of Libyan Jewish prisoners sent from Fossoli to Bergen-Belsen, in *Benghazi—Bergen-Belsen* (Heb., 2013) English translation by Yardenne Greenspan, *Benghazi—Bergen-Belsen* (San Bernadino: Createspace, 2016). Also Eugenio Iafrate, *Elementi indesiderabili*, passim; Carlo Greppi, *L'Ultimo treno: Racconti del viaggio verso il lager* (Rome: Donazelli, 2012), especially. All heartbreaking to read.

17. Information obtained by Ariel Paggi from the International Tracing Service.
18. Ibid.
19. See Betti, et al., *Banda*, pp. 234–235.
20. See Luciana Rocchi, Appendix to *Ebrei in Toscana*, p. 321. The main source of information on Rosenfeld is *Banda*, ibid. Paggi has a different story for Rosenfeld in *Il Muro*, but due to the considerable detail in the other sources, I intend to give them credence here. Paggi describes Ernesto as a former pharmacist from Milan, taken in the second transport, and escaping along the way. See p. 226 for his valiant attempts at tracing the family.
21. Liliana Picciotto, *Il Libro della memoria: Gli Ebrei deportati dall'Italia (1943-45)* (Milan: Mursia, 1991) and the Survivors' Registry at USHHM.
22. Further details are given based on documents examined by Luciana Rocchi, "Ebrei nella Toscana Meridionale," in Collotti, *Ebrei in Toscana* vol 1, p. 299. These details do not clarify whether they survived. Ariel Paggi has tried to trace them, via the International Tracing Service and the Survivors' Registry at USHMM, and AMIA in Argentina, with no success. A different Edith Singer, a survivor, published a book of Holocaust memories in the United States, and possibly the two have at some point been confused. Liliana Picciotto has several accounts of the rather chaotic last attempted transfers from Fossoli area to Verona, after the bridges had been bombed, during which numbers of prisoners managed to escape. See *Salvarsi*, pp. 251–252.
23. Paggi, *Bambino*, p. 69. They were protected by the director Dr. Bruscalupi and the chief surgeon, Dr. Bognomini. See also Picciotto, *Salvarsi*, p. 243.
24. Census data reported by Michele Sarfatti in *Mussolini contro gli ebrei*, Turin, 1994, p. 136, and reproduced in the booklet accompanying an exhibit, *1938, La Scuola ebraica di Livorno* (Livorno: Museo ebraico, 1997), p. 12.
25. The testimony was provided by Frida Misul, a survivor from Auschwitz who knew the family from Livorno. A corroborating file on the story of the Finzis, including Misul's testimony, exists in the Archivio di Stato di Grosseto (with thanks to Laura Paggini). Fascicolo Finzi: Letter from Natale to Capo della Provincia, requesting for his wife to receive treatment in a maternity home, since she is in the last month

of pregnancy December 26; and December 30, 1043, Report from the Comune of Castell'Azzara on their arrest; January 11, Report on Finzi Natale, ebreo internato; January 12, Telegram to the director of the Camp of Roccatederighi; January 26, Medical report by Dr. Livio Salghini of Roccatederighi; February 17 Natale asks for an extension of his leave to assist his wife; Feb. 19 (Gigliola's birth certificate), 1944. The file ends with the death certificates. Also recounted by Edda Servi, *Child*, pp. 193 and 304, who reports that her own mother would mumble to herself the terrible news she had heard. Since the Jews from Roccatederighi, both foreign and Italian, had been taken in the same two convoys, there could have been more eyewitnesses who were among the few survivors.

26. Leone Paserman was one of several Jews who were reunited with the families of their protectors, in a special ceremony held in Pitigliano, July 19, 2015. The groups also visited the exhibit in Ribolla. With thanks to Gabriella Pizzetti, curator of the museum in Ribolla, for showing me photos of this reunion. Marcella Servi was also able to be present.

27. Recounted by Marcella Servi on information from her father, Azeglio.

28. Marcella's conversation with me on August 19, 2015. Ariel Paggi in *Il Muro* also mentions beatings (p. 101). As already discussed, these so-called Frenchmen were mostly Algerian Muslims, combatants and prisoners-of-war from the Free French army who had been mistaken for African Jews. On "African Jews" see Yossi Sucary, English trans., "Benghazi—Bergen-Belsen," cit.

29. *Child*, pp. 271–272.

30. Rocchi, ibid., p. 299, quoting an interview with "Ganna," Aristeo Banchi, another partisan leader. In the postwar years, a story of a battle would definitely enhance the partisans' reputation. Azeglio also said that "qualche internato" (an internee or two) had fled with the guards, complicating the situation.

31. See also Laura Paggini, *Pesante come una piuma,* p. 33: "There's a stone tablet on a small hill at the back . . . it says that there was a boy and they shot him right here" ("'C'è una lapide' . . . su una piccola collina a ridosso . . . 'c'è scritto che era un ragazzo e che gli hanno sparato proprio qui'"). This is one of the first signs the fictional young campers find at Roccatederighi, though the memorial stone is not fictional, in 2002. Thus, they have little understanding of the event at that point.

32. Conversation with Heide Moldenhauer, June 12, 2018.

33. Betti et al., *Banda*, p. 237. Also Luciana Rocchi, "La Liberazione di Grosseto: Storia di una Resistenza breve e di un lungo antifascismo nel primo capoluogo toscano liberato" ISGREC, n.d., published first on www.toscananovecento.it, and found on the ISGREC website. Rocchi emphasizes that there was a long, suppressed tradition of anti-Fascism in these rural areas, but the actual Resistance fighting lasted only a short time.

34. Betti et al., *Banda*, chapter on the battle of Pitigliano, pp. 172–179; and Franco Dominici, "La Battaglia di Pitigliano: 10–11 Giugno 1944," *Corriere del Tufo*, December 30, 2016, in Pillole di storia (http://www.nctufo.it/corriere/rubriche/pillole-di-storia/) da Eredazione (http://www.nctufo.it/author/admin/).

35. On the Fascists' escape northward, see Marco Grilli, *Per noi il tempo si è fermato all'alba*, pp. 111–112.

36. The rethinking of the bishop's role actually began around 1996, as Carlo Groppi, Luciana Rocchi, and other researchers at ISGREC began to publish their work.
37. A point made by Rocchi, ibid., p. 301.
38. Paggi, *Il Muro*, p. 34.

*Chapter 8*

# Post War: The Search for a Return to Normal

## *For Jews, a Future of Virtual Judaism*

### THE SEARCH FOR A RETURN TO NORMAL

After the war's end, which came early to southern Tuscany, as to be expected, everyone was desperately trying to return to normal. It was small mercy for the province that the end to the bloodshed came early. To say there was so much to be done is only to state the obvious. Individuals and the state and country were devastated by the tragedy that had occurred, both on the national level and in terms of individual lives shattered in death, injury, mourning, loss, and trauma. Immediate violent revenge and summary justice gave way to postwar trials. The harsh sentences given notorious Fascists, however, were gradually commuted over the years. What has been described as a too-early amnesty failed to heal all the wounds, especially among Jews. The racial laws against Jews, which have sometimes been characterized as the salient feature of Fascism, were not quickly repealed. In fact, the Vatican in 1943 continued to maintain that there was some good in them. "At the end of that year [1943], the Racial Laws had not yet been revoked even in the liberated zone, perhaps due to the intervention of the Holy See, according to which the legislation 'has measures that should be abrogated, yet contains others as well that are worth confirmation.'"[1] In Italy in 1945, after the final Fascist defeat, it took a number of laws, nineteen in fact, until the 1950s, to abrogate all the anti-Jewish measures. "In total, five laws restored the Jews' civil rights, seven restored their property rights, four laws enabled them to resume their careers, two provided benefits to racial persecutees, and one law ruled against racist propaganda."[2]

At the war's end, the foreign Jews who had been imprisoned in Roccatederighi and had survived seem to have scattered. Of the thirty or forty who were sent to Auschwitz, which was not liberated until January 27, 1945, most perished there. Only four, or in other accounts six, survived. Those who were sent to other Nazi camps, such as Bergen-Belsen, had a greater chance of survival. We have already discussed the fates of several families. Others whose names have not come up yet are discussed here. Some of those who survived or may have survived ended up in far-flung destinations. Katherine Sattler, not discussed previously, went to Australia. Edith Singer, if she survived, may have reached the United States and her uncle Ernest Rosenfeld, perhaps, reached Argentina. Arthur Zeller was sent from Auschwitz to Dachau, and survived, while Frederick Berman was sent directly to Dachau in 1944 and survived. Moshe Gorniki, a Polish Jew from Zgieva, had been in Teramo and Arcidosso, then Roccatederighi. He was in Convoy 10 that left from Fossoli and was later traced to Buchenwald, Terezin, Deggendor, Winzer, Ostenhofen, and Hamburg. On January 9, 1949, Gorniki took the "Ballou" from Bremerhaven to the United States. He was known to have an address in Springfield, Massachusetts.[3] Almost no foreign Jews returned to the area of southern Tuscany.

A reception center was set up in Milan after the war for returning Italian Jews and other survivors, and data were accumulated about survivors.[4] One other family of foreign Jews besides the Pasermans may have avoided arrest and remained in our area. Both were sheltered in caves and never entered the camp, and both families moved to Rome after liberation.[5] The second family is probably Walter Mundstein's family with whom he reunited in Rome and whose saga is recounted in the American Jewish Joint Distribution Committee publication.

In the provincial capital, Grosseto, the Office of the Prefect (Prefettura) had much to do concerning local Jews after liberation. A thorny issue that the Grosseto authorities dealt with was compensation to local Jews who had been divested of their possessions.[6] The Fascist EGELI organization kept fairly good records, though some confiscated assets had been directed to the wrong recipient or misappropriated. After the war, Jews began to make claims for restitution. The 1946 folder contains a number of documents with such titles as "Sequestri Beni Baldacci" and "Società Paganico," a company that had been seized although only one co-owner of the three was Jewish. Properties that had been sold had new owners who had paid good cash for their acquisitions. Restitution promised to be a long drawn-out and frustrating process, as it indeed turned out to be.[7] On a national level, restitution and reparation came up against the Catholic concept that all were sufferers. Michael Livingston writes:

> If the Race Laws teach us important lessons about the power of law, they also remind us of its limitations. Nowhere is this more apparent than in the story of postwar reparations—or the lack thereof—for damage sustained by Jews

during the Race Laws and Holocaust period. Here the legal system that proved so creative in extending and expanding the Race Laws proved equally if not more creative in delaying or avoiding compensation, so that the issue remains largely unresolved almost seventy years after the event, and may remain so indefinitely.[8]

There was still talk of "campi di concentramento," but as an option for returning "repubblichini," or former Fascists returning home from the north after the war. A May 1945 document of the Questura (police headquarters) calls a meeting, on the initiative of the mayor of Grosseto, to discuss the advisability of such a "campo di concentramento."[9] It is not clear whether the Fascists would be confined there to await trial or whether housing was simply not available for them.

In September 1945, a letter and questionnaire arrived from the post-Liberation Ministry of the Interior addressed to all "Prefetti del Regno."[10] It stated that a certain Signorina Lachlin, who had seen an article published in London stating that 28,000 Jews had been deported from Italy, would like to know if this were true. The minister was requesting information about the Jews of Italy from all provinces and localities. He emphasized that the people and the clergy of Italy had done all they could to save Jews, often putting their own lives in danger. He also asked for particular cases that were interesting or tragic. The postwar minister was hoping to hear a narrative he wished to create. By mid-November, a response from our province to the minister's request was drafted; by December 10, 1945, a final report entitled "Questione ebraica in Italia" had been prepared by an official of the carabinieri of Orbetello. The report refers to a total of sixty-four Jews in Pitigliano and five Jews in Manciano before the war. Nineteen Jews from Pitigliano were interned in Roccatederighi, of whom fifteen returned to Pitigliano and four were transferred to Carpi (Fossoli) and then to Germany. It states that there is no more information about these four. It was obviously still possible in late 1945 to plead ignorance about the fate of Jews who had been deported. The report addresses the foreign Jews: twenty-four Jews, all German or Polish, had been interned in Arcidosso between October 1941 and March 1944. All stayed with private families and received subsidies from the Italian government. There is no mention of their fate after that and no mention of Roccatederighi (figure 8.1).

A different version of the report mentions another Jew from Pitigliano who was interned in Germany and that there were no news of him (see note below regarding Goffredo Paggi, Ariel's uncle, who died at Auschwitz). This report continues that there were no suicides among these Jews. Forty Jews from Pitigliano, four from nearby Manciano, and one from Magliana were in "latitanza," that is, had gone into hiding. In addition, twenty-five Jews of German and Polish citizenship in internment are noted. Then on June 9, 1944,

**Figure 8.1  Overgrown Sign Board at Entrance to Roccatederighi Seminary, Announcing Plan to Turn It into a Rest Home for Alzheimer's Patients.** *Source*: Photo by Judith Roumani, 2018.

all the Jews fled to the "macchia" or forest to await the arrival of the Allies. It states that almost all the Jews of the province returned, except for five, and of those who returned their economic situation was "non molto brillante," not very good. The food supply in the "campi di concentramento" had left much to be desired and their economic situation was now modest as they had lost much of their "materiali e merci": some had been taken by Nazi and Fascist troops, and some was destroyed by bombings. There is no mention of official confiscations.[11]

Though this report is factual, as far as it goes, the deportations and deaths are glossed over. The fate of the foreign Jews is ignored. The role that any Italians may have played in arrests or deportations is omitted. I conjecture that this is one of the earliest postwar documents laying the groundwork in November 1945 for the "Italiani brava gente" narrative.

In 1946, the Grosseto authorities were interested in any political activity or involvement on the part of the church. The Grosseto carabinieri, therefore, had a report drawn up on "Attività politica del clero." It concluded that "the clergy does not demonstrate any particular political activity, but displays an aversion to the parties of the Left, because the latter are known to be hostile to them." Thus, despite the country's veering to the Left, and the rise of the Communist party, partly due to its important role in the Resistance, the church maintained its hostility to the parties on the Left after the war.[12]

Even the more liberal and less dogmatic Bishop Battistelli of Pitigliano and his superior, the cardinal in Florence, shared in this aversion to the Left. The documents in the Archivio Storico Diocesano of Pitigliano relating to Bishop Battistelli, previously cited, also attest to the same political attitude. For example, on August 16, 1949, the cardinal of Florence wrote officially to his bishops that the marriage of an excommunicated person should be treated the same as the marriage of two people of mixed religion.

Other local attitudes lingered too. Over the next decade, 1945–1955, trials of major Fascist leaders, including Alceo Ercolani, the Fascist prefect and head of the province, and Michele De Anna, the Fascist colonel, took place. Ercolani had been so zealous as to set up his own internment camp for Jews and appointed a head of camp before the Ministry of the Interior had issued instructions to the provinces. He had been reprimanded for his haste, as the ministry had its own procedures and its own candidates for camp commander positions. Ercolani had left the province of Grosseto and fled north as the Allies approached. He became the head of the Fascist RSI government's refugee administration in Milan as the war ended. The irony is that the man who had coldly arranged and supervised the deportation of foreign Jewish refugees was himself now supposedly helping refugees.[13]

Arrested in May 1945, Ercolani was held until he was tried in Grosseto for the serious crimes of collaboration and of absconding with state funds. He received thirty years, appealed, and finally received a twenty-one year sentence in February 1949. In May 1950, he was released to house arrest and freed to "libertà vigilata" (probation) in 1951. He eventually retired comfortably on a state pension in his home province of Viterbo. Thus, the person most responsible for the Fascist crimes committed in the province of Grosseto served less than five years in prison, mostly before his sentencing.

Other local high Fascists, some with blood on their hands, such as Ercolani's assistants Scotti and Barberini, and propagandists such as Ferdinando Pierazzi, editor of the weekly newspaper *La Maremma*, received extended sentences and even death sentences. But all of them were eventually lightened or commuted, until they received amnesty in what has been described by many as a too-hasty forgiving which did not give justice its due. Italians who lost loved ones felt this inequity most keenly. The Togliatti Amnesty was declared by the Communist Minister of Justice Palmiro Togliatti who believed, correctly, that many former Fascists would become Communists. The series of amnesties were greeted with reactions ranging from anger and a sense of injustice, to cynicism, irony, and satire. The following is an example of the satirical mode, reflective of many Italians' postwar attitudes:

> "In Florence . . . they say that those who salute with their fists closed [i.e. the Communist salute] do so in order to ensure that their Fascist pins do not slip from their fingers."
>
> In most cases, people went to great lengths to bury a past that no one wanted to remember. Erasing collective memory was convenient to all, even to those who had the most to gain by pinpointing blame.[14]

One of the most hated and feared among local Fascists was Colonel Michele De Anna, the perpetrator of the mass execution of draft evaders at Istia. Eight families lost their young sons on one day (for a total of twelve deaths, thus several of siblings). De Anna fled north in 1944 with other local Fascists. He turned up in Milan where he served as a doctor in the refugee administration run by Ercolani, and later fled to Switzerland. He was found guilty in absentia and sentenced to death by firing squad, immediately commuted to *ergastolo*, a life sentence. At De Anna's later appeal in 1955, in Perugia, also in absentia, several people who had witnessed the events testified to his guilt. Bishop Galeazzi was called to the witness stand and testified in De Anna's defense. He swore that another Fascist, someone who had in the meantime been killed, had confessed to him that he was responsible. De Anna's previous sentence of *ergastolo* was confirmed by the Perugia Court of Appeal.

The bishop's testimony shocked and angered local people, especially as actual witnesses reported seeing De Anna order the murders. De Anna had also received a commendation at the time for his behavior from Prefect Ercolani.[15] Galeazzi's testimony was in direct contradiction to other testimonies, and "provoked among family members of the victims and civil lawyers present at the trial some unfavorable comments about the bishop. The victim's families reported in Grosseto about the debate and commented unfavorably on the bishop's statements."[16] Though the bishop seems to have committed perjury, this affair does not seem to have made a lasting dent on his public reputation. De Anna lived on in Switzerland and later Rome, where he continued to practice as a medical doctor. Even as late as 1960, letters were being received at the provincial Prefettura urging the arrest of the notorious criminal De Anna, confirming a popular desire that justice be served. In 1966, he was pardoned; he never served a day in prison.

On a national level, Italians today still sometimes lament the rush to amnesty for former Fascists that occurred after the war's end. The earliest, more limited amnesty was created by the Decreto di Amnestia Generale of 1946, known as the Togliatti Amnesty. It was followed by other, more extensive amnesties, in 1948, 1953, and the final one in 1966.

Many, like Ariel Paggi, believe that the turn to Communism of former Fascists may have led to the early amnesties, which came too soon for the country to heal and justice to be achieved. During the war, his uncle Goffredo Paggi who had taken refuge in Pitigliano had left and returned to his job in Florence. There he was informed on by a colleague, deported to Auschwitz, and was murdered there. Paggi discusses the family's attempts to have the colleague prosecuted after the war. Since he had later became a Communist partisan, their efforts were not successful:

> My dad and my aunts tried to have the colleague who had denounced Uncle Goffredo prosecuted; the attempt was in vain because that gentleman had achieved the status of Communist partisan and was an activist in the party. I

Figure 8.2 **Ariel Paggi Pointing Out Plaque Listing Holocaust Victims from Pitigliano, Next to Synagogue, During His Interview.** *Source*: Photo by Jacques Roumani, 2011.

heard this years later from my uncle Mario Paggi of Milan, who had been our family's lawyer.[17]

Justice was frustrated in many spheres in Italy; this incident, in particular, brought it home to the Jews of Pitigliano (figure 8.2).

In 1994, documents were discovered by the prosecutor working on the Erich Preibke case in a cache dubbed "l'armadio della vergogna," the cabinet of shame. They were found in a storeroom in the military prosecutors' offices in Rome, in a cabinet whose doors were suspiciously turned against a wall. The documents detailed the charges against notorious Nazis with Italian blood on their hands who were supposed to be brought to Italy for trial but largely had not been. Preibke was the Nazi SS officer responsible for the massacre of 335 people, including seventy-five Jews, at the Fosse Ardeantine in Rome. He was discovered living in Argentina, extradited in 1995, and brought to Italy for trial.[18] His initial absolution in 1996 led to popular protests, and he was tried again in 1997. Priebke received fifteen years *ergastolo,* extended sentence, which was commuted to house arrest because of his advanced age. Preibke died in 2013 at the ripe age of 100. He was one of the few Nazis put on trial in Italy.

Another Nazi who did go to trial in Italy right after the war was Herbert Kappler, head of the SS and German police for Italy. He was responsible for the same incident. He also extorted the ransom of gold from the Jewish Community of Rome (which the Jews thought was buying them safety) and was responsible for the subsequent deportation of about 2,000 Jews from Rome. Kappler was found guilty and given a life sentence, to be served in an Italian prison. He was imprisoned, and eventually moved to a hospital because of cancer. In 1977, six months before his death, he was smuggled out in a suitcase by his wife and taken to Germany.[19]

The 13,000 pages of documents and nine hundred files in the cabinet of shame deal with many other sensitive and potentially embarrassing issues related to the postwar handling of trials, their outcomes, and the many amnesties. The latest documents in the files are from the early 1970s, indicating that that must have been when the cabinet was closed and supposedly forgotten.

While the Roccatederighi incident and its consequences have been occasionally noted in Italy, there does not seem to be any information about it and the role of any Nazis deployed there in the "cabinet of shame." Documents from another case that occurred nearby were relegated to this cabinet of amnesia. In Castelnuovo just across the border in the province of Pisa,[20] approximately one hundred non-Jewish Italians taken from San Niccioleta and Massa Marittima, nearby towns in Grosseto province, were executed in June 1944, by a joint division of German Nazis and Italian Fascists.[21] The Italian civilians were arrested in their homes and force-marched north as hostages with the withdrawing Nazis and Fascists. When it was decided that they were too much of a burden, they were executed behind the local geothermal electrical station, whose sounds masked those of the shots and cries of the victims. Two Fascists were convicted in 1949 to thirty-year sentences for this crime against humanity.

In April 1971, Simon Wiesenthal wrote to the Italian government with a list of victims' names to ask who were the Germans involved in this incident. Instead of responding, the Italian Ministry of Defense wrote to the Italian Ministry of Foreign Affairs in June 1971, with a document of perfect obfuscation: No one remembered . . . the victims were from out of the area (actually from about thirty kilometers away) . . . the Germans had fled immediately and no one had dared ask their names . . . the names of the victims were not enough evidence, and the names of the perpetrators were unknown.

In 1971, among the survivors who could have helped with information were the two Fascists who had been found guilty in the Italian court.

Unfortunately, neither Simon Wiesenthal nor the German government ever received any answer from the Italian ambassador to Vienna or anyone else in Italy. The entire file, after the back-and-forth between three ministries and two prefectures, was sealed up in the cabinet of shame. The myth of the "good Italian" required, in the 1970s, that the willing collaboration of Italian Fascists in Nazi-led atrocities had to be covered up, at least until the archaeologists of future generations, who would see this as remote history, something like an act of war of the ancient Romans, might discover it. All credit goes to the courage of the Italian parliament in 2015–2016 in releasing these documents, and even putting them online, while some of those who were present might conceivably still be alive, and justice might still be served—or, if not justice, at least the cause of transparency.

Immediately after liberation, in September 1944, Bishop Galeazzi of Grosseto had claimed the rent for his seminary at Roccatederighi, which the Fascist administration of Ercolani had never actually paid him. The new postwar prefect of Grosseto, De Dominicis, directed the bishop to follow official procedures and apply to the Ministry of the Interior. He refrained from pointing out Galeazzi's colossal gaffe in not understanding that the postwar government could not be held responsible for financing of Fascist internment camps. Galeazzi persisted and wrote immediately to the ministry to claim his unpaid rent. Perhaps he failed to grasp the official lack of continuity between the Fascist administration and the postwar government. When he sent a copy of the informal letter-lease for the seminary, he did cross out the phrase concerning his "special homage" to the Fascist government. He stated that he had been forced to open the seminary under duress and implied that he did not want reopen the summer seminary for the winter because of the inconvenience rather than because he had had any moral qualms.[22] There is no evidence that the bishop received the rent that he thought was owed to him.[23]

Apart from one postwar incident, Bishop Galeazzi's career continued without a setback. According to Ariel Paggi, an attempt by Tranquillo Servi to rehabilitate the bishop's reputation after the war, while inappropriate, bore some fruit. However, the behavior of Tranquillo himself was criticized by other Jews. In turn, Tranquillo's daughter Carla emphatically defended her father, saying that he only wanted to protect his family. She quotes her father as saying that there was no prior arrangement made with the bishop before they entered the camp. The fact remains she was a small child while in the camp herself, probably little able to comprehend events of the time. Much of her book relies on published and archival sources, thus, the "eye-witness" is often superseded by the "researcher."[24]

Ariel Paggi gives his own views regarding the bishop:

He [Bishop Galeazzi] was a person of high prestige, busy providing the developing Maremma with churches and other structures needed for its strong demographic growth. He had contacts with the highest levels of the regime, in particular with Mussolini's private office and even with Galeazzo Ciano [Mussolini's son-in-law and minister of foreign affairs]. One cannot say whether his great power was used in favor of or against the Jews: it is not simple to evaluate his spirit and motivations that led him to act. The fact remains that Roccatederighi was the only church structure in Europe that was handed over to be a concentration camp.[25]

Roccatederighi was not exactly the only ecclesiastical structure in Europe used to imprison Jews. The others, according to all indications, had had to be requisitioned, whereas Roccatederighi was actually rented out under a legal contract, to the expected financial benefit of the church. The uniqueness of this situation is confirmed by conversations with Martin Dean and Geoffrey Megargee, of the United States Holocaust Memorial Museum.

Indeed, the bishop had high contacts in the Fascist government. As a powerful and prestigious local figure in his own right, he confronted the provincial authorities in 1933 and had gone above them to Mussolini himself.[26] After the war, he continued his persuasive techniques in order to raise funds, and few dared oppose him.

Adolfo Turbanti, of ISGREC, Istituto di Studi Grossetani sulla Resistenza e l'Epoca Contemporanea, puts forward another assessment of the bishop's attitudes and career:

He guided the church of the Province of Grosseto with a firm hand for over thirty years, over a period during which no form of dissent was conceivable; during Fascism, as the head of the diocese, he was a pillar of the local power system. The civil authorities (prefect, mayor, federal secretary of the National

Fascist Party) all had to take account of his views and programs. Though he had continual differences with the civil authorities, he never opposed the regime and he was always ready to promote the values typical of Fascism: nationalism, militarism, etc. He did not hesitate to recognize the legitimacy of the RSI [Italian Socialist Republic established by Mussolini under Nazi auspices in Salò] and approve its policies in practice, which were based on a close alliance with Nazi Germany. So was he a Fascist bishop? I don't believe so. His goal was to extract from his relations with the regime the greatest advantages for the church. He was a bishop perfectly aligned with the church of the Concordat and the Lateran Pacts and he took longer than others did, perhaps also because of his authoritarianism, to become aware of the crisis in the Fascist regime and especially of the responsibility of Fascism for the war that had brought conflict and destruction to Italy. What Galeazzi was interested in above all was receiving permits and financing from the Fascist authorities to build churches and seminaries. By putting pressure on those authorities, who perhaps would have preferred other projects, he managed to achieve his goals.[27]

Adolfo Turbanti relates that as a child he met the bishop; it was toward the end of his career and Galeazzi was very ill. He seems to have been impressive nevertheless. Despite his long postwar career Galeazzi was a man of another age, of the time of the church's agreements with Mussolini, the 1929 Lateran Pacts, and its coexistence with Fascism.

The bishop has been described as a "razzista inconsapevole," "unconscious racist," (Pezzini), but he could also be described as a "fascista inconsapevole," "unconscious Fascist," a person capable of rash actions in support of his rigidly held principles. This characterization seems to have veered away from the ethical positions usually expected of a religious man. A certain congruence between Fascism and the high officials within the Italian church at the time made these institutions and their leaders comfortable together, comfortable in their mutual condemnation of Jews and Judaism's unwillingness to accept Christ, and therefore in persecuting Jews, and also in their authoritarianism. Galeazzi and Ercolani shared too many values in common not to work together. Laura Paggini's imaginative portrayal of Bishop Galeazzi as a man of stone seems appropriate in a symbolic way. After the war, in the province of Grosseto, there was no introspection and no discussion with regard to this issue, only silence. For many decades, Roccatederighi was obliterated from memory, suppressed like a bad conscience.[28]

Then again, at the highest level in the church, Pope Pius XII may have provided a role model for at least some of the very same attitudes held by the bishop. A recent assessment of Pope Pius XII views his stance toward Jews who were in danger during World War II as a "moral failure."[29] Certain bishops might have taken a cue from this unspoken example. The debates continue between those who are critical of Pope Pius XII's silence in the face of the Holocaust and lack of action to save the Jews of Rome, of Italy, and of Europe, and those who are intent on proving that Pope Pius XII was pro-Jewish and pro-Zionist, that he did take action to save Jews, and that he should be not only canonized but also beatified and made a saint.[30]

## JEWS OF THE PROVINCE OF GROSSETO TRY TO RETURN TO NORMAL LIFE

The Jews of Pitigliano who returned home did not find the process easy. All had lost material goods. Some had trouble reclaiming their homes from squatters. As we saw, EGELI's job during the war was to confiscate Jewish property, possessions, bank accounts, and even insurance policies in a clear indication that these Jews were not expected back. In the province, there had been some unseemly haste, based on a network of willing volunteers, to redistribute or sell these assets. The EGELI administrator for the specific area of Pitigliano, however, was not unduly active. Whether from humanitarianism or a wish to wait out the conflict and see who would come out on top, the local EGELI administrator had a "hands-off" attitude, we are told.[31] Paggi discusses the lack of or long-drawn-out reparations for Jews who suffered career disruption and other damages, like his father, unlike the prompt reimbursement for damages experienced by the former partisans and political deportees. He hints at the frustration involved in the processes for supposedly reintegrated Jewish citizens.[32] All this, despite an initially warm welcome from neighbors in Pitigliano, confirms the statements of Guri Schwarz, on a national level, about the Jews of Italy:

> The survivors had to face a process of reintegration which was anything but immediate and painless. . . . [They] were often regarded with suspicion and treated with impatience, almost as if they were illegitimate usurpers in claiming the homes or property of which they had been deprived, the jobs they had lost, the rights and dignity which had been wrested from them.[33]

Besides property claims, immediately after the war in central and northern Italy there were "denuncie," denouncements, of those who had harmed Jews. A particularly interesting and very early case was filed by the Jewish community of Pitigliano, under the leadership of Arrigo Sadun, in a long letter dated July 28, 1944, to the Comitato di Liberazione Nazionale di Pitigliano, one of the committees that took over from the many Resistance groups and coordinated with the Allied forces. It describes a Secretario del Fascio, Giuseppe Barone, who was particularly zealous in persecuting Jews, and schoolteachers who incited "la ragazzaglia," gangs of urchins, to insult and throw stones at Jewish children. Barone also undertook a campaign to have the SIAT bus company fire its Jewish employees, an action not required by the racial laws, and also no longer to transport Jewish goods (essential for small businessmen to make a living). He also requested Christians to stop socializing with Jews in public or in private. Barone, the letter alleges, tried to pressure one of the Jews to burn down the synagogue, as the price for having his identity card returned to him. The report states that no other such anti-Jewish campaigns occurred in any other part of the province, even Grosseto.[34] It does not appear that the letter received any response.

Jews found it difficult to reintegrate into the life of Pitigliano on several levels: economic, social, and even more so, psychological. The postwar provincial administration made slow gestures at compensation.[35] Azeglio Servi's family returned to reclaim their home occupied by squatters, who were evicted by the fourteen-year-old Marcella. The Servis found that many of their possessions had disappeared. Manlio Paggi received payment by the Comune for being a school examiner or commissioner on July 10, 1945, and again in October. He was paid, but these were obviously minor, short-term assignments, far from a reinstatement into his former professional status.[36] Azeglio Servi applied for a subsidy from Grosseto, but was twice denied (on December 21, 1944, Grosseto informed the Comune that what he asked could not be granted, and on the 24th the Comune answered Azeglio; he applied again and was rejected again on January 25, 1945).

There were few means to make a living. The Servis' precious sewing machine, which had been looted, was miraculously retrieved from the ruins of the bombing, while their black cat seems to have turned up again, and they hosted Signora Clara Piperno, until she could return to her home in Rome. Ten-year-old Mario repaired the sewing machine, and the sisters set their skills to work to create a tailoring and dressmaking business, which helped their family survive. Their older brothers, in the meantime, initially found construction work. It does not seem that their father managed to find work.

The randomness of war is shown in the story of the elderly Enrichetta Paggi, who had been hidden throughout the war by local doctors in Pitigliano's hospital. Returning to the center of town to check on her apartment, Enrichetta had arrived just in time to be killed by one of the Allies' errant bombs.

The Servis also mourned their friend the dentist, who had been killed in the bombing, while two Finzi children were killed by a booby-trap they found after the Germans had fled. Abramo Moscati, the former adviser to the mayor, now bereft of his daughter, son-in-law, and grandchildren who had died in Auschwitz, was also bereft of his house. He remained homeless in Pitigliano, sleeping in a shop. His fourteen-year-old granddaughter Marissa had managed to trek in from her village to check on him, while the Nazis were still in control, a very risky excursion. Abramo eventually moved away to his other daughter Ulda in the village, where he died shortly after.[37] The family buried him hastily in the Jewish cemetery of Pitigliano, without obtaining the requisite permission.

Despite the Servi family's joy at being reunited, there were sad thoughts of so many others who had disappeared or were known to have lost their lives, both Jews and non-Jews. Azeglio, once a carefree and cheerful man, became a shadow of his former self, not only physically but in terms of lost ideals and, in the opinion of his daughters, though he lived for another twenty-five years, never really recovered. Other family members, such as the ebullient Uncle Guido, whose smile had been almost larger than his face, were also affected psychologically: Guido spent his last years in a mental hospital in Florence.

Both the two Servi families and the Paggis experienced great embarrassment when they had to interact with the former Fascists of the town. These were people who had boycotted, insulted, and isolated them for six years. Paggi writes, almost apologetically, that for years when the ex-seminarian who had pointed him out to a German soldier became a shopkeeper, he could not bring himself to frequent his establishment. Gino Servi describes his embarrassment vis-à-vis the townspeople as if what had happened were somehow his own fault. The four Servi siblings received certificates of participation in the Resistance, which ostensibly should have entitled them to a certain respect. It did not seem to ease their psychological discomfort, however.

Paggi also recalls how Jews, such as Livio Servi's family, who returned to Pitigliano after the war dealt with known informers:

> The Contis found out that the family's presence had become known to those who should not have known; they had been spied on by a neighbor who was not on good terms with the Contis. Elena Servi refused to reveal the name of the informer because his children were still living in Pitigliano: "I can't reveal it because the children of the one who spied are still living in Pitigliano." After the war, her father Livio did not [formally] accuse him, and limited himself to a verbal reproach, confronting him to his face, and he answered that he had had nothing against the Servis, but did have something against the Contis, his neighbors.[38]

Eugenia Servi, the teenage daughter of Tranquillo, seems to have been particularly uncomfortable in Pitigliano after the end of the war. She states that she took every opportunity to leave and visit relatives in Florence. On her return to Pitigliano, as she neared the town she would experience an oppressive, nightmarish feeling, "un incubo," which increased the closer she got. Eventually, Eugenia moved to Florence for good. Her younger sister, Carla, suffered from anorexia while the family was in the camp, and subsequently, when they were in semi-hiding until the war ended. Her 2012 autobiography has an indicative title, *Una infanzia perduta* (A lost childhood). Much of the memoir is devoted to defending the reputation of her father. There seem to have been some lingering recriminations among some of the Jewish families after the war.

Is it possible that in addition to personal trauma there was survivors' guilt, or even, in the apparently civilized and initially less dangerous environment of Roccatederighi, there had been some whiff of Primo Levi's "gray zone" that held sway in the German death camps? The moral compromises of the period affected many, victims, collaborators, bystanders as well as actual perpetrators, not only at the time, but long after. Roccatederighi was merely an ante-chamber to an ante-chamber of the Holocaust. Nevertheless, something of the evil wafted back in the form of deceit on the part of Fascists and their sympathizers and shame and fear in the hearts of all Jews of the region.

In recent years, Primo Levi's rather precise concept of the moral gray zone in the Nazi death camps,[39] where brutalized and starving prisoners had little scope for making moral decisions and many who were making them suffer, such as the kapos, were themselves impelled by fear and under the threat of death, has, according to Robert Gordon, been logically extended to cover the behavior of most Italians who were not obviously committed to one side or the other in the conflict.[40] Though this expansion of Levi's original intention may distort or dilute it, it does help to explain some of the behaviors that the Jews of the province experienced and encountered. Gordon describes the attitude of "atendismo" or "attetismo," impelling a vast number of Italians, who were not ideologically loyal to Fascism but anxious to survive, to wait for as long as possible and see which way the wind would blow. He mentions the conscripts of 1943–1944 as the main group of Italians who were not able to succeed in sitting on the fence. As we have seen in our province, they sometimes paid with their lives for "renitenza," draft avoidance.

As Edda and Marcella Servi recount, along with kindnesses they received during the persecution years, they had also knocked on many doors that people had refused to open out of fear.[41]

Carla Servi recalls that their family eventually went into hiding. Their father turned to one of the doctors at the hospital who sent them to a family who were his tenant farmers where they received cold treatment, designed to induce them to leave. The six-year-old Carla was locked in a room full of cobwebs and told not to speak. The farmers thought that planes overhead were eavesdropping on their conversations and could tell they were harboring Jews. This Jewish family, loyal to Fascism, soon left for a more hospitable situation, leaving all their possessions behind.[42]

The other young Servi refugees, Azeglio's children, developed a technique of knocking on one door and asking for a little food, which they said they would eat elsewhere. Then they would go to another farm and ask if they could just sit down to eat their food. If they were allowed, they would then ask if there were a place where they could sleep.

It was well known that if the partisans succeeded in killing a German, the Germans would stage a revenge attack, exacting ten lives for one German one from the hapless farmers. The young Servis were not only refugees, they were also partisans, which increased the danger for anyone helping them. Robert Gordon describes the farmers (in Nazi-occupied central and northern Italy as a whole) as adopting a policy of being friendly to everyone, but of helping no one. On the other hand, to confuse the moral picture even more, there is also the fact that the more it became obvious that the Germans were losing, the more even convinced Fascists would plan for how they would look once the war was over.

It is evident when one considers the range of behaviors in the province of Grosseto, that the local story of "italiani bravi" all protecting the Jews has been due for a reassessment. The fear that prevailed, and the urge to survive, led many who were not convinced Fascists to avoid doing the most courageous thing. All the more credit, then, to the minority who ignored their personal fear and did protect Jews and to the partisans who actively resisted. Luciana Rocchi, Michele Sarfatti, David Bidussa, all of them historians, like Alberto Moravia in the literary sphere, describe the moral corruption, hypocrisy, and conformism of Fascism, which did not need any importations from Germany to flourish and wreak its own damage, in this civil war that had broken out between Italians.[43] Michele Sarfatti has examined how foreign historians (writing mainly in English) after the war credited the Italians with largely resisting the Nazis and trying to prevent the deportation of Jews, when that was not the case. In fact, from 1938 on propaganda tried to show that Italian Fascism had always been racist (considered a positive thing), that there was no pressure from the Germans, and that the antisemitic laws were actually a native Italian product, as Matard-Bonucci shows.

There is a spectrum of behavior, and of moral responsibility, from the extreme Fascists who, even two days before they themselves fled, found a way to deport another bus-load of Jews from Roccatederighi, to those who obeyed because they were part of the system, but might, when undetected, do something to save a Jewish life (especially that of a local Jew who could speak in their favor in the coming reckoning after the war), to those who sat on the fence for as long as possible, and finally to those who without hesitation or apparent fear from the beginning offered all the help they could to save Jews, whether foreign or local. Perhaps "spectrum" is too nuanced a term, in a war situation, and does not do justice to those who knowingly risked their lives to oppose Fascism, and in many cases lost them.

As discussed above, we do not hear a great deal about Nazis being put on trial in Italy. Richard Evans states that Nazis were supposed to be tried in the countries in which they had committed their crimes. He refers to a "series of trials in countries formerly occupied by the Germans, including Italy, Norway and Poland."[44] According to Yad Vashem, only minor actors were tried in Italy (exceptions would be Herbert Kappler, and the later Priebke trial and retrial in the 1990s and 2000s, as well as a few early trials discussed by Robert Katz).[45] The "cabinet of shame" documents, discussed at the beginning of this chapter, give a good illustration of why Nazis were seldom charged for crimes committed in Italy: their trials would necessarily have implicated too many local collaborators.

## FOR JEWS, A FUTURE OF VIRTUAL JUDAISM

In Pitigliano, the synagogue and Jewish community premises perch on the edge of a tufa cliff, notoriously unstable rock. Soon after the war, it was discovered that the synagogue was unsafe, destabilized by the bombing, with "enormous cracks" according to Marcella Servi. For a few years, her father held services on Rosh Hashana and Yom Kippur and the Jews of Pitigliano, who by now had mostly drifted away, would return briefly. The school rooms and the old library, which contained precious ancient books[46] were also declared unsafe. The library contained a rare incunabulum, four manuscripts, and many rare sixteenth-century books, attesting to the once high cultural level of this small community. The nucleus may even have been the books brought by David De Pomis, held to be the first Jew to settle in Pitigliano. Piatelli writes that a few works included in inventories from 1918 and 1950 did not arrive in Rome when the books were transferred in 1953.[47]

Though Elena Servi, Marcella Servi, and a few others eventually moved to Israel, it does not seem that Jews from the province, in particular Pitigliano, were especially caught up in young Italian Jews' enthusiasm for Aliyah to Israel immediately after the war. Marcella Simoni describes the wave of Aliyah from Italy known as the Generation of 1948, exactly the peers of these young Pitigliano Jews. The young people of our three families were intent on other concerns. There was even a training farm, Hachshara, of the Halutz movement where young Jews would spend a year, not far away from Pitigliano on the other side of Lake Bolsena in the Province of Viterbo, before they moved on to Israel during the early postwar years. It was mainly for foreign Jews passing through Italy and is reported to have been sheltering arms, at which the postwar police of Viterbo winked.[48]

Azeglio Servi's family managed to move to Florence, intent on having the young people continue their education and develop professional futures.

When they tried to sell their apartment, they discovered that despite having lived there for generations, according to Edda, it did not actually belong to them but rather to the Jewish Community of Livorno. They salvaged some of the ritual objects from the synagogue before they left Pitigliano, in view of its impending collapse, for safekeeping.[49]

Both of the two Servi sisters, Marcella and Edda, later moved to America and married American Jews, while the rest of the family remained in Florence. Elena Servi's family had also dispersed. She herself moved to Israel. The Paggis had also since left, first for Grosseto, then for Livorno, and Milan.

Most of the Jews who owed their lives to the protection of local farmers returned to the area from time to time. Edda Servi went back to the farms immediately after the war and met the daughters of the farming families who had sheltered the young siblings, as we see in her book. Ariel Paggi tells how his family used to visit their rescuers the Perugini family as long as they, themselves, lived in Pitigliano, but later a sort of lassitude and silence took over:

> As long as we stayed in Pitigliano we maintained contact with the Perugini family and we attended Rosita's marriage to the son of Narcisi. My parents, after we left Pitigliano, cut off ties with those who rescued them, as if they wanted to forget a period of anguish, and did not return to the town except for funerals. Subsequently, they almost never spoke about that period; perhaps it was the only way for them to reconstruct their lives and go on. I have noticed that most of the Jews who survived behaved like my parents.[50]

Much later, though, Elena Servi and Ariel Paggi spearheaded a movement among the Jews to recognize and acknowledge their gratitude to their saviors: "All those who helped us, or their children or grandchildren, have received a letter of recognition and thanks from Yad Vashem (Elena Servi)."[51]

With regard to Roccatederighi, total amnesia took over among the local population, either deliberately or unwittingly. In June 2018, the villa was just as neglected as ten years earlier when the plaque was installed, and the grounds and steps leading up to it totally overgrown (figure 8.3). An attempt had been made to convert it into a rest home for Alzheimer's sufferers. Apparently, the company had gone bankrupt, and the renovations were abandoned. Construction materials and overgrown signs still lie around, attesting to a lack of incentive to see the project through and of anything to replace it. In the meantime, the forest is taking over.

After 1948, when the synagogue in Pitigliano ceased to function, the unused Torah Ark that held the Torah scrolls was sent to a kibbutz in Israel. A sad photograph from the 1950s shows the bricked up gap where it had stood for centuries. Finally, in 1960, the abandoned synagogue of Pitigliano

**Figure 8.3  Plaque at Roccatederighi Seminary in Memory of Holocaust Victims Deported from the Camp.** Installed in 2008, it does not list the victims' names and is now covered in lichen. *Source*: Photo by Judith Roumani, 2018.

collapsed down the hillside, followed in 1963 by the school premises, leaving only the rear wall of the synagogue and small portions of two side walls, all open to the sky. The *geniza*, repository of old, damaged books, apparently completely disappeared.[52] Thus, the synagogue of Pitigliano was in ruins or had disappeared, the library dispersed, and almost all of the Jews made lives elsewhere.[53]

It seemed as if all had ended for the Jewish community of Pitigliano, when events took an unexpected turn (figure 8.4). Around 1985, the Comune [municipality] decided to restore the old synagogue and the buildings of the Jewish community. The long-term mayor of the town, Augusto Brozzi, led this commendable effort together with the few Jews who maintained contact with Pitigliano, including Elena Servi, who as a widow returned from Israel with her son Ernesto; Ariel Paggi; Leone Paserman; and a few others. The meticulous

**Figure 8.4** Door to Former Jewish Home Next to Synagogue in Ghetto of Pitigliano.
*Source*: Photo by Judith Roumani, 2002.

restoration of the synagogue was really a reconstruction, on the basis of old photographs, since most of the building had disappeared down the hillside. It was finished and reopened in 1995 (figure 8.5). The restoration of the old community oven, used to bake matza, the school and library premises, ancient mikva, a wine cellar, and more, was completed around 2000, under the direction of architect Massimo Francardi. This was partly almost a work of archaeology as it involved digging out much debris and fallen masonry. A celebration was held at which Rabbi Mino Bahbout, from Rome, announced a plan for "Il ritorno ebraico nella Piccola Gerusalemme" (the Jewish return to Little Jerusalem). He specializes in reviving old Jewish communities to the extent possible, and has also been active in Trani and Sicily in the south. One of the wines of Pitigliano,

**Figure 8.5** **Pitigliano's Synagogue, Interior.** *Source*: Photo by Judith Roumani, 2002.

which have received kosher designation, is called "La Piccola Gerusalemme." The bakery named Il Forno del Ghetto bakes "sfratti," the traditional Jewish pastries and the traditionally shaped lace-like oval matzot.

These major works have brought new life to the town, which is striving to distinguish itself from other Tuscan hill towns that are equally beautiful, but without an overtly Jewish dimension. A Jewish-Christian organization, La Piccola Gerusalemme, founded by Elena Servi, takes care of the synagogue and the newly opened Jewish museum, including a conference room, the former butcher's shop, and the former kosher oven. A well-stocked little shop sells souvenirs, books, and kosher products.

With the passage of time and the passing of rescuers and witnesses alike, it has not been possible to meet all the requirements and honor all who have deserved recognition as Righteous Gentiles. The ambassador, consuls, and cultural attaches of Israel have visited Pitigliano several times to confer this status on rescuers or their descendants. Other descendants who did not meet the strict requirements of Yad Vashem, but nevertheless saved Jews, have received more informal certificates and medals of recognition.

All of these very laudable steps have not led to the Jewish community's return or revival, though. I founded a non-profit organization, the Jewish Institute of Pitigliano, to honor the history of the town and its Jewish community and encourage foreign Jews to visit. Other Italian and foreign Jews who may or may not have had some historical link with the town have purchased vacation properties there. Jewish-themed events such as La Giornata della Memoria (European Holocaust Remembrance Day, in January) and a day in September (the European Day of Jewish Culture) are held regularly, when synagogues all over Italy and Europe open their doors for visitors. Pitigliano's annual Petilia Festival includes Jewish food and music, such as (when we attended) a visiting Klezmer band. Travel magazines and gourmet food magazines (inspired by the cookbooks of Edda Servi) regularly send reporters to write about Passover in Pitigliano and other similar subjects. An exhibit of Italian Jewish arts in Pitigliano was organized in the synagogue before the museum existed.[54] "Pesach in Pitigliano" which would bring a group of Americans and Israelis proved too challenging due to the lack of facilities for *kashrut* food preparation. A travel agent in Tel Aviv specializing in "destination weddings" sometimes brings Israeli couples to celebrate their nuptials in Pitigliano.

What does all this add up to? The municipality has been extremely cooperative and respectful of Jewish sensitivities. For example, the synagogue is always closed on Shabbat and Jewish holidays, unless a visiting Jewish group seeks to have services there. Despite good will on all sides, the Jewish presence in Pitigliano today is largely virtual.[55] The Jews who trace their origins to Pitigliano, nevertheless, continue to remember both the good and the bad. They still hold the people of the province of Grosseto to account for their dualistic history, which grew most complicated during the time of greatest testing, the Fascist and Holocaust years. The people and the province, as a whole, are perhaps only now finally coming to terms with the past, their historical treatment of the Jews, and the less-than-stellar behavior of the local Fascists, such as Alceo Ercolani, and their fellow-travelers, such as Bishop Galeazzi. On the other hand, they can also be extremely proud of those who did indeed risk their lives to save Jews. In this sense, the case of the province of Grosseto as a test of the "Italiani brava gente" myth is not strictly typical. It embraces two extremes: non-Jewish Italians who fearlessly protected their local Jewish neighbors and other non-Jewish Italians of the province who set up a concentration camp from which they callously and hypocritically sent Jews, some Italian, some foreign, on their way to the death camps.

## NOTES

1. Gregorio Nardi, trans. Harvey Sachs, "The 'Aryanization' of Italian Musical Life," *Printed Matter*, December 11, 2017, reproduced from an Orel Foundation publication. Something comparable had happened in Algeria, where the watchword in 1942 was "The Jews will have to wait" after the Allies had liberated it but the *Statut des juifs*, the Vichy government's antisemitic laws, were left in force.

2. Klein, *Italy's Jews*, pp. 183–184.

3. Data from Ariel Paggi's "Elenco Salvati." See also Paggi's "Elenco degli ebrei presenti al Campo di Concentramento di Roccatederighi e loro destino." Also Ariel Paggi, file on the fates of the Rosenfeld/Singers. Ariel Paggi has been trying without success to contact these survivors and/or their descendants.

4. Today, the outgrowth of this and other centers is the International Tracing Service, and such institutions as the Survivor's Registry. See Suzanne Brown-Fleming, *Nazi Persecution and Postwar Repercussions: The International Tracing Service Archive and Holocaust Research* Lanham, MD: USHMM and Rowman and Littlefield, 2016.

5. See Betti, *Banda*, p. 243, the second (in this source unnamed) family of Polish Jews.

6. Files relating to Jews after the war, many of them about restitution of confiscated property to the Jews, are in the Archivio di Stato of the province.

7. A document that supposedly lists amounts of compensation paid to Jews of Pitigliano has either gone missing or never existed. (See Dominici, "La Persecuzione degli Ebrei a Pitigliano" where readers are invited to view it.) It is neither in the municipal Archive of Pitigliano, nor in the Jewish Museum of Pitigliano, when I searched in 2019. Restitutions to Jews that are listed in the Pitigliano Archive concern minor household items.

8. Livingston, *Fascists and the Jews of Italy*, p. 231. Livingston also states "That the courts and especially the bureaucracy were often staffed by the same people who administered the Race Laws, and who were perversely clever in finding reasons to deny compensation, made things still worse" (p. 232).

9. Archivio di Stato, Grosseto (ASG) Filza Questura, Ebrei 14/5/1945. A handwritten note to eight people, including the Sindaco (mayor) of Grosseto. With thanks to Dr. Gemini and her staff for facilitating access to these documents and providing photographs.

10. ASG, 21/9/1945, letter from Ministero dell'Interno to all "Prefetti del Regno."

11. The first report was signed by a capitano comandante of police, the second one by the prefect, who added that in terms of numbers, the Jewish population, meaning the local Jewish population, was the same as it was before the war. ASG reports dated 15/11/1945, from the Orbetello carabinieri to the Questura of Grosseto,

and 12/10/1945, signed by the Comando Campo Orbetello, and by the Prefect of Grosseto.

12. "Il clero . . . non esplica palese attività politica, ma dimostra avversione ai partiti di sinistra, perchè questi gli sono notariamente ostili." Carabinieri di Grosseto. Note from Tenente Colonnello Comandante to Regia Prefettura di Grosseto, April 28, 1946.

13. Marco Grilli, *Per noi il tempo si è fermato all'alba*, pp. 110–111.

14. From Lorenzo Del Boca, trans. Ilaria Marra Rosiglione, *Italy's Lies: Debunking History's Lies so that Italy might become a 'Normal Country'* (New York: Bordighera Press, 2014), p. 172. This same work contains a long list of prominent postwar Italians who had participated in some way with the Fascist regime.

15. See Rocchi's email. Further elaborated in Marco Grilli, *Per noi il tempo s'è fermato all'alba*, pp. 115–116.

16. "Destava fra i presenti familiari delle vittime ed avvocati di parte civile commenti poco favorevoli nei riguardi di Mons. Vescovo. Le famiglie delle vittime hanno portato in Grosseto l'eco del dibattimento e hanno commentato sfavorevolmente la disposizione del Vescovo" in Grilli, ibid., quoting from a Questura report, "De Anna Michele," 26/6/1955.

17. "Il babbo e le zie cercarono di fare processare il collega che aveva denunziato lo zio Goffredo: il tentativo andò a vuoto perché quel signore aveva avuto la qualifica di partigiano comunista ed era attivista del partito. Questo particolare me lo raccontò anni dopo lo zio Mario Paggi di Milano, che era stato l'avvocato della nostra famiglia" *Bambino*, p. 71.

18. On Priebke, see Robert Katz, *The Battle for Rome: The Germans, the Allies, the Partisans, and the Pope*, 2003 (New York: Simon and Schuster, 2004) and https ://it.wikipedia.org/wiki/Erich_Priebke. On Kappler, see idem, *Black Sabbath: A Journey through a Crime against Humanity* (New York: Macmillan, 1969), p. 310.

19. Trials of a few other Nazis are discussed in Robert Katz, *The Battle for Rome* 2003, pp. 334–344.

20. The Val di Cecina where this occurred may be partially visible from the hill on which Roccatederighi stands.

21. See MAE (Ministero Affari Esteri) 103/9; this file consists of requests for information and responses in early 1971 among the Ministry of Foreign Affairs, Ministry of Defense, Ministry of the Interior (all at the level of the minister), the Prefectures of Grosseto and of Pisa, and the Embassy of Italy in Vienna, responding to the original request for names of German perpetrators from the Simon Wiesenthal Center in Vienna. It does not seem that Vienna ever received a response. All the pages were carefully numbered and stamped "Riservato" (confidential) and "Doc. Segreto" (Secret document), placed in the cabinet, and not declassified until the Chamber of Deputies ordered it in 2015.

22. Reproductions of the documents in Luciana Rocchi, ed., *La Persecuzione degli ebrei nella provincial di Grosseto, 1943–44* (Grosseto ISGREC, 1996, 2002): Letter to the bishop from the new prefect, A. De Domicis, 15/9/1944; letter from Galeazzi to the new minister of the interior, 19/9/1944, pp. 52–54. The documents are well

analyzed in Paolo Pezzini, "Ebrei in seminario," www.larivistadeilibri.it/2002/05/pezzino.html.

23. Email from Luciana Rocchi November 9, 2014.

24. When sources are missing, for example when she asserts that the bishop saved Jewish lives, her account does not have any overwhelming credibility.

25. "Fu una persona di alto prestigio, impegnato nell'attività di corredare la Maremma in via di bonifica di strutture civili e chiese all'altezza del forte sviluppo demografico; mantenne contatti con i più alti livelli del regime, in particolare con la segretaria privata di Mussolini e perfino con Galeazzo Ciano. Non si può dire se il suo grande potere fu usato a favore o contro gli ebrei: non è infatti semplice valutare lo spirito e le motivazioni per cui lo fece. Rimane il fatto che Roccatederighi fu l'unica struttura ecclesiastica in Europa adibita a campo di concentramento." Paggi, *Bambino*, p. 58. In *Il Muro*, p. 98 Paggi mentions the camp at Asti. But it was requisitioned from the church by the Germans and priests were hiding some Jews in other parts of the building.

26. See Valeria Galimi, ed., *Il Fascismo a Grosseto*, pp. 89–90, chapter by Marco Grilli, "Il Governo della città e della provincia."

27. "Aveva guidato la Chiesa grossetana con mano ferma per più di 30 anni, in un periodo in cui non era concepibile alcuna forma di dissenso. Durante il fascismo era stato di fatto, come capo della Diocesi, un pilastro del Sistema di potere locale. Di lui, delle sue aspettative e dei suoi programmi, le autorità civili (prefetto, podestà, segretario federale del Partito Nazionale Fascista) dovevano tenere conto. Benché avesse continui contrasti con le autorità civili, non si oppose mai al regime e fu sempre disposto a esaltare alcuni valori tipici del fascismo: nazionalismo, militarismo, ecc. Non esitò infine a riconoscere la legittimità della Repubblica Sociale Italiana (cosiddetta Repubblica di Salò) e ad approvarne di fatto la politica, fondata sulla stretta alleanza con la Germania nazista. Fu dunque un vescovo fascista? Non credo: il suo obiettivo fu quello di ricavare nel rapporto con il regime fascista i maggiori vantaggi per la Chiesa. Fu un vescovo perfettamente allineato con la Chiesa del Concordato e dei Patti Lateranensi e tardò più di altri, forse anche a causa del suo autoritarismo, ad accorgersi della crisi del regime fascista e soprattutto della responsabilità del fascismo per la guerra che aveva portato in Italia lutti e distruzioni. Ciò che a Galeazzi interessò soprattutto fu di avere dalle autorità del fascismo permessi e finanziamenti per costruire chiese e seminari. Questo riuscì a fare, forzando a volte la volontà di quelle autorità, che magari avrebbero preferito impegnarsi in altri progetti." Personal email from Adolfo Turbanti, of ISGREC, March 22, 2015. Luciana Rocchi also mentions in an email a rumor that Paolo Galeazzi may have been involved in helping the notorious De Anna flee to Switzerland, perhaps with Vatican help. Email from Luciana Rocchi, November 9, 2014. Rocchi emphasizes that these are only indications, not historically proven facts, as church archives are not available for consultation.

28. Both Luciana Rocchi and Ariel Paggi emphasize this in Vera Paggi's documentary, *Roccatederighi, Campo di Concentramento*.

29. A subject beyond the scope of this book. For this judgment, see Jacques Kornberg, *The Pope's Dilemma: Pius XII Faces Atrocities and Genocide in the*

*Second World War* (Toronto: Toronto University Press, 2015), p. 8. An original text examining the topic is Giovanni Miccoli, *I Dilemmi e i silenzi di Pio XXII*, a recent documentary film on the subject is *Holy Silence*, dir. Steven Pressman, 2020.

30. For example, the press release "Pave the Way Foundation Reveals Surprising Documents that show Pope Pius XII's Role in Establishing the State of Israel," Mar. 19, 2014, https://www.prnewswire.com/newsreleases. The Vatican has promised to release all documents from the period of Pius XII, which may perhaps clear up the issue. It will take some time for sections of the archive covering his papacy and opened in March 2020 to be sufficiently analyzed.

31. Paggi, *Bambino*, p. 56.

32. Documents in the Archivio Comunale di Pitigliano from 1944 and 1945 reveal how Ariel Paggi's father had to accept short-term examiner positions, and how Azeglio Servi, who twice applied for a "subsidy," was denied it. See below.

33. Guri Schwarz, *After Mussolini: Jewish Lives and Jewish Memories in Post-Fascist Italy* (Edgeware and Portland: Vallentine Mitchell, 2012), pp. 3–5. See also the moving essay by Giacomo Lichtner, which includes the story of his mother in Rome and Pitigliano: "That Latent Sense of Otherness: Old and New Anti-Semitisms in Postwar Italy," *Modern Italy* 23.4 (2018): 461–472.

34. The original letter is in ISGREC; the report is published in Enzo Collotti, ed., *Ebrei in Toscana, vol. 2, Documenti*, pp. 332–334.

35. See ASG, Questura, 1946 files. Jews entitled to government pensions or restitution payments struggled for many years to get their rights as they had not been political prisoners (Paggi, *Muro*, p. 132). The Archivio Storico Comunale di Pitigliano contains few references to restitutions. I found only references to Gino Servi's receiving back a table from the Casa del Partigiano. Abramo Moscati received back a mattress. The Casa del Partigiano was obviously a center housing partisans who entered the town at the end of the war.

36. p. 466, vol. 20 of Deliberazioni della Giunta municipale 1943–1946. Also for the second session, October 18, 1945.

37. Marissa's dramatic journey is recounted in Celata, *E poi la Salvezza*, pp. 72–73, as well as Abramo's death and burial.

38. "I Conti venne a conoscenza che la presenza della famiglia era nota anche a chi non avrebbe dovuto saperlo: c'era stata una spiata ad opera di un vicino che non era in buoni rapporti con i Conti. Elena Servi si è rifiutata di rivelare il nome del delatore in quanto i suoi figli abitano ancora a Pitigliano; 'Non posso rivelarlo perché i figli di chi fece la spia abitano ancora a Pitigliano.' Livio dopo la guerra non lo denunciò limitandosi ad uno scontro verbale, dopo la guerra glielo rinfacciò, e lui rispose che non ce l'aveva con i Servi, ma con il Conti di cui era un vicino" (Paggi, "Famiglie coninvolte," and *Il Muro*).

39. Primo Levi, *The Drowned and the Saved* 1986; trans. Raymond Rosenthal (New York: Vintage, 1989) chapter 2, "The Gray Zone," pp. 36–69.

40. Robert Gordon, *The Holocaust in Italian Culture, 1944-2010* (Stanford: Stanford Univ. Press, 2012), chapter 8, "Grey Zones and Good Italians," pp. 139–156. See review by Jacques Roumani, *Sephardic Horizons*. https://www.sephardichorizons.org/Volume2/Issue4/jacquesroumani.html

41. Gino Servi remembers differently from his sister, Edda; he explicitly said that "Non ho ricordi di una porta chiusa," "I do not remember any door being closed." Gino is listed as a member of the seventh group of the "Monte Amiata" band of partisans, serving from March 1, 1944, to July 20, 1944, under the battle name/nom de guerre "Ebreo" ("Jew"). He took part in the battle for Sovana, and perhaps other skirmishes.

42. Carla Servi, *Una Infanzia perduta*, p. 37.

43. See Michele Sarfatti, "Did the Germans Do it All? The Italian Shoah in International Historiography (1946–1986)," *Quest: Issues in Contemporary Jewish History* 7 (July 2014), www.quest-cdecjournal.it/focus.php. See also moked.it/blog/2015/06/10/libri-storie-di-indesiderabili which is Sarfatti's review of Eugenio Iafrate, *Elementi indesiderabili* on Italian collaboration with the Nazis' project. Marie-Anne Matard-Bonucci, "L'Antisemitismo totalitario del fascismo," pp. 141–168 in *Storia della Shoah in Italia: Vicende, memorie, rappresentazioni* vol. 1 (Turin: Utet, 2010).

44. Richard J. Evans, "The Anatomy of Hell," *New York Review of Books* July 9, 2015, p. 54, a review of six books on the death camps and subsequent trials of Nazis.

45. www.yadvashem.org Shoah Resource Center, "Trials of War Criminals," http://www.yadvashem.org/odot_pdf/Microsoft%20Word%20-%205887.pdf.

46. See Servi's *Child*, p. 312, for a partial list made in about 1950 of the contents of the library of Università Israelitica di Pitigliano, such as an ancient manuscript of *Ha-Kuzari* by Yehuda Halevi. About seventy old books and manuscripts are now in the National Library of Israel. See the online catalog, National Library of Israel, http://merhav.nli.org.il/primo_library/libweb/action/search.do?dscnt=0&dum=true&indx=1&tab=default_tab&dstmp=1465150722283&srt=rank&vl(freeText0)=pitigliano&vid=NLI&fn=search&ct=search&mode=Basic&vid=NLI&backFromPreferences=true. For a scholarly treatment of the libraries of Pitigliano, see Angelo Piatelli, "I Quattro manoscritti e l'incunabolo della Biblioteca di Pitigliano, oggi presso il Centro Bibliografico dell'UCEI," *Rassegna mensile di Israel*, 3rd series, 57, 1991. Nine hundred books from three Jewish libraries in Pitigliano were transferred to Rome in 1953 following a decision by the Community of Livorno and its section in Pitigliano and were placed in the UCEI library.

47. Elena Servi mentioned in her interview with us in 2011 that after the war some boxes of old books were mailed to Livorno, but had never arrived.

48. Marcella Simon, "Young Italian Jews in Israel, and Back: Voices from a Generation" (1945–1953), in *Italian Jewish Networks from the Seventeenth to the Twentieth Century: Bridging Europe and the Mediterranean*, eds. Francesca Bregoli, Carlotta Ferrara degli Uberti, Guri Schwarz, pp. 173–200 (London: Palgrave Macmillan, 2018).

49. For example, the *parochet,* Torah Ark curtain for Shavuot, was donated to the Jewish Museum of New York, in honor of Azeglio Servi. It is viewable online at: https://artsandculture.google.com/culturalinstitute/beta/asset/torah-ark-curtain/bwF6MVHtLV211g and is reproduced herein.

50. "Fino a quando rimanemmo a Pitigliano mantenemmo i contatti con la famiglia Perugini e partecipammo alle nozze di Rosalba con il figlio di Narcisi. . . . I miei genitori, dopo aver lasciato Pitigliano, hanno tagliato i rapporti con chi li ha salvati,

come per dimenticare un periodo di angosce, e non sono più tornati al paese se non in occasione di funerale. Di quel periodo non hanno quasi mai parlato negli anni successive; era forse l'unico modo per potersi ricostruire una vita e andare avanti. Ho potuto verificare che la maggioranza degli ebrei sopravvissuti si sono comportati come loro." *Bambino*, p. 72.

51. One can affirm that Ariel Paggi's later research quest more than makes up for his parents' silence.

52. Photographs of the devastated state of the ghetto area can be seen in *Gli Ebrei a Pitiglano: La Piccola Gerusalemme* ed. Angelo Biondi, trans. Steve Siporin (photos taken in 1976 by Carlo Fè).

53. See a moving article from 1970, lamenting the community that had once been. Ugo Ayò, "Pitigliano viva, Pitigliano ebraica," *Rassegna mensile di Israel,* 3rd series, 36:3 (March 1970), 147–153.

54. See Antonello Carrucoli, "Pitigliano: Una mostra dedicata all'arte della stampa degli ebrei." *Corriere di Maremma* 78 (June 30, 2002); and Giuseppe Celata, "Pitigliano: La Piccola Gerusalemme del Tufo." *La Nazione Grosseto* 144.176 (June 30, 2002).

55. See Ruth Ellen Gruber, *Virtually Jewish: Reinventing Jewish Culture in Europe* (Berkeley: Univ. of California press, 2002) on the existence of "virtual Judaism," empty synagogues but full museums and cemeteries scattered across Europe, and now part of many locations' tourism strategy.

# Bibliography

Absalom, Roger. *A Strange Alliance: Aspects of Escape and Survival in Italy 1943–45*. Florence: L. S. Olschki, 1991.

Absalom, Roger, Paola Carucci, Arianna Franceschini, Jan Lambertz, Franco Nudi, and Simone Slaviero. *Le Stragi nazifascisti in Toscana: Guida alle fonti archivistiche: Gli Archivi italiani e alleati*. Rome: Carocci, 2004.

American Jewish Joint Distribution Committee. "Saga of a Child." *JDC Digest*. 4.3 (July 1945). (NY_AR3344_00033_00139.Pdf).

Ayò, Ugo. "Pitigliano viva, Pitigliano ebraica." *Rassegna mensile di Israel* 3rd Series. 36.3 (1970): 147–153.

Bartezzaghi, Stefano. *Una Telefonata con Primo Levi (A Phone Conversation with Primo Levi)*. Translated by Jonathan Hunt. Turin: Einaudi, 2012.

Bassani, Giorgio. *Five Stories of Ferrara*. New York: Harcourt Brace Jovanovich, 1971.

Bassani, Giorgio. *Il Romanzo di Ferrara*. 2 Vols. Milan: Arnaldo Mondadori, 1991.

Bassani, Giorgio. *The Garden of the Finzi-Continis*. Translated by William Weaver. Edited by Tim Parks. New York: Knopf, 2005.

Bauer, Yehuda. *A History of the Holocaust*. New York: Franklin Watts, 1982.

Ben-Ghiat, Ruth. *Fascist Modernities: Italy, 1922–1945*. Berkeley: University of California, 2001.

*Besa: The Promise*. Dir. Rachel Ghoslins. JWM Productions, 2012. DVD.

Betti, Giulietto, and Franco Dominici. *Banda armata maremmana 1943–44: La Resistenza, la guerra e la persecuzione degli ebrei a sud di Grosseto*. Arcidosso: Effigi, 2014.

Bettina, Elizabeth. *It Happened in Italy: Untold Stories of How the People of Italy Defied the Horrors of the Holocaust*. Nashville: Thomas Nelson, 2009.

Biondi, Angelo. *Gli Ebrei nel marchesato di Piancastagnaio*. Pitigliano: Laurum, 2002.

Biondi, Angelo, ed. *Gli ebrei a Pitigliano: La Piccola Gerusalemme*. Grotte Di Castro: Tipografia Ceccarelli, 2009.

Biondi, Angelo, and Franco Dominici. *Pitigliano: Discovering the City and Its Territory*. Arcidosso: Effigi, 2015.

"Bishop Paolo Galeazzi." *Catholic Hierarchy*, n.d. (http://www.catholichierarchy.org/bishop/bgale.html).

"Bishop Stanislao Battistelli." *Catholic Hierarchy*, n.d. (www.catholichierarchy.org/bishop/bbatti.html).

Blouin, Francis X. *Vatican Archives: An Inventory and Guide to Historical Documents of the Holy See*. Vols. 9 and 10. New York: Oxford University Press, 1998.

Bocchini Camaiani, Bruna, and Daniele Menozzi, eds. *Lettere pastorali dei vescovi della Toscana*. Genoa: Marietti, 1990.

Bocchini Camaiani, Bruna, and Maria Cristina Giuntella, eds. *Cattolici, chiesa, resistenza nell'Italia Centrale*. Bologna: Il Mulino, 1997.

Bosworth, R. J. B. *Mussolini's Italy: Life under the Dictatorship, 1915–1945*. New York: Penguin, 2006.

Bregoli, Francesca, Carlotta Ferrara degli Uberti, and Guri Schwarz, eds. *Italian Jewish Networks from the Seventeenth to the Twentieth Century: Bridging Europe and the Mediterranean*. London: Palgrave Macmillan, 2018.

Brown-Fleming, Suzanne. *Nazi Persecution and Postwar Repercussions: The International Tracing Service Archive and Holocaust Research*. Lanham, MD and London: USHMM and Rowman and Littlefield, 2016.

Browning, Christopher R. "When Europe Failed: Europe on Trial, Istvan Deak." *New York Review of Books* 62.13 (2015).

Cansetti, Ilari. "Bibliografia sulla resistenza in provincia di Grosseto." *Grossetocontemporanea* (n.d.): 19 Apr. 2012.

Capogreco, Carlo Spartaco. *I campi del duce*. Turin: Einaudi, 2004. Translated by Norma Bouchard and Valerio Ferme. *Mussolini's Camps: Civilian Internment in Fascist Italy (1940–1943)*. London and New York: Routledge, 2019.

Carrucoli, Antonello. "Pitigliano: Una mostra dedicata all'arte della stampa degli ebrei." *Corriere di Maremma* (30 June 2002): 78.

Cassin, Alessandro. "Memory Buried: In Search of Mussolini's Camps." Interview with Carlo Spartaco Capogreco. *Italy*, 29 Jan. 2010. (www.iitaly.org/magazine/focus/facts-stories/article/memory-buried-in-search-mussolinis-camps).

Cassin, Alessandro. "DELASEM: The Unhailed Organization that Assisted Thousands of Jewish Refugees." Interview with Donato Grosser, 26 Mar. 2014. (www.primolevicenter.org/printed-matter/delasem).

Cavarocchi, Francesca, and Elena Mazzini, eds. *La Chiesa fiorentina e il soccorso agli ebrei: istituzioni, percorsi (1943–1944)*. Rome: Viella, 2018.

Celata, Giuseppe. *Gli ebrei a Pitigliano: I quattro secoli di una comunità diversa*. Pitigliano: Comune di Pitigliano, 1995.

Celata, Giuseppe. *The Jews of Pitigliano: Four Centuries of a Diverse Community*. Pitigliano: ATLA, 2001.

Celata, Giuseppe. "Pitigliano: La Piccola Gerusalemme del tufo." *La Nazione Grosseto* (30 June 2002): 144.

Celata, Giuseppe. *E poi la salvezza: Storie italiane di ebrei strappati all Shoah (1943–1945)*. Florence: Edizioni Medicea, 2014.

Cerroni, Luigi. *A Short History of the Jewish Settlement in Pitigliano/Breve Storia della Comunità Ebraica di Pitigliano*. Pitigliano: La Piccola Gerusalemme, n.d.

Cesare, Ioly Zorattini, Pier, Michele Luzzati, and Michele Sarfatti. *Studi sul mondo sefardita: In memoria di Aron Leoni*. Firenze: L.S. Olschki, 2012.

Chertok, Haim. *He Also Spoke as a Jew: The Life of James Parkes*. London: Vallentine Mitchell, 2006.

Cifelli, Alberto. *I Prefetti del Regno nel ventennio Fascista*. Rome: Scuola Superiore dell'Amministrazione dell'interno, 1999.

Clark, Martin, et al. *Modern Italy, 1871 to the Present*. Harlow, U.K.: Pearson Longman, 2008.

Cohen, Richard I. *The Burden of Conscience: French Jewry's Response to the Holocaust*. Bloomington, IN: Indiana University Press, 1985.

Collotti, Enzo, ed. *Razza e fascismo. La Persecuzione contra gli ebrei in Toscana (1938–1943). Saggi*. Rome: Carocci, 1999.

Collotti, Enzo, ed. *Ebrei in Toscana tra occupazione tedesca e RSI: Persecuzione, depredazione, deportazione (1943–1945)* Vol. 1, *Saggi*, Vol. 2, *Documenti*. Rome: Carocce Editore & Regione Toscana, 2007.

Cornwell, John. *Hitler's Pope: The Secret History of Pius XII*. New York: Viking, 1999.

D'Amico, Giovanna. "Roccatederighi." In Joseph White, volume ed., Geoffrey Megargee, series ed. *Encyclopedia of Camps and Ghettos, 1939–1945*. Vol. 3. *Camps and Ghettos Under European Regimes Aligned with Nazi Germany*. Bloomington: Indiana University Press and USHMM, 2018.

De Felice, Renzo. *Storia degli ebrei italiani sotto il Fascismo*. 1961. Torino: G. Einaudi, 1972.

De Felice, Renzo. *Ebrei in un paese arabo*. Bologna: Il Mulino, 1978. Translated by Judith Roumani. *Jews in an Arab Land: Libya, 1835–1970*. Austin: Texas University Press, 1985.

De Felice, Renzo. *The Jews in Fascist Italy: A History*. Translated by Robert L. Miller. New York: Enigma, 2001.

Del Boca, Angelo. *Italiani, brava gente?* Vicenza: BEAT, 2014.

Del Boca, Lorenzo. *Italy's Lies: Debunking History's Lies so that Italy Might Become a 'Normal Country'*. Translated by Ilaria Marra Rosiglioni. New York: Bordighera Press, 2014.

Di Porto, Bruno, ed. "Un libro di Carla Servi: Esperienza di bambina internata nel campo di Roccatederighi e difesa della memoria del padre." *Hazman ve haraion/Il tempo e l'idea*. 20 (July–Dec. 2012): 13–24, 42–44.

Dominici, Franco. "Ercole Gervasi, storia di un antifascista." *Il Corriere del Tufo*, 10 Feb. 2017a. (http://www.nctufo.it/corriere/rubriche/pillole-di-storia/).

Dominici, Franco. "Temistocle Sadun: Luci e ombre." *Il Corriere del Tufo*, 16 Mar. 2017b. (http://www.nctufo.it/corriere/rubriche/pillole-di-storia/).

Dominici, Franco. "La persecuzione degli ebrei a Pitigliano." *Il Corriere del Tufo*, 22 Mar. 2017c. (http://www.nctufo.it/corriere/rubriche/pillole-di-storia/).

Donati, Giuliana. *Ebrei in Italia: Deportazione, resistenza*. Milan: Centro di Documentazione Ebraica Contemporanea, 1980.

Donovan, Gill. "Bishop Rented Property for Concentration Camp." *National Catholic Reporter* February (2002). The Free Library. (http://www.thefreelibrary.com/Bisho p+rented+property+for+concentration+camp.+(World).a083667066).
Dorfman, Ben-Zion, and Rivka Dorfman. *Synagogues Without Jews*. Philadelphia: Jewish Publication Society, 2000.
Duggan, Christopher. *The Force of Destiny: A History of Italy Since 1796*. Boston: Houghton Mifflin, 2008.
Ebner, Michael R. *Ordinary Violence in Mussolini's Italy*. Cambridge: Cambridge University Press, 2011.
Ellin, Abby. "In Tuscany, a Jewish Heritage." *New York Times* (25 Nov. 2012): 8.
Evans, Richard J. "The Anatomy of Hell: From Dachau to Ravensbruck." *The New York Review of Books* 62.12 (2015): 52–54.
Faccini, Luigi, dir. *Il Pane della memoria*. Perf. Elena Servi, n.d. DVD.
Fanciulli, Pietro. *La Contea di Pitigliano e Sorano nelle carte degli archivi spagnoli di Simancas e Madrid e dell'Archivio di Stato di Firenze Mediceo del principato*. Pitigliano: ATLA, 1998.
Fanciulli, Pietro. *Il Dramma di un paese: Porto S. Stefano 1943–1983. Storia dei bombardamenti e della distruzione del paese in occasione del 40° anniversario del 1° bombardamento, con l'elenco completo delle vittime di guerra, civili e militari*. Pitigliano: Laurum, 2003.
Fanciulli, Pietro. (http://tronkzone.blogspot.com/2009/04/il-dramma-di-un-paese .html).
Flores, Marcello, ed. *Storia della Shoah in Italia: Vicende, memorie, rappresentazioni*. Turin: UTET, 2010.
Galeazzi, Paolo. *Lettere pastorali*. Grosseto: Tipografia Fascista 'La Maremma', 1939, 1941; Grosseto: Tipografia 'La Stampa', 1949, 1953–1954, 1955, 1956.
Galeazzi-Lisi, Riccardo. *Dans l'ombre et dans la lumière de Pie XII*. Paris: Flammarion, 1960.
Galimi, Valeria, ed. *Il Fascismo a Grosseto: Figure e articolazioni del potere in provincia (1922–1938)*. Grosseto: ISGREC and Effigi, 2018.
Galimi, Valeria, and Giovanna Procacci. *"Per la difesa della razza": L'applicazione delle leggi antiebraiche nelle università italiane*. Milan: Unicopli, 2009.
Gillette, Aaron. *Racial Theories in Fascist Italy*. London: Routledge, 2002.
Giusti, Roberto, and Giovanni Greco, eds. *Pitigliano 'La Piccola Gerusalemme': Terra della libertà e dell'accoglienza*. San Giovanni in Persiceto: Banca Di Credito Cooperativo di Pitigliano & Ingrafica, 2010.
Gordon, Robert S. C. *Outrageous Fortune: Luck and the Holocaust/Sfacciata Fortuna: La Shoah e il caso*. New York: Primo Levi Center, CPL Editions, 2010.
Gordon, Robert S. C. *The Holocaust in Italian Culture, 1944–2010*. Stanford: Stanford University Press, 2012.
Grayzel, Solomon. *A History of the Contemporary Jews: From 1900 to the Present*. New York: Harper & Row, 1965.
Greppi, Carlo. Intro. David Bidussa. *L'Ultimo treno: Racconti del viaggio verso il lager*. Rome: Donazelli, 2012.

Grilli, Marco. "I Martiri d'Istia: La strage." *Grossetocontemporanea* (2013), 3 Aug. 2013. (http://www.isgrec.it/).
Grilli, Marco. *Per noi il tempo s'è fermato all'alba: Storia dei martiri d'Istia.* Arcidosso: Effigi, 2014.
Gruber, Ruth Ellen. *Virtually Jewish: Reinventing Jewish Culture in Europe.* Berkeley: California University Press, 2002.
Guerrazzi, Amedeo Osti. "Quei volenterosi spioni di Hitler." *La Stampa*, 26 Jan. 2016. (http://www.lastampa.it/2016/01/26/cultura/quei-volenterosi-spioni-di-hitler-9Xh3Zj3D8Xks6ZXI2COyAN/pagina.html).
Hartman, Geoffrey H. *The Longest Shadow: In the Aftermath of the Holocaust.* Bloomington: Indiana University Press, 1996.
Herzer, Ivo, Klaus Voigt, and James Burgwyn. *The Italian Refuge: Rescue of Jews During the Holocaust.* Washington, DC: Catholic University of America, 1989.
Horowitz, Sara R. *Voicing the Void: Muteness and Memory in Holocaust Fiction.* Albany: State University of New York, 1997.
Horowitz, Sara R., ed. *Lessons and Legacies Conference (10th).* Evanston: Northwestern University, 2008.
"I Lager italiani 1943–1945: Il campo di Grosseto." *Corriere della Sera*, 12 Feb. 2002.
Iafrate, Eugenio, and Elisa Guida. *Elementi indesiderabili: Storia e memorie di un "trasporto" Roma - Mauthausen 1944.* Rome: Edizioni Chillemi, 2015.
Israel, Giorgio. *Il Fascismo e la razza: La Scienza italiana e le politiche razziali del regime.* Bologna: Il Mulino, 2010.
Jacobson, Kenneth. *Embattled Selves: An Investigation into the Nature of Identity Through Oral Histories of Holocaust Survivors.* New York: Atlantic Monthly, 1994.
Jewish Institute of Pitigliano. "Jewish Life in Pitigliano." n.d. (http://www.jipitaly.org).
Jewish Institute of Pitigliano. "Welcome." n.d. (http://www.jipitaly.org/).
Jilovski, Esther. *Remembering the Holocaust: Generations, Witnessing and Place.* London: Bloomsbury, 2015.
Kahn, Eytan. "Pitigliano 1799: Ritrovata la terza filza del processo della Rivoluzione." In *Pitigliano: A True Love Story*, n.d. (www.pitigliano-toscana.com/pitigliano.html).
Katz, Robert. *Black Sabbath: A Journey Through a Crime Against Humanity.* New York: Macmillan, 1969.
Katz, Robert. *The Battle for Rome: The Germans, the Allies, the Partisans, and the Pope: September 1943–June 1944.* New York: Simon and Schuster, 2003.
Kauffman, Richard, and Carol Field. *The Hill Towns of Italy.* New York: Dutton, 1983.
Kertzer, David. *The Kidnapping of Edgardo Mortara.* New York: Random House, 1997.
Kertzer, David I. *The Popes Against the Jews: The Vatican's Role in the Rise of Modern Antisemitism.* New York: Alfred A. Knopf, 2001.

Kertzer, David I. *The Pope and Mussolini: The Secret History of Pius XI and the Rise of Fascism in Europe*. New York: Random House, 2014.
Kertzer, David I. *The Pope Who Would Be King*. New York: Random House, 2018.
Klein, Shira. *Italy's Jews from Emancipation to Fascism*. Cambridge and New York: Cambridge University Press, 2018.
Knowles, Anne Kelly, Tim Cole, and Alberto Giordano. *Geographies of the Holocaust*. Bloomington: Indiana University Press, 2014.
Kornberg, Jacques. *The Pope's Dilemma: Pius XII Faces Atrocities and Genocide in the Second World War*. Toronto: University of Toronto Press, 2015.
Landi, Sara. "Il ritorno dei sopravvissuti alla Shoah: Due famiglie ebree in visita ai luoghi dove, bambini, vissero l'incubo della persecuzione e la generosità dei grossetani." *Il Tirreno*, 28 July 2015 (online).
Landini, Fabio. "Il seminario di Roccatederighi, un campo di internamento in Maremma." *Corriere della Sera*, 18 Feb. 2010. Blog di Dino Messina.
Levi, Lia. *L'Albergo della Magnolia*. Rome: Edizioni e/o, 2001.
Levi, Lia. *Questa sera è già domani*. Rome: Edizioni e/o, 2018.
Levi, Primo. *Survival in Auschwitz*. London: Collier Macmillan, 1986.
Levi, Primo. *The Drowned and the Saved*. Translated by Raymond Rosenthal. New York: Summit, 1988; Vintage, 1989.
Levis Sullam, Simon. *The Italian Executioners: The Genocide of the Jews of Italy*. 2015. Translated by Oona Smyth. Princeton: Princeton University Press, 2018.
Lichtner, Giacomo. *Fascism in Italian Cinema Since 1945: The Politics and Aesthetics of Memory*. Basingstoke and New York: Palgrave Macmillan, 2013.
Lichtner, Giacomo. "That Latent Sense of Otherness: Old and New Anti-Semitisms in Postwar Italy." *Modern Italy* 23.4 (2018): 461–472.
Liska, Vivian, and Thomas Nolden, eds. *Contemporary Jewish Writing in Europe: A Guide*. Bloomington: Indiana University Press, 2008.
Livingston, Michael. *The Fascists and the Jews of Italy: Mussolini's Race Laws, 1938–1943*. New York, Cambridge: Cambridge University Press, 2014.
Machlin, Gia. "The Curious Appearance of the Black Cat in Pitigliano." (http://www.italianjew.wordpress.com/2014/04/25/the-curious-appearance-of-the-black-cat-inpitigliano/).
Mano, Davide. "Ebrei di Pitigliano/Jews in Pitigliano: Sciatini e macellari di fine '700/Late eighteenth-century 'sciattini' and 'macellari' butchers." *Le Colline Oggi/ The Hills Today* 37 (5 Aug. 2009): 9.
Matard-Bonucci, Marie-Anne. *L'Italie fasciste et la persecution des juifs*. Paris: Presses Universitaires de France, 2012.
Meningher, Naor, dir. *Our Hebrews*, 2016. Short film.
Miccoli, Giovanni. *I Dilemmi e i silenzi di Pio XII: Vaticano, Seconda Guerra mondiale e Shoah*. Milan: BUR Storia, 2007.
Michelucci, Riccardo. "Roccatederighi: Il Lager in affitto dalla Curia." 15 June 2014. (http://www.riccardomichelucci.it/italia/roccatederighi-il-lager-in-affitto-dalla-curia/).
Mintz, Alan L. *Popular Culture and the Shaping of Holocaust Memory in America*. Seattle: University Press of Washington, 2001.

Mole, Gary D. *Beyond the Limit-Experience: French Poetry of the Deportation, 1940–1945*. New York: P. Lang, 2002.

Moravia, Alberto. *Il Conformista: The Conformist*. Translated by Tim Parks. London: Prion, 1999.

Morelli, Emanuela. *Pitigliano, Sovana, Sorano, Saturnia and Their Tuff-Rock Cultures*. Translated by Donald Bathgate. Florence: Edizioni Polistampa, 2008.

Myers, David N., Peter Reill, Geoffrey Symcox, and Massimo Ciavolella. *Acculturation and Its Discontents: The Italian Jewish Experience Between Exclusion and Inclusion*. Toronto: University of Toronto Press, 2008.

Nussenblatt, Rosine. "Interview with Flory Jagoda." *Sephardic Horizons* 1.2 (2011). (www.sephardichorizons.org.Volume1/Issue2/Articles_V1/2/Flory_Jagoda.html).

Paggi, Ariel. *Un Bambino nella tempestà*. Livorno: Belforte: 2009.

Paggi, Ariel. *Il Muro degli ebrei: Roccatederighi e la provincia di Grosseto (1943–1945)*. Livorno: Salomone Belforte, 2018.

Paggi, Ariel, and Judith Roumani. "From Pitigliano to Tripoli via Livorno: The Educational Odyssey of Giannetto Paggi." *Sephardic Horizons* 2.4 (2012). (https://www.sephardichorizons.org/Volume2/Issue4/paggi.html). Italian trans. and summary, "Giannetto Paggi da Pitigliano a Tripoli." *Hazman ve Haraion/Il Tempo e l'idea* 21.1–12 (Jan.–June 2013): 23.

Paggi, Vera, dir. *Roccatederighi: Campo di concentramento*. RAI, 2007. DVD.

Paggi, Vera. *Vicolo degli azzimi: Dal Ghetto di Pitigliano al miracolo economico*. Rimini: Panozzo, 2013.

Paggini, Laura. *Pesante come una piuma*. Lecce/Livorno: Edizioniyoucanprint, 2014.

Paioletti, Franco. *Pitigliano dal Risorgimento al primo novecento*. Arcidosso: Effigi, 2011.

Paris, Erna. *The Holocaust's Long Shadows: Truth, Lies, and History*. New York: Bloomsbury, 2001.

"Paul on Pius: The Story of Enrico Galeazzi 1943." n.d., 9 Sept. 2015. (http://paulonpius.blogspot.com/2010/10/story-of-enrico-galeazzi-1943.html).

Perra, Emiliano. "Narratives of Innocence and Victimhood: The Reception of the Miniseries *Holocaust* in Italy." *Holocaust and Genocide Studies* 22.3 (Winter 2008): 411–440.

Perri, Giuseppe. *Il caso Lichtner: Gli ebrei stranieri, fascismo e la guerra*. Milan: Jaca, 2010.

Pezzino, Paolo. "Ebrei in seminario." *La Rivista dei libri/The New York Review of Books*, 2002. (www.larivistadeilibri.it/2002/05/pezzino.html).

Piatelli, Angelo. "I Quattro manoscritti e l'incunabolo della biblioteca di Pitigliano, oggi presso il Centro Bibliografico dell'UCEI." *Rassegna mensile di Israel* 3rd Series. 57 (1991).

Piccini, Daniele. "Demolita la leggenda nera su Pio XXII." *Avvenire Roma Sette* (5 Oct. 2014): 4.

Picciotto, Liliana. *Il Libro della memoria: Gli Ebrei deportati dall'Italia (1943–1945)*. Milan: Mursia, 1991.

Picciotto, Liliana. *L'Alba ci colse come un tradimento: Gli ebrei nel campo di Fossoli, 1943–44*. Milan: Mondadori, 2010.

Picciotto, Liliana. "Il Vaticano e la persecuzione antiebraica in Italia: Una Lettura dei documenti diplomatici della Santa Sede." 11 Oct. 2016. CDEC. Pdf.

Picciotto, Liliana. *Salvarsi: Gli Ebrei d'Italia sfuggiti alla Shoah, 1943–1945*. Milan: Einaudi, 2017.

Pivirotto, Riccardo, and Monica Sideri. *L'Ebreo errante: Guida ai luoghi ebraici tra arte e storia nella Maremma Collinare*. Pitigliano: Rotary International, 1997.

Pizzinelli, Ferrero. *Vocabolario del vernacolo pitiglianese*. Pitigliano: Laurum, 2001.

Pizzuti, Anna. *Vite di carta: Storie di ebrei stranieri internati dal fascismo*. Rome: Donzelli, 2010.

Pizzuti, Anna. "L'Applicazione delle leggi antiebraiche fascisti nella Colonia Libica e l'internamento in Italia." (http://www.annapizzuti.it/public/SLIDELIBIADEF.pdf).

Portelli, Alessandro. *The Order Has Been Carried Out*. New York: Palgrave, 2003.

Portelli, Alessandro. "Oral Memory and the *Shoah*." In *Literature of the Holocaust*. Edited by Alan Rosen. New York and Cambridge: Cambridge University Press, 2013: 193–210.

Reguer, Sarah. *The Most Tenacious of Minorities: The Jews of Italy*. Brighton, MA: Academic Studies Press, 2013.

Rittner, Carol, and John K. Roth. *Pope Pius XII and the Holocaust*. London: Leicester University Press, 2002.

Rocchi, Luciana. "Legge Razziali, L'ordine e stato eseguito: Lo zelo persecutorio del capo della provincia di Grosseto, L'ambiguità del vescovo, la complicità dei dirigenti locali." *Il Manifesto*, 25 Apr. 2001. (http://www.storiaxxsecolo.it/rassegnasta/rassegna_man250401a.htm).

Rocchi, Luciana. "La Liberazione di Grosseto: Storia di una Resistenza breve e di un lungo antifascismo nel primo capoluogo toscano liberato." *Toscana Novecento*, n.d. (https://www.toscananovecento.it. http://www.isgrec.it).

Rocchi, Luciana, ed. *La Persecuzione degli ebrei nella provincia di Grosseto nel 1943–44*. Grosseto: Istituto Storico Grossetano della Resistenza e dell'età contemporanea (ISGREC), 2002.

Romani, Giuseppe. *La Rocca degli Aldobrandeschi e degli Orsini in Pitigliano 1290–1865*. Pitigliano: A.T.L.A., 1983.

Rosen, Alan, ed. *Literature of the Holocaust: A Critical Introduction*. Cambridge: Cambridge University Press, 2013.

Rosenfeld, Gavriel. "Why the Germans?" *Jewish Review of Books* 5.4 (2015): 28–30.

Roth, Cecil. *The History of the Jews of Italy*. Philadelphia: Jewish Publication Society of America, 1946.

Roumani, Jacques. *The Emergence of Modern Libya: Political Traditions and Colonial Change*. Ph.D. diss., Princeton University, 1987.

Roumani, Jacques. "*The Holocaust in Italian Culture, 1944–2010* by Robert S.C. Gordon (review)" *Sephardic Horizons* 2.4 (Fall 2012). (www.sephardichorizons.org/Volume2/Issue4/jacquesroumani.html).

Roumani, Judith. "Review: *And the World Stood Silent: Sephardic Poetry of the Holocaust* by Isaac Jack Lévy." *La Lettre Sépharade* 6 (2001).

Roumani, Judith. "*The Jews of Italy: Memory and Identity* by Barbara Garvin and Bernard Cooperman, editors, University Press of Maryland, (review)." *La Lettre Sépharade* 9 (Apr. 2002).

Roumani, Judith. "Review: *Trading Diasporas and Trading Networks in the Early Modern Period: A Sephardic Partnership of Livorno* by Francesca Trivellato, PhD diss., Brown University." *La Lettre Sépharade* 24 (Apr. 2005).

Roumani, Judith. "Film Review: *Besa: The Promise*." *Sephardic Horizons* 3.3 (2013a).

Roumani, Judith. "Sephardic Literary Responses to the Holocaust." In *Literature of the Holocaust*. Edited by Alan Rosen. New York and Cambridge: Cambridge University Press, 2013b: 225–237.

Roumani, Judith. "Italy's Cabinet of Shame Revealed: One Case of Frustrated Justice." *Sephardic Horizons* 7.3–4 (Summer–Fall 2017). (https://www.sephardichorizons.org/Volume7/Issue3&4/Roumani.html).

Roumani, Judith. "Yossi Sucary's Novel *Benghazi—Bergen-Belsen* in the Context of North African Jewish Literature of the Holocaust." In *Jewish Libya: Memory and Identity in Text and Image*. Edited by Jacques Roumani, et al. Syracuse: Syracuse University Press, 2018, and Italian Translated by *Lucia Finotto* and *Libia Ebraica*. Livorno: Belforte Press, 2020.

Salerno, Eric. *Uccideteli tutti: Libia 1943: Gli ebrei nel campo di concentramento fascista di Giado*. Milan: Il Saggiatore, 2008.

Salis, Renzo Sertoli. "Nazionalità e razza nell'ordine nuovo." *Dottrina fascista* 6 (Feb.–Mar. 1942). Offprint.

Salvadori, Roberto G. *La Comunità ebraica di Pitigliano dal XVI al XX secolo*. Florence: La Giuntina, 1991.

Salvadori, Roberto G. *Breve storia degli ebrei toscani*. Florence: Le Lettere, 1995.

Salvadori, Roberto G. *1799: Gli ebrei italiani nella bufera antigiacobina*. Florence: La Giuntina, 1999a.

Salvadori, Roberto G. *La Notte della Rivoluzione e la Notte degli Orvietani: Gli ebrei di Pitigliano e i moti del 'Viva Maria' (1799)*. Pitigliano: Comune di Pitigliano, 1999b.

Sarfatti, Michele. *Mussolini contro gli ebrei: Cronaca dell'elaborazione dei leggi del 1938*. Turin: Silvio Zamorani Editore, 1994.

Sarfatti, Michele. *Le Leggi antiebraiche spiegate agli italiani di oggi*. Turin: Einaudi, 2002.

Sarfatti, Michele. *The Jews in Mussolini's Italy: From Equality to Persecution*. Madison, WI: University of Wisconsin, 2006.

Sarfatti, Michele. "Did the Germans Do It All? The Italian Shoah in International Historiography (1946–1986)." *Quest: Issues in Contemporary Jewish History* 7 (2014). (www.quest-cdecjournal.it/focus.php).

Sarfatti, Michele. "Libri: Storie di Indesirabili." *Moked*, 10 June 2015. (moked.it/blog/2015/06/10/libri-storie-di-indesiberabili).

Schwarz, Guri. *Ritrovare se stessi: Gli ebrei nell'Italia postfascista*. Laterza, 2004. Translated by Giovanni Noor Mazhar. *After Mussolini: Jewish Life and Jewish Memories in Post-Fascist Italy*. Edgeware and Portland: Vallentine Mitchell, 2012.

Semelin, Jacques. *Persécutions et entreaides dans la France occupéé: Comment 75% des juifs en France ont échappé à la mort*. Paris: Les Arènes-Seuil, 2013.

Servi, Carla. *Una Infanzia perduta: Fra storia e memoria (Grosseto, 1943–1944)*. Empoli: Ibiskos Ulivieri, 2012.

Servi Machlin, Edda. *Child of the Ghetto: Coming of Age in Fascist Italy*. Croton-on-Hudson: Giro, 1995.

Shapiro, Michael. "Women and Hidden Jews under Fascist Rule: Roberto Bassi's Evidence." *Shofar: An Interdisciplinary Journal of Jewish Studies* 31.3 (2013): 103–114.

Signer, Michael Alan. *Humanity at the Limit: The Impact of the Holocaust Experience on Jews and Christians*. Bloomington: Indiana University Press, 2000.

Sindacato Interprovinciale dei Giornalisti Lombardi. "Intro. Joseph Goebbels." In *Perfida Inghilterra*. Lombardy: Sindacato Interprovinciale dei Giornalisti Lombardi, 1943.

Snowden, Frank M. *The Fascist Revolution in Tuscany, 1919–1922*. Cambridge: Cambridge University Press, 1989.

Sorrenti, A., E. Tromba, and S. N. Sinicroppi. *Il Kaddish a Ferramonti: Le anime ritrovate*. Catovillan: Edizioni Prometeo, n.d.

Spizzichino, Giancarlo. *Il Mo'èd di piombo*. Milan: Morasha, 2008.

Stille, Alexander. *Benevolence and Betrayal: Five Italian Jewish Families Under Fascism*. New York: Summit, 1991.

Sucary, Yossi. *Benghazi--Bergen-Belsen* (Heb.). Tel Aviv: Am Oved, 2013. (Eng.). San Bernadino: Createspace, 2016.

Suedfeld, Peter. "Life after the Ashes: The Postwar Pain, and Resilience, of Young Holocaust Survivors." Mona and Otto Weinmann Lecture Series, 15 May 2002. Washington, DC: USHMM, 2002.

Sullam, Simon Levis. *The Italian Executioners: The Genocide of the Jews of Italy*. 2015. Translated by Oona Smyth. Princeton: Princeton University Press, 2018.

Thomson, Ian. *Primo Levi*. London: Hutchinson, 2002.

Traverso, Enzo. *Le Passé, modes d'emploi: Histoire, mémoire, politique*. Paris: La Fabrique, 2005.

UCEI. "Qui Roma: L'Incontro con Kertzer e Canali: Confrontarsi con verità scomode: Il Fascismo e la sfida degli storici." *L'Unione Informa*, 24 Feb. 2016. (info @ucei.it).

Ventresca, Robert. *Soldier of Christ: The Life of Pope Pius XII*. Cambridge, MA: Belknap of Harvard University Press, 2013.

Vitarello, James. "In World War II, Italian Army Refused to Persecute Jews." *Washington Jewish Week* (27 May 1999): 17.

Viterbo, Lionella. *Le Comunità ebraiche di Siena e Pitigliano nel Censimento del 1841 ed il loro rapporto con quella fiorentina*. Livorno: Belforte, 2012.

Wieviorka, Annette. *L'ère du témoin*. 1998. Paris: Pluriel, 2013.

Wistrich, Robert. "Antisemitism, the World's Obsession." Interview with Barry Rubin and Judith Roumani. (http://www.covenant.idc.ac.il/en/vol1/issue3/Antisemitism-The-World-Obsession.html).

Yad Vashem Righteous Among the Nations. (http://www.yadvashem.org/yv/en/righteous/statistics/italy.pdf).

Yad Vashem Shoah Resource Center. "Trials of War Criminals." (http://www.yadvashem.org/odot_pdf/Microsoft%20Word%20-%205887.pdf).

Zieve, Tamara. "Saviors of Italy's Jewish Past." *Jerusalem Post*, 6 July 2017. Reproduced in www. esefarad.com, 7 July 2017.

Zuccotti, Susan. *The Italians and the Holocaust: Persecution, Rescue, and Survival.* New York: Basic, 1987.

Zuccotti, Susan. *Under His Very Windows: The Vatican and the Holocaust in Italy.* New Haven: Yale University Press, 2000.

# Index

Page references for figures are italicized.

Archivio Storico Diocesano, Pitigliano, 85, 88, 163
Arcidosso, xviii, 112–18, 126–27, 128, 147, 160, 162
armistice, September 1943, 52, 65, 91, 112

bagnetti degli Ebrei, Jewish baths, 17, 76
Balbo, Italo, 28, 33, 44n1, 44n6
Barone, Giuseppe, 170–71
Battistelli, Bishop Stanislao, xix, 51, 75, 83, 84–86, 98, 124–25, 144, 153, 163
Betti, Giulietto, 108n46, 155n19, 156n33–n34, 181n5
Biondi, Angelo, xvii, 21nn3–4, 21n7, 22n16, 59, 74–76, 83, 87, 98, 186n52
Bravo, Ana, 37, 46n27

cabinet of shame 166–67, 175
camps, 3, 29, 83, 90–92, 98, 103, 106n20, 112–13, 139, 142, 167; Civitella del Tronto camp, 147; Ferramonti, xviii, 98, 112–13, 116, 118, 121–22; Fossoli dei Carpi transit camp, xvii, xviii, xix, 1, 91–92, 94, 102, 115, 119, 133–44, 145, 146, 150, 152, 154n6, 154n9, 155n16, 155n22, 160, 162; Scipione provincial camp, 2, 140, 142–44, 146; Tricarico internment camp, xvi, 42, 112
Capogreco, Carlo Spartaco, 3, 106n20, 142
Cava/Moscati family, xvi, 120, 144–45
Cavarocchi, Francesca, 84, 86
Celata, Giuseppe, 14, 21n10, 22n17, 132, 154n13
Civitella Marittima, 112
Civitella Paganico, 33, 112, 118, 143
Collotti, Enzo, 52, 63–64, 90, 106n21, 108nn43, 154n13–n14, 155n22, 184n34
Conti family, xviii, 69, 79n9, 172, 184n38
Convoy 10, 134, 143–44, 160
Convoy 13, 143

Dainelli family, xvii, 66, 76, 78n2
De Anna, Colonel Michele, 132, 163–64
De Felice, Renzo, 33, 45n18, 137
Del Boca, Angelo, 2, 4
Delegation for the Assistance of Jewish Emigrants (DELASEM), 75, 77, 82, 85

De Pomis, David, 7, 8, 9, 21n4, 175
Disegni, Rabbi Avraham, 18, 43, 65
Di Segni, Umberto, 33, 44n6
Dominici, Franco, 47n37, 48n40, 108n46, 156n34, 181n7, 188
Donati, Giuliana, 154, 155

Ercolani, Prefect Alceo, xix, 89, 90, 92–93, 98, 100–102, 103, 107n28, 108nn40–41, 109n48, 112, 115, 118, 123–24, 132–34, 140, 152, 153n2, 163, 164, 167, 169, 180

Felici, Pietro and Marina, xvii, xviii, 55, 57, 66, 73, 121
Finzi family, xix, 145, 156n25
forced conversions, 13, 22n18

Galeazzi, Bishop of Grosetto, Monsignor Paolo, xvii, xix, 36, 82–83, 85, 86–89, *87*, 90, 92, 95, 97–100, 102–3, 106n37, 108n38, 108n47, 123–25, 128n23, 133–34, 139–40, 142, 146, 151–53, 164, 167–69, 180, 183n27
Galeazzi, Count Enrico, 88, 89, 105n16
Galeazzo, Ciano, 36, 87, 92, 168, 183n25
Gasbarri, Monsignor Primo, 99, 108
Gillette, Aaron, 28, 39
Gordon, Robert, 173, 174, 184n40
Grilli, Marco, 45n13, 156n35, 182n13, 182n15–n16, 183n26
Guazzerotti, Agostino, xvii, 28, 58–59, 66, 73

Iafrate, Eugenio, 140, 154n11
Istia, 101–2, 132, 134, 164
Italiani brava gente, 2, 3, 46n27, 78, 162, 174, 180

Jews of Yugoslavia, 91–92

Kappler, Herbert, 166, 175

Kertzer, David, 2, 4, 47n27
Kornberg, Jacques, 183n29

La Lente, 17–18, 60
*La Maremma*, 33, 50–51, 163
*La Settimana israelitica*, 18
Lattes, Rabbi Dante, 17, 35, 40, 42, 45
Levi, Fabio, 37
Levi, Lia, 38
Levi, Primo, 96, 137, 139, 155n16, 173
Libya, 11, 16, 27–28, 33, 62, 91, 147
Lichtner, Giacomo, 2, 5
Lichtner family, xix, 122
Livorno, xvi, xix, 4, 10–12, 15, 17–18, 23n24, 34, 43, 58, 73, 97, 101, 120, 127, 134, 144–45, 153, 156n25, 176, 185n47

Machlin, Edda Servi, xv, 19, 23, 24n34. 49, 52–54, 59–60, 73–74, 77, 91, 103, 141, 147, 149, 154, 154n13, 156n25, 176
Maremma, 8, 36–37, 56, 87, 168
Modigliani, Amedeo, 14, 23n24
Modigliani, Rachele, 14, *15*, 23n24
Moravia, Alberto, 31–32, 34, 174
Mosbach, Egon, xviii, 114–15, *114*, 127nn10–11, 142–43
Moscati, Abramo, xvi, 16, 24n30, 30, 34, 48, 120, 144, 171–72, 184n35

Nunes, Cesare, xvi, 132, 134, 139
Nunes family, xvi, 61, 99, 132, 143, 151
Nuremberg Laws, 29, 37, 101

Orsini, Count Niccolo, 7–10, 21n7

Paggi, Ariel, xvi, xvii, 16, *20*, 23n23, 42, 52, 53, 55, 57–58, 62, 65–67, 68, 71, 73–74, 77, 83–84, 94–95, 100, 107n35, 117, 120, 121, 126n6, 141, *165*, 165–66, 168, 176, 181n3, 184n32

Paggi, Giannetto, 17, 27–28
Paggi, Manlio, xv, xvii, 42, 66–68, 112, 171
Paggi, Mario, 41–42, 166, 171
Paggi, Osvaldo, 17, 19, 24n33, 34, 41, 60, 72
Paggi, Vera, 19, 41, 79n15, 94, 107n31
Paggini, Laura, 5, 115, 127nn9–10, 131–32, 149–50, 156n31, 169
Paioletti, Franco, 16, 141
Paserman family, xvii, xviii, 120–21, 122, 146, 156n26, 160, 177
Pellegrini, Ernesto, 55, 66, 68–69
Perugini family, xviii, 57, *57*, 66, *68*, 176, 186n50
Pezzino, Paolo, 96, 99–100
Pitigliano: ghetto, 10, 14, 93; Jewish Institute of Pitigliano, 3, *178*, 179; Liberation, 151–52; *Parochet* (Torah Ark curtain), 14, *15*, 185n49; Piccola Gerusalemme, xvi, 16, 34, 78n6, 178; Synagogue, 176–79, *180*
Pizzuti, Anna, 111, 113, 126n7
Pollak family, xix, 111, 118, 140, 143
Pope Pius XI, xi, 38–39, 81, 123
Pope Pius XII, xii, 4, 39, 81, 88, 123, 169–70
Portelli, Alessandro, 62, 67
Preibke, Erich, 166
Purim Katan, 14

racial laws, 1938, xv, 2, 20, 27–29, 35, 39–40, 42, 45n16, 46n27, 49, 51, 79n7, 94, 106, 145, 159, 160–61, 171
resistance, xv, xvii, xix, 35, 37, 56, 60, 63n3, 63n7, 72, 77, 82, 101–2, 105n7, 139, 141, 146, 150–51, 156n33, 163, 170, 172
restitution, claims for, 160, 181n7, 184n35
righteous gentiles, xvi, 55, 73–75, 80, 179
Risorgimento, 14, 16, 29, 35–36

Rizziello, Gaetano, xix, 93, 97–98, 125, 134, 140–41, 150–51
Roccatederighi camp, xvi, xvii, xviii, 5, 53–54, 74, 83–84, 89–93, 102–4, 107n28, 107n31, 109n48, 115, 118–20, 123–25, 126n6, 131–34, 139–41, 143–45, 146–49, 151–52, 154n6, 156n25, 156n31, 159, 160, *161*, 162, 166–69, 173, 176, *177*, 183n25
Rocchi, Luciana, 36, 51–52, 63n12, 82, 88, 94, 96, 101, 141, 149, 152, 154n14, 156n33, 174, 183n27
Rosenfeld/Singer family, xix, 119–20, 143–44, 149–50, 155n20, 160, 181
Roumani, Jacques xii, xxii, 21, 64n17–n19, 64n26, 70, 79n11, 80n20, 165, 184n40

Sadun, Arrigo, 16, 23n29, 170
Sadun, Dina, xvi, 95
Sadun, Temistocle, 43, 48n40
Sarfatti, Michele, 2, 35–36, 37–38, 42, 72, 174
Servi, Azeglio, xv, xix, 19, 35, 42–43, 54, 58, 62, 70–71, 92, 93–94, 96–98, 103, 119, 121, 125, 134, *135–38*, 140, 143, 146, 148, 150, 171, 172, 175, 184n32
Servi, Elena, 16–18, 53, 58–59, 63–64, 68–70, 75, 78–79, 172, 175–77, 179, 184
Servi, Eugenia, xvii, 52, 95, 98–99, 103, 119, 172–73
Servi, Gino, xv, 52, 75, 172, 184n35, 185n41
Servi, Livio, xvi, xviii, 23n29, 48, 68, 78n7, 172
Servi, Marcella, xv, *15*, 19, 56, 58, 70, 79, 85, 95–96, 106, 156, 173, 175
Servi, Marco, 13, 19, 51
Servi, Tranquillo, xvii, 48n40, 94–96, 119–20, 132, 134, 168, 172
SIAT Bus Company, xvii, 141, 154n14, 171

Singer, Edith, xix, 94, 119, 120, 144, 149, 150, 151, 155n22, 160, 181
Sonno, Francesco, 69
Sorano, xvii, 9, 10–12, 22n14, 50, 59, 74; ghetto, 10–11
Sovana, xvii, xix, 9, 12, 22n17, 50, 185
Spina, Alessandro, 32, 45n9
Sullam, Simon Levis, 23, 124

Tittmann, Harold, 2, 86

Togliatti Amnesty, 163–65
Turteltaub family, xviii, 115–18, 128n12, 143

Waisborg family, xix, 142, 146
Waldman family, xix, 118, 143
Wiesenthal, Simon, 167

Zuccotti, Susan, 4, 80n23, 81, 104n2–n4, 107n26, 126n4

# About the Author

**Judith Roumani**, Ph.D., has published numerous articles about Sephardic literature, particularly literature of the Holocaust. She is author of *Albert Memmi* (1987); a journal editor (www.sephardichorizons.org); and the translator of Renzo De Felice's *Jews in an Arab Land: Libya 1835–1970* (1985) and Albert Memmi's novel *The Desert: Or, the Life and Adventures of Jubair Wali al-Mammi* (2015), as well as co-editor of *Jewish Libya: Memory and Identity in Text and Image* (2018), published as *Libia ebraica* (2020). She is also founder and director of the Jewish Institute of Pitigliano.

www.ingramcontent.com/pod-product-compliance
Lightning Source LLC
Chambersburg PA
CBHW070829300426
44111CB00014B/2501